T0330949

Income Inequality in Singapore

The World Bank, 1993 conferred on Singapore the status of 'tiger economy' because of its two miraculous characteristics: high growth and reduced income inequality. Expansion of educational provision is one of the major policies the government of Singapore has followed since 1975, particularly to enrich the human capital endowment of the country, which has been crucial to the success of Singapore. This book makes a coherent study of these extremely important issues to examine the trends and patterns of income inequality in Singapore.

The book delves further into the trends and patterns of income inequality in Singapore and their implications for the future. It attempts to analyse the links between social welfare and inequality in the light of a rapid economic growth phase and adduced important policy implications. The concepts and methodologies used in this book, as well as the novelty of analyses and policy implications, make this a coherent and in-depth study of extremely important issues, with up-to-date observations.

In the last three decades no such book on Singapore has been written, and this book fills that gap in the existing literature. It is crucial reading for anyone who is interested in learning more about the tiger economy of Singapore.

Pundarik Mukhopadhaya is an Associate Professor at the Department of Economics, Macquarie University, Australia. Dr Mukhopadhaya has published widely on income distribution analysis and various other issues in development economics. Some of his major publications have appeared in *Journal of Contemporary Asia*, *Researches on Economic Inequality*, *Advances in Econometrics*, *Applied Economics*, *Journal on Income Distribution*, *Journal of Asian Economics*, *Asian Economics Journal*, *Journal of World Investment and Trade*, *Netherlands International Law Review*, *Oxford Development Studies* and *Economic Record*. Dr Mukhopadhaya has also provided consultancy to UNESCO, the World Bank and WHO.

Income Inequality in Singapore

Pundarik Mukhopadhaya

LONDON AND NEW YORK

First published 2014
by Routledge
2 Park Square, Milton Park, Abingdon, Oxon OX14 4RN

and by Routledge
711 Third Avenue, New York, NY 10017

Routledge is an imprint of the Taylor & Francis Group, an informa business

British Library Cataloguing in Publication Data
A catalogue record for this book is available from the British Library

Library of Congress Cataloging in Publication Data
Mukhopadhaya, Pundarik.
Income inequality in Singapore / Pundarik Mukhopadhaya.
    pages cm
  Includes bibliographical references and index.
  1. Income distribution—Singapore. 2. Income—Singapore.
  I. Title.
HC445.8.Z9I515 2015
339.2'2095957—dc23   2013036607

ISBN: 978-0-415-50489-8 (hbk)
ISBN: 978-1-315-79797-7 (ebk)

Typeset in Times New Roman
by Sunrise Setting Ltd, Paignton, UK

To my parents
Who inculcated me with the ethical principles and moral values

Contents

Figures

Tables

Acknowledgements

In 1999 when I joined the Department of Economics at the National University of Singapore (NUS) I had the opportunity to work with Professor Bhanoji Rao as a colleague. On the very first day of our meeting he presented me with a copy of his co-authored book *Income Inequality in Singapore*, which drew on information for the period 1966 to 1975. During my four years' stay in Singapore I noticed a number of changes in perception about disparity of income at the ministerial level, and consequently various measures were adopted in the growing economy. I started further investigation on the disparity of income independently and with Professor Rao, and with other colleagues in the Department of Economics. As a result, a number of research papers were published in various journals. I left Singapore in 2003, but I did not stop my investigations into income inequality in that country. In 2010 I spent a couple of months at the Global Asia Institute of the NUS. During that stay, while discussing income disparity issues with various academics, government officials and members of the general public, I realized that a new book on inequality in Singapore needed to be written with more recent analyses. I express my gratitude and thanks to Professor Rao for introducing me to the *miracle* situation of Singapore. I also thank Professor G. Shantakumar, with whom I have written a few research papers particularly related to older women, for sharing with me his insightful observations on Singapore, which proved especially useful.

The study represents the past ten or so years of my research on income distribution in Singapore, and some of the analysis contained within it has been drawn from a number of articles published in *The Developing Economies*, *Journal of Asian Economies*, *Asian Economic Journal*, *Journal of Asia Pacific Economy* and *Singapore Economic Review*. I briefly spoke with Ms Usha Desai on the primary education system in Singapore. She very generously collected valuable data for my research and I thank her for that. Sunil Venaik and I are currently involved in a research project related to old age poverty in Singapore that has revealed a number of interesting findings and prescriptions to reduce such poverty. I haven't specifically used those findings in this book, however. I thank Sunil for the passionate discussions that I have had with him on this subject over the last four years. I have presented my research on Singapore at various conferences that have generated a lot of discussion and I am grateful for all the comments and criticisms that I have received from the discussants and audience. I thank my students Al-Amin Pramanik, Sigit Triandaru and Srinivas Kolluru for helping me out with the collection and processing of some relevant material and data. Laura Billington and Marion Moffatt have been of tremendous help in copy editing and reference checking.

I thank my wife, Chandrama, and daughters Proteeti and Prajusha, for their patience with my absence from duties to them, and for providing moral support in my hours of despair throughout the whole project.

Pundarik Mukhopadhaya
November, 2013

1   Introduction

In all countries social policy-makers generally have goals and values that inform the making of social judgments and guide the formulation of social decisions. Typically, these are likely to include attaining an efficient use of scarce resources and the promotion of equitable and just distribution of those resources. Philosophically, notions of equitable distribution dissolve into an endless sequence of semantic issues. Examples of some of the issues that relate to economic inequality could be: Tom and Dick might both earn the same amount of money, but Dick may be physically handicapped while Tom isn't; Eleanor is richer than Emma, but Eleanor lives in a country that denies her freedoms such as the right to vote or travel freely; Chow earned more than Kim until they were both forty, thereafter Chow earns more. These examples make it obvious that the concept of economic inequality is complex and ultimately linked to other concepts such as freedom, age, personal capability etc. The concept of disparities in personal income is narrow compared to the broader issues of liberty, capabilities etc., but it is easier to quantify and measure. Furthermore, income is typically studied on the basis that it is a reasonable indicator of individual well-being.

Economists, philosophers and policy analysts have been concerned with income inequality issues for over a century. In the mid-1980s there was a paradigm shift in realization by social scientists that the problem of income inequality was universal rather than specific to developing countries. Income may be earned from various sources. Due to a lack of available information for Singapore, in this book we will measure income inequality in terms of earnings only and we will use the terms income and earnings synonymously.

From the early twentieth century, social scientists have been looking for a reliable and satisfactory theory to explain the income/earnings inequality. The human capital model (Becker, 1964; Mincer, 1970; and followers) provides one explanation of income differences in the labour market. In this model each individual is viewed as making an investment decision on how much schooling and training to acquire, with the assumption that both schooling and training increase the productivity of the worker and thus their future wages. Proponents of this theory have identified the relevant costs of the human investment process; they have analysed school and post-school investment, spelled out optimizing decision rules for such investments and derived implications for income differentials among skill categories, across occupations and by age categories. Thus, income differential depends on what degree of schooling and training reached, is sufficient to compensate for the costs of education and training (human resource development), accounting for working life, uncertainty of earnings, unemployment and other non-financial benefits.

Empirical research has established that average income increases with the level of schooling attained, confirming the predictions of human capital models. It has been found that with age, average income first increases and, after a certain point, starts decreasing. This would suggest that there exists some income inequality arising from the age factor. With age, individuals acquire new skills and upgrade old skills through on-the-job training. At the same time, old skills depreciate over time through obsolescence and, after a certain age, the average income starts decreasing. Another interesting observation is that the average income increases faster with age for the more educated workers. To explain the reason for this finding, Mincer (1970) argued that for the more educated workers, income increases at a higher rate because of the positive association between schooling and post-schooling (on- the-job training) investment. There is ample opportunity for on-the-job training for jobs taken by more highly educated workers; however, less-educated workers have little opportunity for the on-the-job training.

An analysis of the human capital model to explain earnings inequality provides some guidance to social policy. In developing countries (sub-Saharan Africa and Latin America in particular), underinvestment in education could explain the high earnings inequality. A study by Psacharopoulos (1985) on the comparison of rates of returns to society from education indicates that in all regions of the world social returns are higher from primary education than from secondary education; and when secondary and tertiary (higher) education are compared, the returns are even greater for secondary than for higher education. The study also reveals that returns to society from education are substantially higher for low-income regions of the world, than middle- and high-income countries. Results for advanced economies indicate that education is still a good investment for increasing productivity and decreasing income inequality. As a result, many government programmes aim to increase schooling and training for low-earning populations. In a number of countries, basic education has been made compulsory, and in some others it is a constitutional right. Efforts have also been made to reduce dropout rates among various age levels. Student loan programmes have been designed to encourage college-age students from low-earning families to attend higher education institutions by way of scholarships, and bursaries are provided for school-age children from poor families.

According to the ability theory (e.g., Taussing, 1915; Roy, 1950; Mandelbrot, 1962), differences in workers' productivity, and hence their earnings, are due to differences in their abilities. It was widely believed that abilities were distributed *normally*, like other physical characteristics. The seemingly natural conclusion to be drawn from this is that income too is distributed normally. In 1897 Pareto's empirical examination revealed that income was not distributed *normally*, instead it had a flat long tail to the right, implying substantial unequal distribution in the labour market. Researchers are sceptical of the direct role ability has in earnings; some have expressed concerns about the indirect effect of education and training, some point out that measuring ability only captures certain components, while others contend that ability depends largely on a person's immediate environment.

From a policy point of view, if ability determines income disparity, it will be interesting to explore the determinants of ability. From the early 1970s, a number of studies tried to resolve whether ability (intelligence in particular) is inherited or affected by the environment. Empirical research on identical twins tried to separate the influence of genetic factors from environmental factors. The crucial role of environment in the development of intelligence is widely accepted. However, there is little agreement concerning the relative contribution of heredity and environment. Some of those who support the heredity position[1] have suggested that selective breeding of the population be used in an attempt to increase the average intelligence level of a society and thus reduce income inequality. This view arises from the contention that certain ethnic groups are genetically inferior. The majority view among social scientists is that nurture (a child's environment, upbringing, parents' education etc.) rather than nature is the prime influence behind various components of ability. Thus, certain research suggests that social policies should be aimed at improving nurture-related outcomes for the betterment of the intelligence level of poor children (Selowsky, 1976).

In the human capital model, it is shown that individuals with more schooling receive higher incomes because education increases their productivity. It is, however, usually noted that subjects taught at more advanced levels of schooling are less relevant to the skills required in the work place. In reality there is imperfect information in the labour market (the human capital model assumes a perfect labour and capital market), and employers have no direct way of assessing prospective employees' productive abilities. In such cases, schooling is viewed as an information (cut-off) device. Employers pay more to applicants with higher levels of schooling and tend to hire them in favour of less-educated applicants, not solely because education enhances productivity, but because it identifies and anticipates more productive workers. This is the main point raised in various signalling or screening models.[2] The argument in screening models is directly contrary to the human capital model. Empirical researchers favour human capital models over screening models; however, it is difficult to establish concretely the superiority of one model over another, because of the observational equivalence of human capital theory and screening models (Blaug, 1989). From the viewpoint of social policy-makers, whatever the (right) argument over models, more schooling commands higher wages, and education disparity is one important reason behind income disparity. Thus improvement in educational attainment in society as a whole is one way to reduce disparity of income.

There could be other forms of market imperfections. Bowles (1972) was of the view that the education system was one way of preserving class background. Children from higher social classes are channelled into one part of the education system and segregated from lower social classes. Children of rich people develop contacts and literally walk into higher paying jobs, while children of poor parents may never access such networks and this becomes the major obstacle to getting jobs at the upper levels of the hierarchy. Bowles estimated empirically that 52 per cent variation in schooling achievement was explained by family background variables. Furthermore, family background accounted directly for 13 per cent of variation of income, and indirectly for another 15 per cent through its impact on schooling achievement. When using family background as a control, it was found that achievement in schooling explained only 2 per cent of the variation of income (Bowles and Nelson, 1974). Behrman and Taubman (1990) on a panel survey estimated that there was a 50 per cent correlation between children's adult income and their parents' income.

Thus parents can assist children to earn higher wages directly by influencing job-search or indirectly *via* education. They can motivate their children to succeed at school and inform them about educational opportunities. Even where entry to higher education is limited (for example, in medicine and law), parents can be instrumental in securing their children's access. These are some examples of the violation of restrictive assumptions of the human capital model. Another important assumption of the human capital model is the existence of a perfect capital market, where everyone is able to borrow money at the same interest rate. This assumption is vital since the cost of investment in schooling at any phase of life in terms of direct costs and opportunity costs can be very high. In reality, the capital market for student loans is not perfect. There are limitations on borrowing as well. Lenders, in most cases, need some security; human capital cannot be held as collateral, and individuals from poor family backgrounds have nothing else to show as security. Children from rich families often have parents to pay for college financing, while others do not have this option. Different students face different market interest rates depending on their circumstances, arising from the imperfect capital market. Therefore, students may make different schooling decisions despite having the same potential rate of return from a college education. Inequality in access to borrowing and consequently access to education may lead to income differentials in excess of those predicted by a simplistic human capital model.

A number of studies have examined reasons for wage differentials in industrialized countries, and many concluded that labour unions have played an important role in wage determination. Freeman (1991) noted that less unionized countries had higher wage inequality in the 1980s, and that between 1978 and 1987 inequality decreased with increasing unionization. Gittleman and Wolff (1993) found evidence to show that the greatest increases in industrial wage inequalities are in areas where there are low levels of unionization. Although unions tend to raise wages of members compared to non-members, evidence shows that overall inequality of income decreases with unionization.

Gender wage difference is another dimension of income disparity. Women typically have fewer years of work experience than men of the same age and educational attainment because of interrupted careers. Also women receive less on-the-job training than men of the same age because employers have less incentive to invest in female workers. However, over the years, all around the world, educational attainment and labour force participation rates for females have increased, leading to a narrowing of the gender wage gap from what it was a few decades ago. Government anti-discrimination programmes have played an important role in improving the economic status of female workers.

The human capital model and its extensions and variants influence social policy to a great extent, and this supports the view that through the expansion of education and training programmes, income inequality can be reduced. These policies affect the supply side of the economy. On the other hand, structural change may shift employment among industries, affecting the demand for labour and the distribution of wages. Industrial concentration, market power, firm size and unionization have important effects on industry wage differentials. Empirical evidence suggests that profitability, employment growth and productivity of various industries all have a significant role to play in inter-industry income diversity. Furthermore, the efficiency wage theory advocates that paying higher wages helps to increase firm profitability. To rectify an adverse income inequality stemming from structural and institutional factors, social decision-makers may influence industries through the implementation of competition policies, company laws and also by generating rules governing public procurement. In every society's labour market, low-paid jobs always exist, however, in some countries (for example, USA and the UK), legislation related to a minimum wage may protect people from acute destitution. Singapore, instead of taking this route, hires people from neighbouring excess-labour countries, thus protecting the interest of the countries in question. However, this selective immigration procedure works adversely on income distribution as it depresses the domestic wage rate at the lower end and consequently unskilled/low-educated individuals in the country are pushed into poverty (relatively speaking).

Over the past decade it has been observed that income inequality had been increasing all over the world. In order to reduce income inequality, some governments have considered providing benefits to individuals and families in two forms: transfer payments, and expenditure on goods and services. Today more than half of the families at the bottom end of the income ladder are found in female-headed households. Children also have very high incidences of relative inequality, because many of them live in single-parent households. The elderly, on the other hand, who are already in the bottom decile of income distribution indicators, have experienced a very sharp decline in their income. Mostly non-working families are found in the lowest-income group, however, almost half of this group is made up of working families. One reason for their low income is that family members may be earning low wages because they have minimum skills and low education, experience discrimination, or are employed in seasonal or service industries. An examination of these situations shows that government transfer payments are made to unemployed people, to single-mother families and to the elderly, and are protected by some social security systems. These programmes provide benefits to retired workers and their dependents and to survivors of insured workers. Besides these transfer payments, government expenditure on health, education etc. provides support to the low-income group and improves the income inequality in a country.

The effect of redistributive policies on the reduction of income inequality is quite complex. In a very poor country, redistribution may bring down the rate of savings which eventually will reduce the investment rate and, in turn, the growth rate will be reduced in the medium or long run. The reason for this is that with redistribution, the fraction of the population (however small) that has the desire and means to save will be frustrated. Thus, for social policy-makers the choice is difficult: whether or not to accept inegalitarian policies in the interest of growth. For a medium-income country the choice is quite straightforward; for these countries redistributive policies may increase savings at the national level. This is because these policies create a large middle class with high aspirations, and this raises the average savings rate.

Although traditionally it is held that initial inequality may have a beneficial impact on growth, this view is being increasingly questioned, both on theoretical and empirical grounds. Empirically, many studies based on cross-country evidence find that the addition/increase of a measure of income inequality as an explanatory variable has a significant negative impact on growth. Various theoretical reasons for this have been proposed. For instance, Alesina and Rodrik (1994) argue that when distribution of capital (that is income-generating assets) is more equal, the median voters prefer a lower tax on capital, generating a lower disincentive effect, than when the distribution is more unequal. Murphy *et al.* (1989) argue that greater equality in income distribution implies an increased domestic demand for output from the industrial sector, thereby stimulating growth in that sector.

This book attempts to measure and interpret the income inequality scenario in Singapore. The World Bank (1993) conferred on Singapore the status of 'tiger economy' because of its two miraculous characteristics: high growth and reduced income inequality. To control any higher rate of growth in income inequality, the Singapore government considered various policies, for example, attempts were made to create equal opportunity through education that may reduce gender imbalance in the long run. The provision of the Central Provident Fund (CPF) was introduced to Singaporeans to provide social protection in old age. In this book we will discuss the trend in income inequality in Singapore and the effectiveness of a number of government policies in that respect.

Singapore in perspective

Singapore is a city-state of around five million people, and it recorded the world's eighth highest GNP per capita of US$32,875 of the 104 countries covered in the World Bank's World Development Indicator for 2011. However, an alternative set of estimates using purchasing power parity (PPP) criteria ranked Singapore as fourth. Singapore has been able to combine rapid economic growth with low inflation, increasing foreign exchange reserves, low level of external debt, and an appreciating currency in relation to the US dollar.

It is among the most internationalized economies in the world (Mirza, 1986; Rodan, 1989; Peebles and Wilson, 1996). The international orientation began as a result of a well-planned development strategy by the government based on export-led growth and foreign direct investment (FDI), which attracted multinational corporations (MNCs) to set up their production and marketing bases to expand their activities in the region. In response to the government's strategy, these MNCs have not only increased their presence over the years, but have also diversified their operations towards R&D, management development, warehousing and distribution, fund management and technical support. These factors, combined with a central location in the Asia-Pacific region, linking the Indian Ocean Rim countries, Australasia and countries along the Pacific Ocean, have given Singapore the status of a hub or a centre of international economic activity. Thus, Singapore has now become a leading manufacturing, logistics and IT hub in the global market.

Singapore has served as a centre for regional entrepôt trade since the early nineteenth century due to its locational advantages combined with a natural deep harbour, connecting the region with Europe and North America. Since the middle of the last century, as other neighbouring countries were developing their own ports and engaging in direct trading of their products, this function has been gradually diluted, and after independence in 1965, Singapore has embarked on a process of industrialization through promotion of export growth strategies. Mukhopadhaya *et al.* (2011) explained that Singapore experienced growth in various phases. The early 1970s were characterized by low growth rates in comparison to the rates achieved in the preceding years. Recovery from the global oil shock began in 1976 and robust growth continued thereafter (though not at double digit levels) until the slowdown in 1985. The period between 1974 and 1985 witnessed a rise in the investment rate to levels close to 50 per cent, and a reduction in the savings–investment gap. In this period Singapore's economy experienced labour shortages and rising costs, which necessitated a shift in the industrial structure towards capital-intensive sectors. As a result, the Singapore government's emphasis shifted to human capital development and technology-intensive products.

Singapore's investment ratio doubled from 20 per cent of GDP in 1965 to more than 40 per cent in 1984. This is because of massive private sector investment in machinery, transportation equipment, and the construction of manufacturing plants and petrochemical complexes. Public sector investment also increased through housing and infrastructure development (including seaports, airport terminals, roads, and mass rapid transport and telecommunication systems).

Singapore's economy went into recession in 1985/6. Robust growth resumed in 1987 and continued through to the start of the Asian Financial Crisis in 1997. In 1991 the Strategic Economic Plan was formulated. This involved promoting Singapore as a total business centre by diversifying its industrial structure towards high-tech value added manufacturing and promoting the service sector as the *twin* engines of growth, as a response to the changing domestic and global economic environment. Services became prominent from the late 1980s to the early 1990s, resulting in a substantially large surplus of saving over investment, mostly due to the surpluses in the government sector. Thus, Singapore's high level of investment was facilitated by high levels of savings.

Since the late 1990s Singapore has experienced a number of external shocks, which reduced the average real GDP growth rate to 5–6 per cent. The more globalized an economy, the more it is prone to external shocks. However, the Asian Financial Crisis did not affect Singapore to the extent that its neighbours Thailand and Korea suffered (see Tables A1.1 and A1.2 in the appendix of this chapter). There were some retrenchments, but the unemployment rate rose only slightly to 4.6 per cent in 1999. Despite the slumps in 2001 and 2008–09, the average unemployment rate for the whole period did not experience any noticeable change.

With effective and timely implementation of manpower policies, and with continued political stability, Singapore today is one of the most internationally oriented and integrated economies in the world. Its ability to attract huge FDI flows has turned the economy into a manufacturing base for foreign multinationals, and a major international financial, logistics, trading and transportation hub in the global economy.

Singapore is characterized by enormous economic achievement, large policy changes and the hegemonistic exercise of state power. The government of Singapore in its growth and development process was able to define a long-term goal. During the initial phase of development when emphasis was more on the creation of full employment, the government did not place much importance on skill formation. 'These made minimal demands on the education and the training system, and indeed investment in education was behind that of some of the other NIEs [newly industrialized economies]' (Ashton and Green, 1996: 161).

During the late 1970s, Singapore started focusing more attention on secondary, vocational and technical education, and developed a training infrastructure. However, on the one hand the projected growth rate was very high, but on the other, a large proportion of the population had only lower primary education. Nevertheless the government had to employ its adult, under-educated population and so several on-the-job training programmes were made available. The 1990s and beyond marks the expansion of higher education (and work-based skills training). Due to the lack of highly skilled workers during the high growth period of the 1980s and 1990s, and in the development of the knowledge-based economy in the late 1990s and 2000s, the government encouraged the hiring of foreign-skills at very high competitive levels (comparable to other industrialized countries), which had some adverse effects on the distribution of income. Furthermore, with the expansion of and emphasis on education, participation rates in lower-paid jobs decreased and the government realized that it was advantageous to hire low-paid workers from the labour excess in neighbouring countries. This added another element to the increase in income inequality.

Extending dimensions: from gross national income to human development

Singapore's Human Development Index (HDI) value has been very high (0.866 in 2011). Since 2000 Singapore's HDI value increased at an average annual growth rate of 0.7 per cent. Singapore ranks twenty-sixth out of 187 countries and territories in the United Nations Development Programme (UNDP, 2011). Between 1980 and 2011 Singapore life expectancy at birth increased by 9.5 years and mean years of schooling increased by 5.1 years. However, Singapore's 2011 HDI is below the average of 0.889 for countries in the very high human development group, despite the fact that Singapore's gross national income (GNI) per capita (PPP $US) is 1.57 times higher than that of very high HDI countries (on average). Singapore's HDI is lower than that of the high HDI countries (on average) because Singapore's performance in terms of education compared to high HDI countries is poor. Statistics in 2011 show that while Singapore's mean years of schooling is 8.8 years, for very high HDI countries that figure is 11.3 years, with the expected years of schooling being 1.5 points less compared to the very high HDI countries.[3]

To unmask the inequality in the distribution in human development across the population of a country, the 2010 Human Development Report introduced the inequality adjusted HDI (IHDI). The IHDI takes into account inequality in all three dimensions (income, education and health) of the HDI. The Singapore government does not publish relevant data that would enable a calculation of the inequality adjusted HDI, however, information is available for Singapore to compute gender-based inequality using the Gender Inequality Index (GII). The GII considers three dimensions – the reproductive health (measured by maternal mortality and adolescent fertility rates), empowerment (measured by the share of parliamentary seats held by each gender and attainment of secondary and higher education by each gender) and economic activity (measured by the labour market participation rate by each gender). While the average GII value of very high HDI countries is 0.224, Singapore's GII value was 0.086 in 2011. Singapore has achieved a substantially high rank in terms of health indicators for both genders, however, in terms of gender disparity, it is yet to achieve more. Furthermore, the proportion of the female population with at least secondary education in Singapore is 57.3 per cent, while that of very high HDI countries is 82 per cent (UNDP, 2011). So, with respect to educational achievement of women, Singapore needs further improvement.

This book does not attempt to analyse different dimensions of inequalities other than income for Singapore because of the lack of available data. However, while analysing the dispersion of income we explain the role of education and explore the gender dimension of inequality using the available information. The lack of data does not allow us to scientifically analyse the effects of different policies of the Singapore government on income inequality, however, we do provide a discussion of government policies where possible.

Methodology used

A common measure of income inequality as used in this book is the Gini coefficient, developed by Corrado Gini in 1912/14. This is essentially a statistical or descriptive measure of dispersion of income, although it can be interpreted in terms of an aggregation of human feelings such as unfairness or relative deprivation.

Decomposition of the inequality index by subgroups of population (for example, by geographical location or by ethnic background, or by educational status) is widely used to enumerate the respective inequality components. From the policy perspective an additive decomposable inequality measure has some practical convenience (for example, in identifying the target group etc.). A decomposable inequality measure in this case would mean that the inequality index can be decomposed into 'between' and 'within' subgroups. The Theil index, another inequality measure, has very strong support from among social scientists because of its decomposability properties. For the purpose of decomposing the income inequality in Singapore we have used the Theil index.

A note on the available data related to income distribution

There are three regular sources available for the income data of Singapore: the report on the quinquennial Household Expenditure Survey (HES); the report on the annual Labour Force Survey (LFS); and the annual report of the Inland Revenue Authority of Singapore (IRAS). Each data source has advantages and limitations with regard to analyses of income inequality.

In general, one would expect the most comprehensive data to come from the HES. First, since both household income and expenditure data are obtainable through the HES, there is the opportunity to crosscheck income data against expenditure, and hence there is a relatively greater chance of obtaining quality data. Second, the surveys try to capture all types of income (wages and salaries, as well as income from interest, rent and dividends). One drawback is that the survey is conducted every five years and there is always a considerable lapse of time before the published report is available in the public domain. One further limitation is that income component does not include single-person households for the periods 1987–8, 1992–3 and 1997–8. Another limitation in the computation of income disparity from published HES income data arises from the clubbing of households of differing sizes in each income class. Thus, in the household income group, say, \$1,000 to \$1,999, there may be households of size 2, and 3 as well as 4, 5, 6 and so on.[4] In the household of size 3, the income per person will be \$500 (if we assume that there is no inequality within the group), while income per person in the household of size 5 is \$300. Clearly, households with the same household income but of different sizes do not enjoy the same economic status. There is widespread agreement that as the size of the household increases, economies of scale can be realized (see Buhmann *et al.*, 1988). Furthermore, both adults and children have different needs (Coulter *et al.*, 1992). To account for the variation in the number of children and adults among families, an adjustment of household income is needed. Hence, measures of household income inequality computed without accounting for the variation in household size and composition at each income level do not accurately capture the underlying inequalities.

Thus, if one considers inequality, one has to arrange the households by adult equivalent income. From the published data on Singapore's household income, such computations are not feasible for the year 1987/8. The Singapore Department of Statistics (DOS, 2000) attempted to compute income inequality without making any adjustment for household size. And five years later DOS (2005) reported various characteristics of households arranged by quintile groups without any adjustment of household size. Such problems with these data make the results and their interpretations totally useless. Other HES provides average household size for each income group, which enables some meaningful interpretable calculations of inequality.

An additional limitation of all available data is the inadequacy of income coverage. The *2007/08 Household Expenditure Survey*, for instance, estimates an income per capita of $2,268 per month, which happens to be only 38.4 per cent of the corresponding estimate from National Income Accounts. Mukhopadhaya *et al.* (2011) demonstrated that income estimates of HES explain less than 40 per cent of the total National Income. To be able to explore realities, there is a need to reconcile the data with the national accounts, which are based on income aggregates. In addition, if tabulations were made available on per capita household income as well as per household expenditure, some detailed investigation on income inequality could be conducted.

The LFS data are generally collected annually on gross monthly income of employees, which includes wages and salaries, allowances, overtime, commissions, tips, bonuses and the mandatory employee contribution to the CPF. The income of employers and own-account workers refers to the total receipt from sales and services performed *less* operating expenses. Thus these surveys exclude all income from property (rents, interest and dividends as well royalties).[5] The income coverage of the Labour Force Surveys is therefore inadequate. However, employee income coverage in the Labour Force Surveys has improved over the years (see Table 1.1). LFS information is used to compute income inequality for most of the cases in this book. Additional information gained from LFS data is that it permits the identification of income of the members of the labour force. Since the reports contain cross-tabulations of income by personal characteristics such as age, education, occupation etc., the data are helpful in a study of the factors that explain income gaps.[6]

Table 1.1 Incomes compared: labour force surveys and national accounts

Income source	1980	1985	1996	2011
(1) Estimated employee income from LFS ($ million)[a]	5,809	11,384	41,905	108,558
(2) Wages and salaries in cash and kind from NA ($ million)[b]	8,336	15,921	48,960	138,406
(3) (1)/(2) in %	69.7	71.5	85.6	78.4

Notes
[a]Estimated from the income distributions for employees from *Labour Force Surveys*, various years.
[b]Compensation of employees reported in Department of Statistics, *The Income Approach to Gross Domestic Product*, July 1998, and *Yearbook of Statistics* 2011.

The annual reports of IRAS provide an excellent tabulation on the distribution of taxpayers by assessed income class. The merits of the data are that they are free from sampling errors, respondents (taxpayers) are well aware of the need to report income accurately, and the data covers all income categories. The main drawback is that there is not enough information on the characteristics of the taxpayers for analytical purposes. Also, several of the low-income earners may not be enumerated in the taxpayer group.

As a matter of fact, HES and IRAS collect data on each household/person, but the published data in reality are arranged within income classes. According to standard laws governing data collection, divulging specific information on individuals is strictly prohibited. In the case of the LFS, it would seem that data were collected via income classes. That is, each respondent states the income group to which he/she belongs. To compute the income inequality in such situation is to assume 'no inequality' in each income group. Consider, for example, the 1,946,500 working people in the monthly income group $500–999 (LFS, 2011). Since there is no individual information on the number of persons for this income group, one has to assume that there is no income inequality within the group. The assumption is not necessary when one has access to the full data set with the income of each and every person or household.[7]

For classes such as the $500–$999 income group, it is common practice to assume the average for the class to be $750 (average of the lower and upper bounds, rounded for convenience). The problem arises with regard to the first and last income classes in the LFS and HES, as these two classes are open-ended. Clearly for the class, 'below $500' ($1,000 in recent years) in the HES or 'below $400' (or 'below $500' for recent years) in the LFS, it is not appropriate to assume the minimum income as zero and take the mean of the class as $250 ($500 for recent years) or $200 ($250 for recent years) respectively. Usually one assumes a non-zero income, based on extraneous information such as the minimum allowance the government may grant to destitute families. The lower limit for the lowest open-ended group is not quite critical since the group generally contains only a small proportion of the total households/persons. Crucial problems arise with the last income class, which is also open-ended: '$7,000+' in the HES and '$6,000 and over' in the LFS ($10,000 and over for both HES and LFS in recent years). Fortunately for the HES, since the overall mean income for the entire sample is given, it is possible to derive the mean of the last open income class.[8] Such is not the case for the LFS and some estimation procedures have to be used. For the calculations in this book, we have used the IRAS data to judge the mean income for the last open-ended income class for the LFS data by appropriately matching the two sets of data.[9]

Organization of the book

Besides the Introduction (Chapter 1) and the final concluding chapter (Chapter 8), there are five chapters (Chapter 3 to Chapter 7) dealing with income inequality in Singapore. In Chapter 2 we discuss the concepts and measurement of income inequality in general. Chapter 3 provides an overview of the trends of inequality from 1984 to current records. A brief discussion of the long-term relationship between growth and inequality is also made in this chapter. Chapter 4 evaluates the Singapore government's attempt at the provision of educational opportunities and its effect on income inequality. Chapter 5 discusses the gender dimension of inequality in Singapore, and Chapter 6 extends the issue to older women. Chapter 7 brings a new theory on evaluating social welfare in terms of equity and efficiency and examines the Singapore case in light of that.

Appendix

Table A1.1 Indicators of economic growth and structural change: Singapore, Korea, Hong Kong and Taiwan, 1990–2012

Singapore

	1990–95	1996–98	1999–2007	2008–10	2011–12
GDP Average annual growth %	8.9	4.9	8.5	5.1	3.25

As % of GDP	1990–1995	1996–1998	1999–2007	2008–2010	2011
Share of industry	33.1	32.5	31.6	27.8	NA
Total consumption	53.9	50.4	55.3	49.9	73.5
Gross investment	35.8	35.0	24.2	26.8	22.9
Exports	142.3	148.7	171.1	214.8	229.7

Korea

	1990–95	1996–98	1999–2007	2008–10	2011–12
GDP Average annual growth %	8.1	1.3	5.7	2.9	3.15

As % of GDP	1990–1995	1996–1998	1999–2007	2008–2010	2011
Share of industry	37.7	36.9	37.3	37.5	39.2
Total consumption	63.2	63.5	67.1	69.3	68.3
Gross investment	37.5	33.3	29.8	28.9	29.5
Exports	27.1	35.5	40.6	51.7	56.2

Hong Kong

	1990–95	1996–98	1999–2007	2008–10	2011–12
GDP Average annual growth %	5.3	1.3	5.0	2.2	3.25

As % of GDP	1990–1995	1996–1998	1999–2007	2008–2010	2011
Share of industry	16.36	14.3	11.3	7.4	NA
Total consumption	72.1	72.6	68.5	70.4	73.5
Gross investment	29.0	31.5	23.1	21.8	22.9
Exports	113.6	134.0	139.9	210	229.7

Taiwan

	1990–95	1996–98	1999–2007	2008–10	2011–12
GDP Average annual growth %	7.0	5.8	4.3	3.2	2.85

As % of GDP	1990–1995	1996–1998	1999–2007	2008–2010	2011
Share of industry	36.0	31.8	28.9	30.6	29.6
Total consumption	72.7	73.8	74.1	72.2	71.9
Gross investment	24.6	24.0	22.3	20.9	21.2
Exports	38.9	40.1	59.1	69.7	75.7

Source: Asian Development Bank, *Key Indicators*, 2011 and 2012. The 2012 figures are estimates from *ADB Outlook* in December 2012.

Table A1.2 External economy indicators: Singapore, Korea, Hong Kong and Taiwan, 1995–2011

	1995	1998	2000	2002	2004	2006	2008	2009	2010	2011
Singapore										
Current account balance (% of GDP)	17.1	22.2	11.6	13.4	24.5	21.8	14.6	19.0	22.2	21.9
Exports (US$ billion)	132.1	119.7	153.2	140.6	200.9	272.1	342.8	273.0	357.9	429.3
External reserves (US$ billion)	68.7	74.9	80.1	82.0	112.2	136.2	172.2	187.8	225.7	237.9
Exchange rate (US$/$)	1.41	1.66	1.73	1.74	1.63	1.53	1.44	1.40	1.29	1.30
South Korea										
Current account balance (% of GDP)	−1.7	11.7	2.4	1.0	4.1	0.6	0.3	3.9	2.8	2.4
Exports (US$ billion)	112.5	172.9	236.2	260.2	359.7	436.6	434.7	358.2	464.3	552.6
External reserves (US$ billion)	32.7	52.0	96.2	121.4	199.1	238.9	201.2	270.0	291.6	306.4
External debt (US$ billion)	85.8	139.3	134.4	141.5	172.3	260.0	317.4	345.4	360.0	398.4
Short-term debt (% of total)	54.3	20.2	31.5	34.1	32.7	43.7	47.2	43.2	37.5	34.2
Debt service (% of exports)	8.0	13.1	10.9	NA	NA	NA	NA	NA	NA	NA
Exchange rate (Won/US$)	775	1,204	1,264	1,186	1,035.1	929.8	1,259.5	1,164.5	1,134.8	1,151.8
Hong Kong										
Current account balance (% of GDP)	—	1.5	4.1	7.6	9.5	12.1	13.7	8.6	6.2	5.1
Exports (US$ billion)	173.6	173.7	202.2	200.3	259.4	316.8	365.2	321.8	394.0	438.0
External reserves (US$ billion)	55.4	89.7	107.1	111.9	123.6	133.2	182.5	255.8	268.7	285.4
Exchange rate (HK$/US$)	7.7	7.7	7.8	7.8	7.8	7.8	7.6	7.8	7.8	7.8
Taiwan										
Current account balance (% of GDP)	2.0	1.2	2.8	8.7	5.7	6.7	6.9	11.4	9.4	8.8
Exports ($ billion)	111.2	112.6	151.9	126.3	150.6	224.0	254.9	203.4	274.4	307.1
External reserves ($ billion)	95.9	95.1	111.4	166.0	246.6	270.8	296.4	353.0	387.2	390.6
Exchange rate (NT$/US$)	26.5	33.4	31.2	34.6	33.4	32.5	32.9	32.0	30.4	30.3

Source: Asian Development Bank, *Key Indicators*, 2011 and 2012. The 2012 figures are estimates from *ADB Outlook* in December 2012.

Note: External debt, external reserves and exchange rate refer to end of year. In the case of HK, however, exchange rate refers to the average for the year.

Notes

1 See Jensen (1969), Herrnstein (1971).
2 See Weiss (1995), Fontana *et al.* (2006).
3 See Smith (1993) on this issue.
4 All references to dollars are Singapore dollars (SGD) unless otherwise stated.
5 The consequence of the exclusion is evident from the rather low percentage (8 to 12 per cent – see Mukhopadhaya *et al.*, 2011) of the non-employment income captured in the LFS.
6 See Rao *et al.* (2003), and Mukhopadhaya and Rao (2002) for such studies.
7 However, there are methods to find the lower and upper bound of the inequality index, some further strong assumptions are to be made in those cases.
8 However, in the HES 1997/98 and 2002/3 instead of average income of the sample, average expenditure of the sample is provided.
9 The IRAS data provide the actual assessed income for each and every income group. An alternative is to fit a Pareto curve as follows: Let the lower income bound of last groups be Y_1 and Y_2. Also let the number of persons with incomes above Y_1 and Y_2 be N_1 and N_2 respectively. The Pareto α can be found as $\Delta \log N / \Delta \log Y$. Then the estimated mean of the last group is calculated from Van der Wijk's law as $(\alpha/(1-\alpha))Y_2$. For our computation we compared this estimate with the IRAS estimate and consider a compromise between the two.

2   Income inequality
A general discussion

Since ethics is mostly concerned with moral values, the question of equality versus inequality is central to moral philosophy. Most analyses have found that individuals are unequal in respect of intelligence, talent, wealth and so forth. Thus it is difficult to provide a precise definition of equality, and so some judgement must be specified. If all human beings have the same 'moral' and 'natural' rights, they are entitled to be treated equally. Therefore, in an equitable society, equality should be the norm and inequality the deviation from that. However, there are differing views in the literature of political philosophy. It is possible to separate these into three different types of thoughts:

1   'Equal treatment of equals', which states that those who are equal in some relevant respect should be treated equally; Aristotle was the main proponent of this reasoning.[1]
2   'Fundamental equality to all' refers to the idea that 'all human beings are of equal worth' and have 'equal fundamental rights' and should be given 'equal treatment'. This notion can be found in the American Declaration of Independence and the French revolutionary Declaration of the Rights of Man and of the Citizen, and in the writings of Rashdall (1907, see pp. 223–39), Tawney (1931, see pp. 35, 37 and 90), Benn (1967), Valtos (1962), Williams (1962) and Berlin (1980).[2]
3   'Social equality of all' refers to economic equality, political equality and also to 'equality of status'.

In social philosophy 'equality' is a controversial concept. To Aristotle equality of treatment was subject to the persons receiving the treatment being equal in relevant aspects. The aspects that are relevant sit somewhere on a spectrum; ranging from the extreme egalitarian approach, in which virtually nothing spares equality of treatment, to other approaches where many things do. In Kantian ethics, equal rights to all human beings to be treated as 'ends' in themselves was the foundation of all morality, however, the application of this ideal was controversial, as it was not clear what counted as a 'departure' from respect for persons as the 'end' in themselves.

Utilitarian and Rawlsian views of distributive justice

Here we do not intend to provide a discussion of all the competing philosophical ideas of distributive justice. Summarily, two broad competing concepts of distributive justice can be identified. First, *a just distribution is any distribution that results from a just process*. This just process entails a marketplace characterized by voluntary participation and free competition. Justice is, therefore, equality of rights and equality of opportunity. This form of distributive justice does not speak about the final form of benefit distributions. Today this understanding of the concept of justice can be used to justify severe inequalities in material conditions. This is the *entitlement theory of justice*. Second, the competing view, is the *social welfare philosophy of justice*, which is defined *broadly* to include the social welfare functions of Bentham,[3] Bergson (1938), Samuelson (1947) and Rawls (1971). The social welfare theory defines justice in terms of its 'end state' distributional results. For utilitarians it is usually evaluated solely in terms of individual utilities. The most significant feature of utilitarianism is that it makes no distinction between what is good and what is just. Actions are deemed just if they raise social welfare in some sense. The only claim that an individual may make against the decision-maker is that it must take as much account of his/her utility in the calculations as it does of anyone else's. Utilitarianism may be thought of as a particularly straightforward attempt to reduce justice to rationality. This view is different from Harsanyi (1975, 1977), in the sense that, whereas utilitarianism relies on the supposed ability to make an 'objective measurement' of pleasure, Harsanyi requires instead that individuals are able to make 'subjective judgements' about whether they would prefer to be one person rather than another. If (a) the 'rational decision-maker' has the ordering of all possible alternative social states, (b) if he/she accepts certain value judgements and (c) if certain 'technical assumptions' are satisfied, then the decision-maker's judgement can be represented by a social welfare function. In this way it is possible to construct social welfare judgement as retaining the theoretical structure of utilitarianism without committing to any assumptions about measurability of pleasure and pain. According to Sen (1979), this approach is called 'welfarism'.

A different view is identified by Rawls (1971) where the concept of social justice is 'justice as fairness'. In elaborating this, Rawls presents a substantial alternative to utilitarianism, which he regards as the dominant moral philosophy. He also offers his own theory as a 'contractarian defence of liberal principles of justice'. Rawls argues that justice as fairness is to be preferred to all other conceptions of justice because it is the one that individuals would choose from a hypothetical starting point (the 'original position'). Here, as he/she would not have any knowledge of his/her own interests, preferences or attachments, he/she would be forced to choose impartially. From behind this 'veil of ignorance', as a rational person, one would reject 'utilitarian', 'intuitionist', 'perfectionist' and 'egoist' alternatives, leaving 'justice as fairness' as the only reasonable option. Moreover, adopting the maximum criterion for making choices under conditions of uncertainty, one would always rank alternatives by their worst possible outcomes, opting

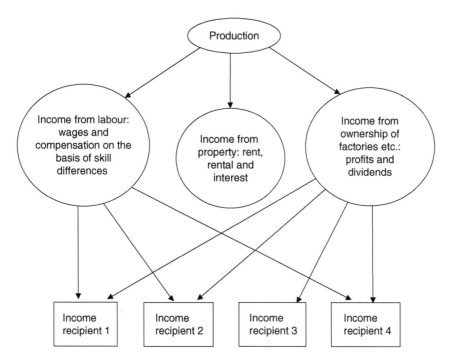

Figure 2.1 Relationship between personal and functional distribution of income.

for the alternative whose worst outcome is superior to the worst outcome of any other.[4]

Personal and functional distribution of income

We study the pattern of income distribution for two main reasons: first, to identify causes of inequality; and second, to suggest measures to achieve an equitable distribution of income to ensure economic justice. The examination of income distribution/income inequality may take at least two directions: functional distribution of income; and personal distribution of income. The former is the distribution of income under three main categories: income from labour with different skills; income from property; and income from entrepreneurship. The personal income distribution provides a description of income flows to income recipients (individuals or households). The relationship between personal and functional distribution of income is shown in Figure 2.1.

The personal distribution of income is studied to measure income inequality in a society and to relate that to various personal characteristics, while functional distribution of income tells us about the relationship between inequality and other features of growth and development. Bertoli and Farina (2007) made an excellent review of the theoretical literature of the functional distribution of income.

In this book our study is on the personal distribution of income (also called the size distribution of income) and more specifically the measurement of income inequality.

Measurement of income inequality: some considerations

The comparison of income inequality rests on the perspective of 'pure distributive justice'. The distributions are not only statistical but also 'actual', and likely to obey certain judgements depending on the structural nature of the considered values. In this section the fundamental ideas, concepts and properties of quantified *income inequalities* will be presented.

The normative judgements

Attempts to measure economic inequality did not start from the premise of 'normative' economics. In the earliest attempts of the measurement of inequality it was viewed as an objective phenomenon. In the statistical sense it was viewed as the dispersion of income or other economic attributes; it was considered an exercise of 'positive' quantitative economics. Nevertheless, this aspect of income inequality does have a normative meaning. Several measures of inequality are widely used as a normative measure in the existing literature. This section examines the question of when a distribution can be called more equal than another distribution, as well as some other properties of inequality measures.

Throughout this chapter, with the discrete distribution of income, it will be assumed that there are N income recipients (families/households/people) labelled $i = 1, 2, \ldots, N$ with the labels chosen so that their incomes, x_i, form an increasing sequence. Thus:

$$x_1 \leq x_2 \leq x_3 \leq \cdots \leq x_N \tag{2.1}$$

and the mean income, $\bar{x}$, is defined as:

$$\bar{x} = \frac{1}{N} \sum_{i=1}^{N} x_i. \tag{2.2}$$

For a given income vector $x = \{x_1, \ldots, x_N\}$ an inequality measure can be defined as $I(x)$ such that if $I(\hat{x}) > I(\tilde{x})$, then the income distribution $\hat{x}$ is more unequal than the distribution $\tilde{x}$.[5]

Symmetry or anonymity or impartiality

This assumes that for an inequality index the identity of the person is immaterial. That means the inequality index is a symmetric function of income. Formally this concept can be written as:

$$I(x) = I(Px) \tag{2.3}$$

where $I(x)$ is the inequality measure and $\mathbf{P}$ is the permutation matrix.[6] It means the inequality will remain the same for any permutation of the income vector. This property is the least objectionable so far as appropriate adjustments (e.g., adjustment of differing family size etc.) are done.

Pigou–Dalton condition of rank preserving transfer

By this condition it is assumed that if there is a transfer of some income from a rich person to a poor person, without interchanging their initial position in the income ladder, inequality in society will decrease. If the original distribution is {2, 10, 14}, any of the following distributions will have lower inequality: {4, 10, 12}, {6, 10, 10}, {2, 12, 12}. All these distributions relate to different definitions of the *weak* and *strong* version of Pigou–Dalton's principle (Foster, 1985). Formally, this condition can be written as:

$$I(\mathbf{Q}x) < I(x) \tag{2.4}$$

for all bistochastic matrices, $\mathbf{Q}$, which are not permutation matrix. The direction of this inequality implies that the inequality measure is an S-convex function of income.[7] From the beginning of this century, economists were convinced that this is the most important property of any inequality measure. However, doubts have been raised about the validity of this principle. Kolm (1966, 1976a, b, 1996, 1999), in an illuminating discussion, casts doubt on the validity of this principle.[8]

> The transfer of one dollar from a richer individual to a poorer has to be labelled just in the appropriate circumstances. It also uncontroversially diminishes the inequality between these two persons' incomes. But in no way can it be said to be *a priori* to diminish income inequality in a larger society where these two incomes are not the extreme ones, since it increases the pair wise inequalities between the receiver and the individuals poorer than her and between the relatively rich and still richer. Although transferring 1 to transform two-person distribution (4, 1) into two person distribution (3, 2) doubtlessly diminishes inequality between these two persons, the same transfer can in no way a priori be said to diminish overall inequality when it transforms the three person distribution (4, 4, 1) into the distribution (4, 3, 2). In the latter case indeed, the transfer also breaks one strict equality, and it increases inequality between the first two persons, transforming the gap from 0 to 1, a very large relative increase. And if there were twenty more fours, this transfer could also be seen as increasing inequality because two persons deviate from the crowd in the end, while only one did initially. Also an interesting psychological effect of equality is that it suppresses envy, but the considered transfer multiplies by two the number of possibly envious people. Nevertheless it is easy to argue convincingly that the resulting distributions can be more just, at least in certain circumstances, for instance because welfare effects

are to have priority over inequality effects, or because unchanging incomes should not be morally relevant.[9]

(Kolm 1999, p. 25)

Temkin (1986, 1993) is concerned about inequality from a moral perspective and equates inequality with injustice. He suggests that people have a 'complaint' if they have less than average income or income less than other people, and that inequality can be formulated in terms of these complaints. For any individual in the population the greater is the gap between his/her income and the income of those above him/her in the distribution, the greater is his/her complaint. Temkin is not clear whether this complaint increases proportionately with the increase of this gap or not. In this context Kolm (references as above) introduced the term 'returns in proximity' and assumed, if inequality depends only on the size of the income gap $g_{ij} = |x_i - x_j|$, the size of inequality measure is $I = F\{g_{ij}\}$. For 'decreasing returns in proximity' the function F is S-convex and for 'increasing returns in proximity' the function F is S-concave. Clearly for decreasing returns in proximity, inequality will decrease for a rich-to-poor transfer and inequality will increase in the case of increasing returns in proximity for such a transfer.

> In the three person society with income distribution $(4, 4, 1)$, a progressive transfer of 1 from the second individual to the third increases inequality, since the new distribution $(4, 3, 2)$ contains no equal pair while the initial one contains one such equality. For instance, the measure of inequality that could be the number of proportion of unequal pairs could decrease as a result of this transfer. With this proportion as measure, inequality decreases when identical populations are joined together. Increasing returns in proximity favour clusters as a cause of low inequality. Increasing returns in proximity is also implicitly quite common in sociological conceptions that focus on groups with certain homogeneity, rather than on individuals.[10]
>
> (Kolm 1999, p. 26)

For the purpose of this study, a rich-to-poor transfer (a 'progressive transfer') of income makes a society more equitable, and we consider this as a decrease in inequality. An infinitesimal transfer from person j to person i can be represented as:

$$dI(x) = \frac{\partial I(x)}{\partial x_j} dx_j + \frac{\partial I(x)}{\partial x_i} dx_i = dx \left[\frac{\partial I(x)}{\partial x_j} - \frac{\partial I(x)}{\partial x_i} \right] < 0 \qquad (2.5)$$

where $dx = dx_j = -dx_i$ (by construction).

Therefore the Pigou–Dalton condition means that the inequality measure is sensitive to transfer. For a more restrictive condition mere sensitivity of transfer is not enough, and it is sometimes thought that a transfer of the same magnitude should be given different weights at different positions on the income scale. Specifically, a transfer from a poorer to a richer person deserves more weight at the lower end of the income scale than at the upper one. This is because the loser at the lower end is poorer than the loser at the upper end, though both losers are poorer relative to their respective gainers. Inequality measures satisfying this condition are called 'transfer sensitive'. Hence for a transfer sensitive inequality measure for a rich to poor transfer, $dI(x)$ is more negative the lower the recipient is on the income ladder.

Population replication

This property states that if the proportion of the population receiving each income configuration is fixed, a change in the population size has no effect on the measurement of the level of inequality.[11] To give an example when considering an income distribution as $\{1, 2, 3, 4, 5\}$, if at each income level the population is tripled, the income configuration becomes $\{1, 1, 1, 2, 2, 2, 3, 3, 3, 4, 4, 4, 5, 5, 5\}$.

The desirability of this property is often questionable. It is not persuasive to imagine that a society having two persons with incomes $0 and $1 million is equally unequal with a society of ten people, five of them having $0 each and the rest having $1 million each. Kolm (1996, 1999) considered a population of n individuals with different incomes replicated m times. Thus initially there are $n(n-1)/2$ pairs of individuals who are comparing their incomes with others. After replication the number of comparing pairs will become $mn(mn-1)/2$ where $m(m-1)/2$ are equal pairs. Thus total number of equal pairs would be $mn(m-1)/2$. Kolm defines an equality index given by the proportion of pairs of equal and unequal income,[12] i.e.,

$$e = \frac{mn(m-1)/2}{mn(mn-1)/2} = \frac{m-1}{mn-1}. \tag{2.6}$$

The inequality index can be given as $i = 1 - e = m(n-1)/(mn-1)$. Clearly, the index depends on m and thus for the inequality index the condition of population homogeneity is violated.

Income replication (also called 'homogeneous of degree zero to all incomes')

It is understood that the inequality ranking reveals a preference about distribution. But what is the meaning of distribution? Here, it means the interpersonal relativities within an income configuration. Let everybody's income in a given distribution be multiplied by some positive term k (say $k = 2$, that is, everybody's income is doubled). There will now be a different income configuration, yet the interpersonal relativities have not changed. In Atkinson's (1980) words a 'shift' has taken place in the income distribution, keeping the 'shape' unchanged. It is the shapes of alternative income configurations that the inequality indices are meant to rank in terms of preferences.[13]

Sen (1973a, p. 36) enquires: 'is this a property we want? Can it be asserted that our judgement of the extent of inequality will not vary according to whether the people involved are generally poor or generally rich?'. He then answers:

> One can argue that for low income levels the inequality measures should take much sharper note of the relative variation. On the other hand, I have heard it argued that inequality is a "luxury" that only a rich economy can "afford", and while I cannot pretend to understand fully this point of view, I am impressed by the number of people who seem prepared to advocate such a position. Though the considerations run in opposite directions then in itself is no justification of making the inequality measure *independent* of the level of mean income.
>
> (ibid., p. 70–1)

Here the considered judgement is given by:

$$I(\lambda x) = I(x), \quad \lambda > 0 \tag{2.7}$$

> In May 1968 in France, radical students triggered a student upheaval which induced a workers' general strike. All these were ended by the Grenelle agreements which decreed a 13% increase in all payrolls. Thus labourers earning 80 pounds a month received 10 pounds more, whereas executives who already earned 800 pounds a month received 100 pounds more. The Radicals felt bitter and cheated; in their view, this widely increased income inequality.
>
> (Kolm 1976a, p. 419)

Dalton (1920, 1925) also felt that a proportionate increase in incomes increases inequality. However, Taussig (1939) pointed out that a proportionate change in incomes has no effect on income inequality. This has been termed 'rightist' by Kolm (1976a, b). An alternative judgement, termed 'leftist' by Kolm, says that for an equal amount increase in incomes, inequality measures remain unchanged: $I(x + \beta e) = I(x)$ for all β, a scalar, such that $x + \beta e \geq 0$, where e is a vector of 1s with N entries. It is also called an 'absolute' measure (as opposed to the previous one which is called a 'relative' measure). However, Dalton (1920, 1925) and Cannan (1930) felt that an equal addition to everybody's income decreases inequality.[14]

Which measure is better on moral grounds is difficult to judge. However, the relative measure of inequality has some practical advantages. This is 'immune' to change in units of income and 'immune to inflation' (hence this measure is called 'scale invariant'). Thus if the income vector is presented in dollars instead of cents, the inequality will not change for relative measure; on the contrary, the absolute measure might show some difference. This is obviously objectionable.

The relative merits of the traditional measures of income inequality are generally discussed from a statistical point of view and these are quite relevant if used for positive purposes. However, efforts have been made to evaluate these measures in terms of broad and general principles. We sketched above some competing views regarding the properties of inequality measures. It is also worthwhile to indicate that by 'a subjective approach' Schokkaert and Overlaet (1989), Amiel and Cowell (1992) and Harrison and Seidl (1994), through their questionnaire method, studied the mental structure and general psychology of people relative to the normative principles of the inequality measures. Their results, in several cases, showed that people responded in different ways from the accepted principles. Does that mean the principles are wrong? Inquiries into these studies

> reveal not properties of inequality but only sentiments, impressions, feelings, or guesses about them or about justice. Assuming that inequality has a property because a sufficient portion of people express this view would largely be like solving a mathematical problem by voting... Also, people commonly give divergent answers because they understand the word inequality differently: some think of injustice and the others of pure logic or of social structure, among the former some think of non-equality and the others emphasise welfare, some see the incomes considered as extra incomes and the others as the examples of global ones, some think of inequality among a subset of incomes and the others take a more global view, some see a more even spread as more equality while others emphasise strict equality, and so on. The perceptional framework also commonly influences the judgement.
>
> (Kolm 1999, p. 30)

Construction of an inequality index

The main task in constructing a measure of inequality is to assign a single number to the distribution $x_1, x_2, \ldots, x_N$ that describes the inequality of the distribution and permits alternative distributions to be ranked. For these measures a normalization is also adapted to bind it within the closed interval [0, 1]; with 0 representing complete equality, and 1 the maximum inequality. In practice there are several measures of inequality in the literature. We will discuss only couple of them here.

The generalized weighted difference indicator gives a general class of inequality measures using absolute difference between all possible pairs of values of income. It can be defined as:

$$\left\{ \sum_i \sum_j |x_i - x_j|^g w(x_i, x_j) \frac{1}{N^2} \right\}^{\frac{1}{g}}, \tag{2.8}$$

where $w(\cdot)$ is the weight function associated with the pair of incomes compared.[15] Quite a number of special cases can be generated from equation (2.8) for different values of g and w. For $g = 1$ and $w(x_i, x_j) = 1$ for all x_i and x_j generates Gini's mean difference Δ. For the same weight and $g = 2$ we will have $\sqrt{(2V)}$ where V is the variance.[16] If specific weights are judged appropriate, they can be introduced by the decision-maker through the function $w(.)$. For instance, the weights can be specified in such a way that the smaller the sum of the incomes compared, the greater the weight. That is:

$$w(x_i, x_j) = \frac{1}{x_i + x_j} \quad \text{for all } i \text{ and } j. \tag{2.9}$$

An inequality index of this kind is, as suggested by Gastwirth (1974), sensitive to the lower part of the distribution. Again the decision-maker can use a weight which is greater the higher the rank orders of the incomes compared differ. One such weight can be:

$$w(x_i, x_j) = |i - j| \quad \text{for all } i \text{ and } j. \tag{2.10}$$

Here in the policy, we employ our value judgement in such a way that differences between extreme incomes receive heavier weights than incomes where rank orders are not very different.

The special measure derived from Δ, the Gini coefficient, has a long tradition in the study of income distribution. This is a normalized form of relative mean difference can be given by $\Delta/2\bar{x}$. The Gini index can be written formally as:

$$G = \frac{1}{2N^2\bar{x}} \sum_{i=1}^{N} \sum_{j=1}^{N} |x_i - x_j| \tag{2.11}$$

(Sen, 1973a, p. 33) interprets this formula: 'In any pair-wise comparison the man with the lower income can be thought to be suffering from some depression on finding his income to be lower. Let this depression be proportional to the difference of income. The sum total of such depressions in all possible pair-wise comparisons takes us to the Gini coefficient.'[17]

The visual nicety of the Gini coefficient is quite clear from its relationship with the Lorenz curve (see Figure 2.2):[18]

$$\text{Gini coefficient} = \frac{\text{Area between Lorenz curve and diagonal}^{19}}{\text{Total area under diagonal}} \tag{2.12}$$

For this reason the Gini coefficient is one of the most widely used inequality indices. From the relationship between the Gini coefficient and the Lorenz curve it follows that the Gini coefficient can be expressed as a measure of individual discontent relative to the absolute egalitarian state where everyone's income is the same (equal to the average income). In fact, Sen (1974, 1976, 1981) was the first to associate inequality measures with the concept of relative deprivation expressing the Gini coefficient as:

$$G = A(\bar{x}, N) \sum_{j=1}^{N} (N + 1 - j)(\bar{x} - x_j) \tag{2.13}$$

where $A(\cdots)$ is the normalization factor.

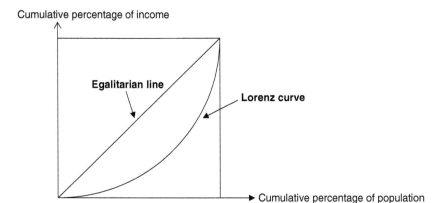

Figure 2.2 Lorenz curve.

Utilizing the concept of ranks of individuals in the income distribution as the weights Fei and Ranis (1974) defines Gini coefficient as:

$$G = A(\bar{x}, N) \sum_{j=1}^{N} (N + 1 - j)(\bar{x} - x_j), \tag{2.14}$$

when incomes are arranged in ascending order. Using this definition it is easy to demonstrate that:

$$G = \frac{2}{N\bar{x}} Cov(i, x_i) \tag{2.15}$$

where $Cov(i, x_i)$ is the covariance of income with its rank, is defined as:

$$Cov(i, x_i) = \frac{1}{N} \sum_{i=1}^{N} (i - \bar{i})(x_i - \bar{x}) \text{ given } \bar{i} = \frac{1}{N} \sum_{i} i = \frac{N+1}{2}. \tag{2.16}$$

Yitzhaki (1979, 1982) and Hey and Lambert (1980) interpreted the Gini coefficient in terms of relative deprivation.[20] They interpreted jth individual's relative deprivation with respect to the ith person as:

$$D_{ji} = \begin{cases} x_i - x_j & \text{for } x_j < x_i \\ 0 & \text{otherwise.} \end{cases} \tag{2.17}$$

Then the Gini coefficient can be obtained by summing up all relative deprivation in the society by $\sum_i \sum_j D_{ij}$ and then by normalizing.[21]

The Gini coefficient is a symmetric and a relative measure of inequality.[22] It can be proved that:

$$\frac{\partial G}{\partial x_{j+h}} - \frac{\partial G}{\partial x_j} = \frac{2h}{N^2 \bar{x}}.$$

(2.18)

Thus it is strictly an S-convex function of income[23] and therefore satisfies the Pigou–Dalton condition of transfer. It can be proved that if the income of any one below median level is raised/reduced without altering the ranking, the Gini coefficient will fall or rise.[24] From equation (2.18) it is clear that for a transfer of income, the number of people in between where the transfer performed affects the Gini coefficient. Here, regarding the property of the Gini coefficient, it is only to mention that for positively skewed uni-modal income distribution (which is the case for most of the income distributions in reality) for a transfer of income from rich to poor, the Gini coefficient is more responsive around the mode of the distribution.[25] In other words, a given amount of progressive transfer is more inequality reducing near the mode of the distribution than at the tails. Some may find this a disadvantage in the use of the Gini coefficient. However, from the normative point of an individual's relative deprivation, the Gini coefficient satisfies most of the accepted ethical codes.[26] For that reason, in this book, the empirical application will mostly use the Gini coefficient as the measure of income inequality.

Decomposition of inequality indices

Investigation of the change in income distribution through time is one interesting issue for consideration. For this reason the decomposition of inequality indices by factor components and by population subgroups is important in order to identify the characteristics of the sources of income and of population.

Decomposition by factor components

In the literature, the decomposition of an inequality index by factor components receives importance because it allows identification of the components through which specific economic policies can be developed so that problems in the overall distribution can be rectified. The problem of decomposing total inequality into the contribution of each of the factor components consists in finding a way of adding the contributions of each source of income. Let us denote x_g as the income from the source g such that:

$$x = \sum_g x_g$$

(2.19)

Then the income inequality index can be decomposed as:

$$I(x) = \sum_g w_g I_g$$

(2.20)

where I_g is the inequality due to the factor g of the total income and w_g is the weight can be written as:

$$w_g = \frac{\bar{x}_g}{\bar{x}}. \tag{2.21}$$

Fei *et al.* (1978), Pyatt *et al.* (1980), Kakwani (1980, 1995), Shorrocks (1982, 1983a), Lerman and Yitzhaki (1985), Silber (1989, 1993) and several others have used this principle to decompose the Gini coefficient into factor components. This process of decomposition takes a very simple functional representation that allows identifying the influence of each w_g and I_g term separately, which is a necessary requirement to determine the relationship between policy prescription and income distribution. Before looking at details of this process it is important to consider the criticisms of Shorrocks (1982) to this kind of decomposition. According to Shorrocks, different and even opposite conclusions about the value of $w_g I_g$ and the proportional contribution of factor g to total inequality (i.e., $w_g I_g / I(x)$) may be achieved, depending on the specific inequality measures. Shorrocks (1983a) has empirically shown that a wide range of different values for those two said components could be obtained for the Gini coefficient and other inequality measures (not discussed here). For this reason Shorrocks (1982) imposed several constraints on the decomposition, by which he derived a rule as:

$$\frac{w_g I_g}{I} = \frac{Cov(x_g, x)}{V(x)} \tag{2.22}$$

which means that the proportional contribution of the factor g to total inequality can be obtained through the ratio of the covariance between factor income and total income, and the variance of total income $V(x)$. Layard and Zabalza (1979), Fry (1984), Cancian *et al.* (1993), Jenkins (1995) among others have followed this principle in order to obtain consistent factor contributions using squared coefficient of variation.[27] Shorrocks (1988) attempts to interpret the proportional contribution of a specific factor to total inequality in four different ways: (i) as the inequality due to the specific source alone; (ii) as the reduction of inequality that would result if the specific income source was eliminated; (iii) as the inequality that would be observed if the specific factor was the only source of income differences and all the other incomes were allocated evenly; and (iv) as the reduction in inequality that would follow from eliminating the differences in the specific source incomes.

The natural disaggregation of the Gini coefficient into factor components, due to Rao (1969) can be given by:

$$G = \sum_g S_g C_g \tag{2.23}$$

where S_g is the income share of the factor g which can be written as:

$$S_g = \frac{\bar{x}_g}{\bar{x}} \quad \text{(which is the same as } w_g \text{ in (2.20)),} \tag{2.24}$$

and C_g is called the concentration coefficient of the factor g and can be defined as:

$$C_g = \frac{2}{N\bar{x}_g} Cov(x_g, F(x)), \tag{2.25}$$

where $F(x)$ represents the rank of income x. Thus it is similar to the Gini coefficient except that individuals are ranked according to x not according to x_g.[28] The value of this coefficient lies between $(-1, 1)$, and most importantly it satisfies the Pigou–Dalton condition of transfer.[29] The deviation of the Gini coefficient from the concentration coefficient (i.e., $C_g - G$) indicates the direction of inequality augmenting or reducing the effect of the component g. Clearly if a certain component of income accrues more to poor people (for example, government cash transfer payments) the concentration coefficient would be negative. On the other hand, if the component of income accrues more to rich people (say, investment income) the concentration coefficient would be positive and more than the value of the Gini coefficient.

In decomposing the Gini coefficient, the empirical research[30] attempts to conclude that $S_g C_g / G$ is the contribution of the gth source of income in total inequality. However, Podder (1993b) and Mukhopadhaya (2013) have demonstrated that such an interpretation of Gini decomposition would be misleading. As an example, let us consider a component which is constant for all households (e.g., the fixed money given to everyone in a society in several countries after the recent financial crisis). The concentration coefficient of the component is then zero. This would be interpreted to mean that the contribution of the component to overall inequality (defined by $S_g C_g / G$) is zero. However, this component, when added to total income, would reduce the total Gini. How could the contribution of the component be zero? Podder (1993b), Podder and Mukhopadhaya (2001) and Mukhopadhaya (2013) have shown that the appropriate interpretation of the contribution should be based on the transformation of the equation to:

$$\sum_{g=1}^{k} S_g (C_g - G) = 0 \tag{2.26}$$

Some authors (e.g., Lerman and Yitzhaki, 1985) represent the Gini decomposition in a more attractive way, as follows:

$$G = \sum_g S_g R_g G_g \tag{2.27}$$

where G_g is the Gini coefficient of the factor component g, which can be written as

$$G_g = \frac{2}{N\bar{x}_g}Cov(x_g, F(x_g)),$$ (2.28)

and

$$R_g = \frac{Cov(x_g, F(x_g))}{Cov(x_g, F(x))}$$ (2.29)

because of the obvious relationship between C_g and G_g.[31]

It has been demonstrated that the Gini coefficient of the total household/personal income can be expressed as the weighted average of the concentration coefficients of each factor component, the weights being proportional to the mean of each factor income. This relationship provides the quantitative framework to analyse the contribution of each of the components of inequality to the total household/personal income.

Decomposition by subgroups of population

Decomposition of the inequality index by subgroups of population, e.g., by geographical location or by ethnic background or by employment status etc., is most widely used to enumerate the respective inequality components. For policy purposes an additively decomposable inequality measure has some practical convenience. Nevertheless, another interesting aspect to observe is whether the inequality measure is changing in the same direction of the inequality of one of its subgroups, *ceteris paribus*, due to some redistribution in that subgroup. The following section will discuss subgroup decomposition considering the definitions of *additivity* and *subgroup consistency*.

Additive decomposable inequality measures

Let the population be divided into subgroups $1, \ldots, g, \ldots, k$ with the population in every group being n_g. An inequality measure is said to be additive decomposable if the total inequality can be found by a weighted sum of the inequality within the subgroups and between the subgroups. Defining x_g as the income vector of subgroup g, $\bar{x}_g$ the mean income of group g and e_g the vector of 1s with n_g entries, decomposability will be captured by the following equation:

$$I(x_1, x_2, \ldots, x_g, N) = \sum_{g=1}^{k} w_g^k I(x_g, n_g) + I(\bar{x}_1 e_1, \ldots, \bar{x}_g e_g, N).$$ (2.30)

With this definition of additive decomposability, the weights are the ratio of the total income of subgroup g to total income in the population. Foster (1983) proved that any relative measure of inequality that is symmetric and satisfies the

Pigou–Dalton condition of transfer is additively decomposable if it is a positive multiple of the Theil's entropy index. Though the Theil index has little economic motivation, it receives very strong support among economists because of its decomposability property.[32]

Is Gini additively decomposable?

The interpretations of the between-group and within-group components of inequality are worthy of discussion. The between-group component can be seen as the value of the inequality index when all within-group income differences are artificially suppressed. Thus it can be said that between-group inequality is the value of the inequality measure for imaginary income distribution, where within-group inequality is smoothed out by assigning each person within a group the mean income of the group. Additionally the within-group component of inequality is a weighted average of inequality for each subgroup only (weights do not necessarily sum to unity).[33]

Rao (1969) was the first to attempt to decompose the Gini coefficient into subgroups of population. Bhattacharya and Mahalanobis (1967) were the first to identify a non-negative 'residual' term over and above the presence of the weighted average of the between-group and within-group Gini coefficient. Mehran (1975) proposed the decomposition of the Gini coefficient as follows:[34]

$$G = \sum_{g=1}^{K} \frac{n_g}{N} \frac{n_g \bar{x}_g}{N \bar{x}} G_g + \sum_{g=1}^{K} \sum_{h=1, g \neq h}^{K} \frac{n_g}{N} \frac{n_g \mu_g}{N \bar{x}} G_{g,h} \tag{2.31}$$

where G_g is the Gini coefficient of group g and $G_{g,h}$ is the ratio of Gini coefficients obtained by taking all pairs of incomes, one in group g and the one in group h. The first term in the right hand side is the weighted within-group inequality and the second the across-group inequality. This can be divided into the between-group term and a residual, R,

$$\frac{1}{\bar{x}} \sum_{g=1}^{K} \sum_{h=1}^{K} \frac{n_g}{N} \frac{n_h}{N} |\bar{x}_g - \bar{x}_h| + R. \tag{2.32}$$

Mehran described R as the 'interaction term'. Pyatt (1976), by his game theoretical approach to decompose the Gini coefficient, separates out three components: within-group Gini coefficient (G_W), Gini coefficient between-group means (G_B), and a term related to 'overlapping' among groups. Thus the Gini coefficient can be expressed as:

$$G = G_W + G_B + R. \tag{2.33}$$

If there is no overlapping income, the residual term vanishes.[35] Yet problems arise in interpreting the residual term. Bhattacharya and Mahalanobis (1967) could not provide any explanation. Pyatt (1976) defines it as an 'expected gain' to some income recipients in a costless hypothetical redistribution. Unlike Mehran, Pyatt allocates R to the within-group Gini component.[36] For Mookherjee and Shorrocks (1982, p. 889) it is 'an awkward interaction effect...impossible to interpret with any precision, except to say that it is the residual necessary to maintain the identity'. Kakwani (1984a, b, c) understood (in the light of Sen's (1973a) interpretation of the Gini coefficient) the overlapping term as the average relative deprivation when all groups have the same mean, and individuals compare their income to all other groups.[37] Lerman and Yitzhaki (1985) argued that the residual term captures 'stratification' and they developed a coefficient similar to the Gini based on the overlapping factors. Lambert and Aronson (1993) derived the Gini decomposition in terms of simple Lorenz and associated concentration curves showing a clear linkage between the residual term and re-ranking. Silber (1989) also found a connection between re-ranking and the overlapping term. Recently Formby *et al.* (1997) made an attempt to interpret the overlapping term as the representation of the degree of mobility of the society. For the disaggregation of the black and white American incomes, the overlapping term has increased over the last few decades, and thus they concluded that the income mobility of the two classes has increased substantially. Chatterjee and Podder (2007) have further demonstrated that normalization of the overlapping term makes it necessary to check the income mobility of various population groups. They derived the normalization factor as:

$$R_c = \left(1 - \sum_{g=1}^{k} \left(\frac{n_g}{N}\right)^2\right) G. \tag{2.34}$$

In the following analysis, a normalized overlapping term is used as

$$R_n = \frac{R}{R_c}. \tag{2.35}$$

Subgroup consistency

An inequality measure is said to be subgroup consistent if any change in inequality of one of the subgroups leaving inequalities in other subgroups constant will change the total inequality of the population in the same direction. Assume an income vector x is divided into two population subgroups z and y. Also assume, due to some redistribution (that is, there will be no change in the number of people in the group as well as no change in the average income) that an increase happens in the inequality in the subgroup z. That is to say symbolically,

$$I(z') > I(z) \tag{2.36}$$

where z' is the new distribution of z then the inequality index $I(x)$ is subgroup consistent if:

$$I(x'\,|\,z',y) > I(x\,|\,z,y). \tag{2.37}$$

Is Gini subgroup consistent in decomposition?

Cowell (1995) showed that the Gini coefficient does not follow the property of subgroup consistency. For instance, if $x = \{1,6,6,7,8,12\}$, $z = \{1,6,12\}$, $y = \{6,7,8\}$ and $z' = \{3,3,13\}$, $y' = \{6,6,9\}$ thus $x' = \{3,3,6,6,9,13\}$ it is seen that:

$$G_x(=0.275) > G_{x'}(=0.267) \text{ though}$$
$$G_z(=0.351) < G_{z'}(=0.386) \text{ and}$$
$$G_y(=0.064) < G_{y'}(=0.095). \tag{2.38}$$

The reason for this kind of inconsistency can easily be determined because of the overlapping subgroup income. Clearly, by defining in the above numerical example $z = \{1,6,6\}$ and $y = \{7,8,12\}$ and then performing some kind of redistribution in the subgroups, the overall Gini coefficient will show subgroup consistency.[38, 39]

It has already been mentioned that the residual term originates because of the presence of overlapping income distribution. Again it has been found that the overlapping income creates a problem in the subgroup consistency.[40]

The Gini coefficient and the Lorenz curve

It has already been discussed that the Gini coefficient also has its appeal because of the fact that it can be shown to be related to the Lorenz curve. Let us define the Lorenz curve for an income distribution specified as an income density function $f(x)$ first. Then a density function $f(x)$ has the following properties:

$$
\begin{aligned}
&x_i \geq 0, \\
&f(x_i) \geq 0 \quad \text{and,} \\
&\sum_{i=1}^{N} f(x_i) = 1
\end{aligned}
\tag{2.39}
$$

(income is considered as discrete random variable).

Assume

$$F(t) = \sum_{i=1}^{t} \frac{i}{N} \tag{2.40}$$

to be the cumulative population share corresponding to the income level t, that is, $F(t)$ is the proportion of population that receives income less than or equal to t.

Also assume

$$H(t) = \frac{\sum_{i=1}^{t} x_i}{\sum_{i=1}^{N} x_i} \qquad (2.41)$$

to be the cumulative income share corresponding to the income level t. The Lorenz curve defines an implicit relation between F and H in terms of the parameter t. The graph corresponding to $F(t)$ and $H(t)$ is said to be the Lorenz curve of the income distribution (see Figure 2.2). The curve actually plots $H(t)$ in the horizontal axis and $F(t)$ in the vertical axis according to increasing x. Denoting $H(t)$ by x_i and $F(t)$ by n_i, we have

$$x_i = H(x) = H(F^{-1}(n_i)) = \varphi(n_i). \qquad (2.42)$$

Alternatively,

$$x_i = H(x) = \frac{1}{\bar{x}} \int_0^{n_i} F^{-1} dF = \int_0^{n_i} F_n^{-1} dF \qquad (2.43)$$

is the mathematical representation of the Lorenz curve.

The Lorenz curve is an attractive presentation of income distribution. In the case of complete equality the curve will attain $x_i = n_i$, and for complete inequality $x_i = 0$ for $n_i \neq 1$ and $x_i = 1$ for $n_i = 1$. The convexity of the curve is an indicator of the deviation of actual income distribution from one of complete equality. Thus from the graphical representation of the Lorenz curve, a measure of inequality can be derived as a ratio of the area between the curves $x_i = n_i$ and $x_i = \varphi(n_i)$ to the area under the curve $x_i = n_i$. The later area is obviously half as it is half of a square having length and width both as one. It can be proved that the Gini coefficient is twice the above-mentioned measure of inequality. Thus it can be said that if the Lorenz curve $x_i = \varphi(n_i)$ is specified the Gini coefficient is:

$$G = 1 - 2 \int_0^1 \varphi(n_i) \, dn_i. \qquad (2.44)$$

For the case of discrete income distribution the Gini coefficient can be calculated by taking the area of the polygon with vertices $(0,0)$, $(F(t_1), G(t_1)), \ldots, (F(t_k), H(t_k))$. Thus the total area below the Lorenz curve can be expressed as:

$$\frac{1}{2} \sum_{i=1}^{N} (F_i - F_{i-1})(H_i + H_{i-1}). \qquad (2.45)$$

From this, the definition of the Gini coefficient can be written as:

$$G = 1 - \sum_{i=1}^{N} (F_i - F_{i-1})(H_i + H_{i-1}), \tag{2.46}$$

with some manipulation this formula turns out to be:

$$G = \sum_{i=1}^{N} (F_{i-1} H_i - F_i H_{i-1}). \tag{2.47}$$

For calculating the Gini coefficient for discrete income distribution, this formula will be used in empirical calculations. Also for the calculation of the concentration coefficient of component g the same procedure may be used.[41]

For many purposes the Lorenz curve is a useful device for comparison of various income distributions. Comparisons between two Lorenz curves would indicate unequivocally which distribution is more equal (the distribution for which the Lorenz curve is more nearer to the egalitarian line is the more equal). In mathematical terms dominance will be indicated. This will be discussed in further detail in Chapter 7.

The entropy measure of inequality

The concept of entropy has been widely applied for measuring inequality because of its decomposability property. In a closed physical system, the elements tend towards an arrangement of maximum disorder, or maximum entropy. In the context of information theory, entropy is interpreted as representing expected information, for example, the degree of uncertainty about the realization of events of variate values in the information system. To introduce the entropy concept in the latter sense, the random variable x needs to be considered, which takes values $\{x_1, x_2, \ldots, x_N\}$ with probabilities $\{p_1, p_2, \ldots, p_N\}$ given $p_i \geq 0$ for all i, and $\Sigma p_i = 1$. As p_i decreases, the information involved in knowing that x takes values x_i becomes more important, and this fact has to be accounted for in the definition of an information function. A measure of the expected amount of information in a value of a random variable with discrete probability density:

$$p' = [p_1, \ldots, p_N] \tag{2.48}$$

can be given by Renyi's α order entropy:

$$I_\alpha(p) = \frac{1}{1-\alpha} \log \left(\sum_{i=1}^{N} p_i^\alpha \right), \quad \alpha > 0, \, \alpha \neq 1$$

$$= \lim_{\alpha \to 1} I_\alpha(p) = \sum_{i=1}^{N} p_i \log p_i^{-1}, \quad \alpha = 1. \tag{2.49}$$

The information measure in the above equation can be derived if some axiomatic conditions on information measures $I_\alpha(p)$ are stated; where p is an element from the set of all finite discrete probability density set. For an application in the context of inequality analysis, $I_\alpha(p)$ with $\alpha = 1$ and $\alpha = 2$ has been used. The minimum value of $I_\alpha(p)$ equals zero, if $p_i = 1$ and $p_j = 0$ for all $i \neq j$, and its maximum equals $\log N$, if $p_i = 1/N$. In income distribution terms it can be interpreted as (if one's income share is unity and all other's are zero), $-I_\alpha(p)$ approaches minimum value – zero. As everybody's income becomes equal (i.e., if income share tends to population share) $I_\alpha(p)$ attends maximum value – $\log N$. These properties suggest that $I_\alpha(p)$ can be used to define inequality measures.

To define an inequality measure, $-I_\alpha(p)$ and its associated normalized equivalent $-I_\alpha(p)/\log N$ can be used. Choices of α equal to 1 or 2 yield different inequality measures. The index $-I_1(p)$ written as $\log \prod_{i=1}^{N} p_i^{p_i}$ with the term after the logarithm is known as the exponential index. Alternatively, the index $-I_2(p) = \log \sum_{i=1}^{N} p_i^2 = \log H$ with $H = \sum_{i=1}^{N} p_i^2$ is known as the *Herfindahl index* and restricted to the interval $[1/N, 1]$.

In the context of income inequality with all N households having different incomes, the relative share of income (say, y_i) can be used for p_is in the above definition of H, and can be expressed as:

$$H = \sum_{i=1}^{N} y_i^2 = \frac{1}{N^2 \bar{x}^2} \sum_{i=1}^{N} x_i^2 = \frac{1}{N^2 \bar{x}^2}(V + \bar{x}^2) = \frac{CV^2 + 1}{N} \qquad (2.50)$$

This demonstrates that the Herfindahl index does not provide us any additional information on inequality as it can be derived from the coefficient of variation.

A somewhat different approach based on (2.49) can be obtained by taking deviations from the maximum value $\log N$, which gives $\log N - I_\alpha(p)$.

By first considering the case for $\alpha = 1$, and $p_i = y_i$:

$$\log N - I_\alpha(p) = \log N + \sum_i y_i \log y_i = \sum_i y_i \log N y_i = \log \left[\prod_i \left(\frac{x_i}{\bar{x}} \right)^{x_i} \right]^{\frac{1}{N\bar{x}}}. \qquad (2.51)$$

This is the inequality measure proposed by Theil (1967). It gives weight to income share more heavily if they are extremely small or large, and is most sensitive to the changes at the low or high income levels.

It is convenient to express the measure as:

$$T_1 = \sum_{i=1}^{K} y_i \log N \frac{x_i}{N_i N\bar{x}} = \sum_{i=1}^{K} y_i \log \frac{y_i}{f_i}. \qquad (2.52)$$

Here, it is assumed that income data is grouped into K classes and there is no inequality within class. The population share in each class is f_i. If the income data is not grouped, f_i means $1/N$ (and $N_i = 1$). According to Theil (1967, p. 95) T_1 is 'the expected information of a message which transforms population share into income share'. For perfect equality each person's income share and population share are equal, and $T_1 = 0$. For perfect inequality, a single person will receive the whole income and others will receive no income. In this case $T_1 = \log N$ and as $x \log x \to 0$ for $x \to 0$ all terms with zero income share will tend to zero.

The alternative measure proposed by Theil is:

$$T_2 = \sum_i f_i \log \frac{f_i}{y_i}. \tag{2.53}$$

T_2 is 'the expected information content of the indirect message which transforms the income shares as prior probabilities into the population shares as posterior probabilities' (Theil, 1967, p. 125). It is not difficult to show that:

$$T_2 = \log_e \frac{\bar{x}}{x_m}, \tag{2.54}$$

where x_m is the geometric mean. Clearly T_2 is not defined for zero income but T_1 is. Both T_1 and T_2 are arithmetic means of strictly convex functions of income. These measures also satisfy Pigou–Dalton's condition of transfer. Despite its wide use, it is difficult to find any normative aspect hidden in this measure. This measure is also the logarithm of a specific geometric mean and can be written as a weighted sum of tangent of the Lorenz curve:

$$\sum_i \frac{y_i}{f_i} \left(f_i \log \frac{y_i}{f_i} \right) \tag{2.55}$$

with $f_i (\log y_i)/f_i$ as weights. The weight is quite complicated and depends both on income share and population share. The weights applied to the relative income shares are heaviest for the classes where y_i/f_i is small or great. Renyi's second order entropy inequality measure has less complicated weights than Theil's measure, which can be defined as:

$$R = \log N - I_2(p) = \log \sum_i \frac{y_i^2}{f_i}. \tag{2.56}$$

A special appeal in measures related to the entropy concept is that these can be easily decomposed. Let us demonstrate how $I_1(p)$ can be decomposed. With $p_i = y_i$, if $y_g = \sum_{i \in subgroup_g} y_i$ the following can be derived:

$$I_1(y) = -\sum_i y_i \log y_i = -\sum_{g=1}^{G}\left[\sum_i y_i \log y_i\right] = \sum_g \sum_i y_i \log \frac{1}{y_i}$$

$$= \sum_g \sum_i y_i \left(\log \frac{y_g}{y_i} + \log y_i\right) = \sum_g y_g \left[\sum_i \frac{y_i}{y_g}\left\{\log y_g \frac{1}{y_i} + \log \frac{1}{y_g}\right\}\right]$$

$$= \sum_g y_g \log \frac{1}{y_g} + \sum_g y_g \sum_i \frac{y_i}{y_g} \log \frac{y_g}{y_i}$$

$$= I_{1,B} + \sum_g y_g I_{1,g} \tag{2.57}$$

where $I_{1,g}$ is the within-group entropy, and the second term in the right hand side of the above equation is a weighted average of within-group entropies, and the first term in the right hand side is the between-group entropies. By considering the data set grouped into G subgroups Theil's entropy measure can be expressed as:

$$T_1 = \sum_{g=1}^{G} y_g T_{1,g} + \sum_{g=1}^{G} y_g \log \frac{y_g}{N_g/N} \quad \text{with } T_{1,g} = y_g \log \frac{y_g}{f_g}. \tag{2.58}$$

The first term in the right hand side is the weighted within-group inequality, the second term is the between-group inequality. Clearly if $y_g = \frac{N_g}{N}$, for all g, the second term of the right hand side vanishes meaning that average income of all groups is equal.

Equation (2.54) above represents the second measure of Theil. Since:

$$\log x_m = \sum_g \frac{N_g}{N} \log x_{m,g} \tag{2.59}$$

this second measure, T_2, can be expressed as:

$$T_2 = \sum_{g=1}^{G} \frac{N_g}{N} T_{2,g} + \sum_{g=1}^{G} \frac{N_g}{N} \log \frac{\bar{x}}{\bar{x}_g}$$

$$= T_{2(W)} + T_{2(B)} \tag{2.60}$$

where the first term in the right hand side is the weighted average of the within-group components, and the second term is the weighted average of the between-group components.

Empirical studies on income distribution

The World Income Inequality Database (WIID) (a data set developed from Deininger and Squire (1996) at the World Bank) provides statistical information on income/expenditure inequalities across time and space. It presents data on changes in income inequality over the period 1950–2008 (for some countries it has gone even to the historical data set of the 1890s). Special focus is given for the 1970s to 2000s for 149 countries, which include developed, developing and transition countries. Mukhopadhaya (2004c) provides a review of the relative quality of data from various sources that are used for income distribution analysis. The relative position with respect to income distribution of the world can be observed from Table 2.1.

Various countries in Table 2.1 are classified in terms of their most recent available Gini. The lowest Gini values, of less than 0.3, are found in the region of the former communist bloc and the welfare states of western Europe. Latin America has always had high Gini, and Malaysia, the only East Asian economy in the group, is in the high Gini category as well. The high inequality in Latin American countries is explained by low growth, poor education, macro-economic volatility and political instability. New research shows that inequality in this region is decreasing. Bridsall *et al.* (2011) analysed the effect of political regime (populist, social democratic, right of centre) to the decline of inequality in Latin America and established that the change in the middle class in the region has had a prime effect on this change in trend.

Link between income distribution and growth

The relationship between economic growth and income inequality has been discussed widely in the literature, but with little consensus on the direction of the relationship. In essence, there exist three streams of thought and empirical findings. Using a diverse sample of developed and developing countries, some argue that a decrease in income inequality will tend to stimulate economic growth (see, for instance, Alesina and Rodrik, 1994; Aghion *et al.*, 1999), whereas others report a positive effect of overall income inequality on successive growth (see, for instance, Banerjee and Newman, 1993; Li and Zou, 1998; Forbes, 2000). There is also another belief, beyond this dichotomy, that postulates a non-monotonic relationship between economic growth and inequality. In a seminal paper Kuznets (1955) suggested that an inverted U-curve describes the relationship between income inequality and per capita income – during the early stages of development income inequality increases – while during the later stages it decreases.

Although the debate on the growth–inequality nexus is unlikely to be resolved any time soon, researchers seem to agree that the ultimate effect of income inequality on growth, as examined in the existing literature, depends conspicuously on the econometric methods employed, the period of time studied, and the sample data considered. Table 2.2 summarizes the recent literature in this respect. Barro (2000) employed a sample of 84 countries during the period between 1965 and 1995, and found no relationship between inequality and economic growth

Table 2.1 Scenario of world income inequality

Gini coefficient			
Less than 0.3	*0.3–less than 0.4*	*0.4–less than 0.45*	*0.45–0.5*	*More than 0.5*

Less than 0.3	0.3–less than 0.4	0.4–less than 0.45	0.45–0.5	More than 0.5
Austria, Australia, Belarus, Belgium, Cyprus, Czech Republic, Denmark, Finland, France, Germany, Hungary, Iceland, Luxembourg, Malta, the Netherlands, Norway, Slovakia, Sweden	Azerbaijan, Bangladesh, Belarus, Bulgaria, Canada, Croatia, Estonia, FYR Macedonia, Greece, Hungary, India, Indonesia, Ireland, Italy, Jamaica, Japan, Kazakhstan, Latvia, Lithuania, Moldova, New Zealand, Norway, Pakistan, Poland, Portugal, Romania, Serbia, Slovenia, South Korea, Spain, Sri Lanka, Taiwan, Tanzania, UK	Armenia, Bahamas, Kyrgyzstan, Romania, Russia Senegal, Singapore, Thailand, Tunisia, Ukraine, Russia	Argentina, China, Costa Rica, Dominican Republic, Hong Kong, Malaysia, Philippines, Turkey, Venezuela, USA	Brazil, Chile, Colombia, El Salvador, Georgia, Guatemala Honduras, Mexico, Panama, South Africa, Guatemala

Source: Computed from UNU-WIDER World Income Inequality Database, Version 2.0c, May 2008.

Table 2.2 Summary of recent literature on the relationship between inequality and growth

Authors (Year)	Sample	Methodology and model specification	Findings
Barro (2000)	84 countries, 1965–95	Three-stage least square estimator. Growth rate of real per capital GDP is the average of each of the three periods, 1965–75, 1975–85, and 1985–95. Determinants of growth include school attainment, fertility, government consumption over GDP, inflation rate, investment over GDP, growth rate of the terms of trade, rule-of-law index, democracy index.	There is no relationship between inequality and economic growth in the entire sample, but a negative relationship in the sample of poor countries, and a positive in the sample of rich countries. More specifically, growth tends to fall with greater inequality when per capita GDP is below around $2,000 (1985 US dollars), and to rise with inequality when GDP is above $2,000.
Forbes (2000)	45 countries (with observations for at least two consecutive 5-year periods), 1966–95	A traditional first GMM estimator to control for country-specific effects: growth, which is averaged over 5-year periods,[42] is a function of initial inequality, income, male and female human capital, market distortions, and country and period dummy variables. Country dummies are to control for time-invariant omitted-variable bias; period dummies are to control for global shocks.	In the medium and short term an increase in the level of inequality in the distribution of income in a country has a positive and significant relationship with its subsequent economic growth rates. That means a country may face a trade-off between reducing inequality and improving growth performance. Suggestion: future work should evaluate the channels through which inequality, growth, and any other variables are related, and include omitted variables (such as share of government spending on health care and education, quality of public education, levels of corruption).

Table 2.2 Continued

Authors (Year)	Sample	Methodology and model specification	Findings
Banerjee and Duflo (2003)	Cross-country data 1965, 1975, 1985, 1995	Non-parametric methods.	The growth rate is an inverted U-shaped function of net changes in inequality: changes in inequality in any direction are associated with lower growth rates. Moreover, in line with the adverse long-run impact of inequality proposed by the theories, they find a negative relationship between growth rates and lagged inequality.
Galbraith and Kum (2003)	150 countries, 1963–99	Introduce a measure of the inequality of manufacturing pay, based on UNIDO's Industrial Statistics. Model: inequality measure is a function of GDP per capita, and GDP per capita square, country-specific effects. Both variables are measured in log forms. Estimation technique: standard OLS with robust standard errors to pooled cross-section data.	Limitations of data sets cannot be overcome by the application of increasingly sophisticated techniques to the raw material. Thus, new information is required. There is a clear downward-sloping relationship between inequality and national income, supporting a core premise of the Kuznets hypothesis that inequality tends to decline with economic progress in the process of successful industrialization. However, the relationship may reverse for the richest countries.

Continued

Table 2.2 Continued

Authors (Year)	Sample	Methodology and model specification	Findings
Knowles (2005)	Cross-country data, 1960–90.	A Barro-style growth regression to test the robustness of consistent data.	When consistently measured data on gross income are included in a cross-country growth regression, there is no evidence of a significant correlation between inequality and economic growth. When consistently measured expenditure data are used, there is evidence of a significant negative correlation between inequality and growth. Taking these results at face value suggests that there is only a significant correlation between inequality and growth, once redistribution of income is taken into account.
Voitchovsky (2005)	25 countries, including a set of eastern European countries, observed for at least two consecutive 5-year periods, between 1975 and 2000.	The first-difference generalized method of moments (GMM) and system GMM estimators. Income (measured by real GDP per capita) is a function of initial income, investment, education, Gini coefficient, and time dummies. (The sample includes only wealthy democratic countries, to increase the degree of homogeneity.)	Inequality in different parts of the income distribution have different effects on growth: a positive effect from inequality in the top quartile of the income distribution, and a negative effect from inequality further down the income distribution. Suggestion for further research: how income inequality influences the functioning of the economy (not only outcomes such as income levels). Thus, research should identify the different channels through which inequality in different parts of the distribution may influence the growth process.

Table 2.2 Continued

Authors (Year)	Sample	Methodology and model specification	Findings
Frazer (2006)	Cross-country study	Method: using overlapping non-parametric regression to explore the relationship between inequality and income level, both in the pooled relation and within and between countries as they have developed. Model: inequality (measured by Gini coefficient) is a function of real GDP per capita, or log of real GDP per capita.	The findings show little support for the Kuznets hypothesis. First, they found examples of low-income countries with significantly decreasing inequality (e.g., India until its income passed $1,700). Moreover, South Korea and Taiwan have achieved considerable advances in per capita GDP despite having relatively small changes in inequality. Second, among high-income countries, they found considerable variety. France and Italy experienced significant and sizeable decreases in inequality as they grew. Norway experienced a small decrease in inequality during growth. On the other hand, the United States and the United Kingdom experienced sizeable and significant increases in inequality during growth, with the United States on trend to reaching high-inequality by international standards.
Castelló-Climent (2010)	Advanced economies or high-income OECD countries	A system GMM estimator to control for country-specific effects and take into account the persistency of the inequality indicators. Inequality is measured in terms of human capital inequality rather than the Gini coefficient.	The results show a different effect of inequality on growth depending on the level of development of the region. A negative effect of income and human capital inequality on economic growth in the whole sample and in the low and middle-income economies, an effect that vanishes or becomes positive for higher-income countries.

Continued

Table 2.2 Continued

Authors (Year)	Sample	Methodology and model specification	Findings
Easterly (2007)	Cross-country data 1960–98	Uses two measures of inequality: the Gini coefficient, and the share of income accruing to the top quintile. Model: regress both measures of inequality on dummy variables capturing the dimensions above, all of which potentially bias the inequality measure. For example, inequality of expenditure is generally less than inequality of income, and of course post-tax income has less inequality than pre-tax income.	The hypothesis advanced by the modern theories is that inequality has an adverse effect on human capital formation and economic development. Using agricultural endowments as an instrument for inequality, in order to overcome concerns about measurement errors and the endogeneity of inequality, his cross-country analysis suggests that inequality has been a barrier to schooling and economic prosperity.
Sukiassyan (2007)	26 transition economies of central and eastern Europe and the Commonwealth of Independent States	Different model specifications with a wide range of explanatory variables for economic growth.	The findings for transition countries indicate a strong, negative contemporaneous growth–inequality relationship for all the specifications in the short to medium run. There is a negative relationship between the change in inequality and initial income, but not a significant relationship between lagged inequality and growth, although our results show a significant, negative effect of lagged inequality on the linear term of the inequality change. There is also some evidence of a significant effect of structural change and liberalization, and policy variables on growth, but this leaves open the question of whether or not these variables are a separate channel affecting economic growth.

Table 2.2 Continued

Authors (Year)	Sample	Methodology and model specification	Findings
Frank (2008)	48 US states, 1945–2004	Models: real state income per capita is a function of initial income per capita, inequality (measure by Gini coefficient, top 1% share of income, top decile share of income), human capital attainment (including the proportion of the population with at least a high school diploma and the proportion with at least a college degree), farming, agriculture services, mining, construction, transportation, trade, finance, insurance, and services.	The findings indicate that the long-run relationship between inequality and growth is positive in nature and driven principally by the concentration of income in the upper end of the income distribution.
Pérez-Moreno (2009)	17 Spanish regions, 1970–2000	Granger causality.	There is no evidence to conclude whether GDP per capita growth either increases or decreases as a consequence of changes in inequality. On the contrary, there is more empirical evidence supporting the hypothesis that growing GDP per capita leads to less inequality more than any other causal relationship. In other words, the results clearly indicate that changes in the GDP per capita cause unidirectional changes in inequality, in a Granger-causal fashion.

Continued

Table 2.2 Continued

Authors (Year)	Sample	Methodology and model specification	Findings
Boix (2009)		Argument: the potential correlation between inequality and development will be always conditional on the (mostly political and institutional) causes that generate the existing income distribution to start with. Hence it is not surprising to find instances in which growth and (mostly temporary) inequality go hand in hand as well as other periods and countries where there is both high and persistent inequality jointly with economic stagnation.	Empirical review: • In the first generation, studies of the impact of inequality on development were generally based on ordinary least squares estimations of cross sections of countries covering a time period of a few decades (normally from 1960 to the 1980s), and inequality was consistently found to reduce growth – with an increase in inequality by one standard deviation decreasing the annual growth rate of per capita income by 0.4 to 0.8 percentage points. • In the second generation, after correcting for omitted-variable bias (such as institutional and legal setups, national cultural traits, and so on) it was found that higher levels of inequality increase growth. • All of these studies assumed that inequality and growth are related linearly. • More recently, studies have moved to estimate a model in which inequality and the growth rate are related through a concave schedule. The author suggests that inequality may be conditionally related to development (either negatively or positively).

Table 2.2 Continued

Authors (Year)	Sample	Methodology and model specification	Findings
Majumdar and Partridge (2009)	48 US counties 1990–2000	Model: Gini coefficient is a function of spatially lagged Gini coefficient, growth rate per capita income and its spatially lagged, educational attainment, population variables (population density, urban and rural proportion, population of different ethnic group), labour market variables (per capital employment, total labour force, sectoral size of labour force), international immigration, and structural change index.	The paper is still in progress.
Tridico (2010)	50 emerging and transition economies experiencing a process of fast growth (grew at an average of more than 2% over the study period) and institutional change, 1995–2006	Model: economic growth during 1995–2006 is regressed against poverty, inequality and human development variables using OLS cross-country regression models. Poverty is measured through a cut-off line of $4 a day. Income inequality is measured as a reduction of Gini coefficient between the years 1993 and 2004.	The results suggest that the economic growth occurring during 1995–2006 contributed neither to a decrease in poverty nor to an increase in human development variables, particularly in life expectancy. Income inequality worsened too: it increased constantly. Countries with a lower level of adult literacy and public expenditure, suffer higher income inequality. Poverty appears to be much lower when countries improved, during the period before the current economic growth, and thanks to public investments, human development variables such as infant mortality and adult literacy. In fact, as the regression results suggest, the public expenditure in education and health increases skills and life expectancy, and provides great opportunities, essential for escaping the poverty trap, and for people to build creative and long lives.

Continued

Table 2.2 Continued

Authors (Year)	Sample	Methodology and model specification	Findings
Rodríguez-Pose and Tselios (2010)	Regional data (in western Europe)	Model: growth of income per capita of the regions of western Europe between 1997 and 2002 is a function of income per capita in 1995; regional income inequality in the same year, educational attainment in 1995, educational inequality in 1995 and a vector of control variables in 1997. Estimation: standard OLS.	The results indicate that both income and educational inequality matter for regional growth. Existing levels of income and education inequality seem to be fundamentally good for socio-economic incentives and thus should be considered as growth-enhancing. The findings also suggest that the association between income per capita and regional growth in western Europe is not clear, as the elasticity coefficient on lagged income per capita is very sensitive to the inclusion of income inequality, education, and other control variables. The results confirm the general belief that educational achievement has a positive connection with economic growth, but also show that, as a whole, the association between inequality in education and growth is stronger than that between growth and educational attainment.

Note: Currency used in this table is US$.

across the entire sample overall, but a negative one in the sample of poor countries, and a positive relation in the sample of rich countries. This result indicates that a decrease in inequality would lead to an expansion in economic growth in poor countries, and deterioration in rich countries. Similar results were reported by Galbraith and Kum (2003) for a sample of 150 countries over 1963–99, and by Castelló-Climent (2010) for a sample of OECD countries.

Forbes (2000) estimated how changes in income inequality are correlated with changes in growth within a given country. He found that in the short and medium term, an increase in a country's level of income inequality has a considerable positive relationship with successive economic growth. That means a country may face a trade-off between reducing inequality and improving economic performance. However, he suggests that, although this relationship is highly robust across samples, it may not apply to very poor countries.

Using a sample of 25 wealthy democratic countries in eastern Europe, Voitchovsky (2005) found that inequality in different parts of the income distribution has different effects on growth: a positive effect from inequality in the top quartile of the income distribution, and a negative one from inequality further down the income distribution.

Frazer (2006) assessed whether the Kuznets hypothesis is applicable to his studied sample and found little support for the hypothesis. In particular, he found that economic development in low-income countries is accompanied by significantly decreasing inequality (e.g., India, until its per capita income passed $1,700). Moreover, a relatively small change in inequality in South Korea and Taiwan has led to a considerable improvement in per capita GDP. The results found among high-income countries vary. France and Italy experienced significant and sizeable decreases in inequality as they grew. In contrast, the United States and the United Kingdom experienced sizeable and significant increases in inequality during growth. Also examining the Kuznets hypothesis, Banerjee and Duflo (2003) suggested that a change in inequality in any direction may be unfavourable to growth.

More recently, Sukiassyan (2007) evaluated the growth–inequality relation using the data from the transition economies of central and eastern Europe and the Commonwealth of Independent States (the former Soviet Republics). Their findings exhibit a negative and strong influence of inequality on growth. Tridico (2010) explored the quality of economic growth in a sample of 50 emerging and transition economies experiencing a process of fast growth and institutional change. The findings suggest that economic growth during 1995–2006 occurred despite the worsening of income inequality. However, this result does not identify an 'inverted U-shaped' Kuznets curve because, even after a consistent period of growth, inequality did not decrease and it remained at higher levels. Furthermore, growth occurred at the expense of an important human development variable (life expectancy), and of an important indicator of democracy (voice and accountability). In a recent study, Vu and Mukhopadhaya (2011) reassessed the relationship between growth and inequality for 74 developed and developing countries using the period 2003–7. To minimize specification and measurement errors, they controlled for differences in initial economic status, education, human development and institutional factors. The study shows that economic growth has a negative connection to inequality in income distribution. More specifically, a decrease in inequality would make low-income countries grow faster than medium- and high-income countries. This implication provides a strong incentive for low-income countries to further aim at eliminating poverty, and income distribution gaps. Their results also show that initial economic conditions and education favourably affect the subsequent rate of growth. However, higher human development measured by life expectancy tends to lower the pace of growth of the economy. Finally, Vu and Mukhopadhaya (2011) found that economic growth does not seem to be accompanied by improvements in governance. However, such a disconnection in the short term may not apply in the long term. Therefore, it is still worthwhile to employ policies and approaches that improve the quality of governance.

More recently, Malinen (2012) examined the relationship between income inequality and economic growth for a panel of 53 countries. His findings suggest that the elasticity of growth with respect to income inequality changes in the process of economic development. In the early stage the effect of income inequality on growth is positive, but turns negative as the economy becomes more developed. Atolia *et al.* (2012) focused on the impact of some underlying mechanisms (such as productivity growth) on the evolution of both economic growth and inequality, and the relationship between them. They found that a gradual productivity change can indeed generate a Kuznets-type inverted U-shaped relationship between inequality and per-capita income, with a diverse set of possible long-run outcomes for inequality across structurally similar countries. Zaman *et al.* (2012) examined the impact of growth and income inequality on poverty for a panel of five selected South Asian Association For Regional Cooperation (SAARC) countries; namely, Bangladesh, India, Nepal, Pakistan and Sri Lanka; over the period 1990–2008. They found that there is a long-run relationship between poverty, growth and income inequality. More specifically, the increase in economic growth and income inequality contributes to a fall and rise in poverty, respectively. They also show that the impact of income inequality in increasing poverty is comparatively greater than that of economic growth in reducing poverty in SAARC countries.

In summary, the ultimate relationship between inequality and economic growth varies from study to study, depending on the estimation methods, data quality and sample coverage. Importantly for a cross-country study, and to obtain a more accurate estimation, it is necessary to control for country-wide differences in economic, social and institutional characteristics.

Conclusion

This chapter brings forth some competing views of distributive justice and discusses measurement and implementation issues of some widely used inequality measures. The focus was to elaborate the Gini and Theil index as a measure of inequality as throughout this book we will mostly use these measures. Although this book will not be using it, we nevertheless provide a brief overview of the Atkinson measure in the Appendix of this chapter. A short discussion on the theoretical and empirical relationship between growth and inequality is also provided to give an overall picture of inequality literature.

Appendix

The generalized Gini coefficient

Yitzhaki (1983) and Kakwani (1980) generalized the Gini coefficient.[43] Yitzhaki introduced an inequality aversion parameter. By using this parameter it is possible to check the robustness of the implied inequality ranking to different distributional judgements. The formula for generalized Gini coefficient can be expressed as:

$$GG = 1 - k(k-1) \int_{p=0}^{1} (1-p)^{k-2} L(p) \, dp, \quad \text{for } k > 2 \tag{A2.1}$$

where k is the inequality aversion parameter. If the value of k is equal to zero the index GG turns out to be the Gini index. Various values of k allow the decision-maker to place different weights on inequality at different parts of the distribution. As p is the proportion of population, at low income level $(1-p)$ is close to 1 and at high income it is close to 0. Thus the greater the value of k, the higher the weight given to the lower income group.

Kakwani (1986) used Sen's definition of the Gini coefficient to propose a generalized version. It can be seen in equation (2.13) that Sen proposed the weight v_i to depend on rank order of all individuals. To Sen $v_i = (N + 1 - j)$. Kakwani introduced a parameter s to define the weight $v_i = (N + 1 - j)^s$. Clearly when $s = 1$, the parameter turns out to be the Gini coefficient and for higher values of s more weight is attached to the lower income group and less weight to the top.

The generalized Gini coefficient has some further normative appeal because of its favourable consideration for the low-income group. However, the mathematical exercise destroys the coefficient's visual nicety.

Welfare-based inequality measures

A convenient approach to measuring the degree of income inequality is the use of a welfare function of income which incorporates normative assumptions concerning the welfare level associated with a certain level of income. The level of welfare corresponds to alternative distributions of the same mean income, and can then be used to derive the degree of inequality. Let W be a fully specified welfare function.[44] Following Dalton (1920) a welfare-based equality measure of prevailing distribution can be defined by comparing the actual welfare level W' with the maximum welfare level W_{max}, obtainable with the given total income $N\bar{x}$ of N units with average income $\bar{x}$. The associated welfare-based inequality measure can, then, be written as:

$$D = 1 - \left(\frac{W'}{W_{max}} \right)$$
(A2.2)

the measure is defined in the interval $[0, 1]$, clearly the maximum equality is defined as the situation in which the optimum welfare level attainable with income $N\bar{x}$ is reached (in this case value of D is equal to 0). Similarly D approaches 1 (i.e., total inequality) as W' approaches 0. Thus, D measures the relative welfare loss associated with a prevailing distribution, as compared with the maximum attainable level. To satisfy the homogeneity (mean invariant) principle by the measure D, the welfare function W is required to be homogeneous of any degree.

The prime problem with this approach is on the specification of the suitable welfare function. The individualistic welfare approach in this context makes use of the interpersonally comparable, cardinal, individual welfare function of income. Then by a complete *a priori*, specification of the mathematical form of W can solve the problem. This approach was introduced by Dalton (1920). If U_i is the individual utility of income of person i Dalton assumed:

1 preferences of all individuals are the same: $U_i(x_i) = U(x_i)$ for all i,
2 utility is twice continuously differentiable, strictly increasing and strictly concave: $\frac{dU(x_i)}{dx_i} > 0$, $\frac{d^2U(x_i)}{dx_i^2} < 0$, for all i, and
3 total welfare is the sum of individual welfare values: $W = \sum_i U_i(x_i)$.

Clearly, assumptions (1) to (3) imply separability i.e., $(\partial^2 W)/(\partial x_i \partial x_j) = 0$, for all $i, i \neq j$.

The class of welfare functions defined from assumptions (1) to (3) is very broad.[45] Atkinson (1970) criticized Dalton's welfare-based inequality measure on the grounds that the measure is not invariant to any positive linear transformation of the individual utility functions. Thus the inequality measures obtained by the positive linear transformations of the utility functions will not be cardinally equivalent.[46] Atkinson (1970)[47] provided an alternative definition of a welfare based inequality measure which has some resemblance to D. It can be written as:

$$A = 1 - \frac{\bar{x}_E}{\bar{x}}$$
(A2.3)

where $\bar{x}_E$ can be implicitly defined by:

$$W' = W(\bar{x}_E, \bar{x}_E, \ldots, \bar{x}_E)$$
(A2.4)

that is $\bar{x}_E$ is a uniform level of income[48] which, if equally distributed among individuals would give the same level of welfare W' as the actual distribution $\{x_1, x_2, \ldots, x_N\}$ with average income $\bar{x}$. Several further additional criteria over

(1) to (3) might be used to restrict the Dalton class of utility functions. Atkinson (1970) restricts the class of welfare functions by using some concepts from the research of risk aversion. In the study of risk aversion a common measure of concavity of utility function at x_i can be given by (see Pratt, 1964):

$$-\frac{U''(x_i)}{U'(x_i)} = \frac{d \log U'(x_i)}{dx_i} = \frac{\varepsilon}{x_i}, \quad x_i \neq 0 \tag{A2.5}$$

where $\varepsilon \geq 0$ guarantees the concavity of the utility function. Atkinson considers the utility function as:

$$U(x_i) = \begin{cases} A + B \dfrac{x_i^{1-\varepsilon}}{1-\varepsilon}, & \varepsilon = 1 \\ \log_e(x_i), & \varepsilon \neq 1. \end{cases} \tag{A2.6}$$

Under this functional form it is easy to derive Atkinson's index of inequality as:

$$I^A = 1 - \frac{1}{\bar{x}} \left(\frac{\sum_i (x_i)^{1-\varepsilon}}{N} \right)^{\frac{1}{1-\varepsilon}}, \quad \text{if } \varepsilon \neq 1$$

$$= 1 - \exp\left(\frac{\sum_i \log_e(x_i/\bar{x})}{N} \right), \quad \text{if } \varepsilon = 1 \tag{A2.7}$$

because of the fact that the geometric mean, x_m, can be defined as:

$$x_m = \frac{\sum_i \log_e x_i}{N}, \tag{A2.8}$$

the Atkinson index for $\varepsilon = 1$ can also be expressed as:

$$I^A(\varepsilon = 1) = 1 - \frac{x_m}{\bar{x}}. \tag{A2.9}$$

In the income inequality context the meaning of ε is relative inequality aversion.[49] In other words, it is the relative sensitivity of transfer of income at different income levels. Atkinson (1983, pp. 56–7) says ε

> represents the weight attached by society to inequality in the distribution. It ranges from zero, which means that the society is indifferent about the distribution, to infinity, which means that the society is only concerned with the position of the lowest income group. The latter position may be seen as corresponding to that developed by Rawls – where inequality is assessed in terms of the position of the least advantaged – where ε lies between these extremes depends on the importance attached to redistribution at the bottom.
>
> (ibid.)

Atkinson interprets ε in the following way:

> suppose there are two people, one with twice the income of the other (they are otherwise identical), and that we are considering taking 1 unit of income from the richer man and giving a portion x to the poorer (the remainder being lost in the process...). At which level of x we cease to regard the distribution as desirable? If...[one] is at all concerned about inequality, then $x = 1$ is...desirable. What is crucial is how far...to x fall below 1 before calling for a stop...The answer determines the implied value of ε from the formula $1/x = 2^{\varepsilon}$. For example, if...[one] stops at $x = 1/2$, this corresponds to $\varepsilon = 1$, but if...[one] is willing to go until only a quarter is transferred, then the implied ε equals 2.
>
> (ibid., p. 58).

Thus as ε increases an increasingly higher weight is attached to transfers at the lower end of the distribution, and less weight to the transfer at the top. If the decision-maker does not want to attach any weight to the distributional consideration, then the value of ε equals zero. Conversely, if he/she is only concerned about the worst-off people, the value infinity will be assigned to ε.

Atkinson used the data collected by Kuznets (1963) covering the distribution of income in seven developed and five less-developed countries, and computed the measure by means of the aforesaid homothetic utility function given by equation (A2.7) for $\varepsilon = 1.0, 1.5, 2.0$. The results indicate that where I^A is sensitive to the choice of ε – the range of variation is considerable, and the ranking of the countries changes considerably with fluctuations in the values of ε as well. Thus the empirical observations of Atkinson raise problems in selecting the appropriate value of ε.[50]

For any value of ε less than infinity, Atkinson's measure is compatible with the Pareto principle. That is, if anyone's income in the society increases without any change in others' income, the welfare of the society will increase, even if it worsens the society's inequality. In Chapter 7 the desirability of the Pareto principle will be discussed. Atkinson's measure is a relative measure of income inequality and is symmetric. This measure satisfies the Pigou–Dalton condition of transfer and avoids the morally arbitrary squaring feature common for variance (which attaches larger weights to the extreme values). Also it avoids the morally arbitrary square root feature common in the coefficient of variance. Although this measure has intuitive appeal, the prime objection always comes regarding the choice of the value of ε.[51]

Atkinson's equally distributed equivalent income, $\bar{x}_E$ can be decomposed using the relation between $\bar{x}_E$ and $\bar{x}_{gE}$s, the equally distributed incomes for the g groups:

$$\bar{x}_E^{1-\varepsilon} = \sum_g \frac{n_g}{N} \bar{x}_{gE}^{1-\varepsilon} \qquad (A2.10)$$

therefore for $0 < \varepsilon < 1$. Hence, it is possible to write:

$$A = 1 - \left[\frac{\bar{x}_E}{\bar{x}}\right]^{1-\varepsilon}$$

$$= \sum_g \frac{n_g}{N}\left[\frac{\bar{x}_g}{\bar{x}}\right]^{1-\varepsilon} A_g + 1 - \frac{n_g}{N}\left[\frac{\bar{x}_g}{\bar{x}}\right]^{1-\varepsilon}$$

$$= A_W + A_B \tag{A2.11}$$

where A_W is the weighted sum of the A indices for each g groups where weights depend on the population share and the income share of the group, and A_B is the between-group component of the A index with n_g persons at income $\bar{x}_g$. One important point to note that Atkinson's index I^A cannot be decomposed in this sense (Anand, 1983).

Research by Blackorby *et al.* (1981) to decompose I^A has taken a different route and come up with a different type of decomposition. They considered four alternative income vectors, (a) the actual income distribution; (b) the distribution where each person receives $\bar{x}_E$; (c) the distribution which assigns each person the equally-distributed-equivalent-income of the subgroup where he/she belongs ($\bar{x}_{gE}$), thus eliminating within-group inequality but leaving each subgroup's social welfare unchanged; and (d) the distribution which preserves each subgroup's inequality but eliminates between-group inequality in such a way that overall social welfare remains constant. Considering that Atkinson's index measures the percentage of total income saved in moving from the original distribution to full equality (with welfare remaining constant), they measure within-group inequality as a percentage saved from (a) to (c) and between-group inequality as the percentage saved in moving from (c) to (b). Thus the within-group inequality can be given by:

$$I_W^A = \frac{N\bar{x} - \sum_g N_g \bar{x}_{gE}}{N\bar{x}}. \tag{A2.12}$$

Moving from (c) to (b) eliminates the rest of the inequality, Blackorby *et al.* (1981) defined between-group inequality as:

$$I_B^A = \frac{\sum_g N_g \bar{x}_{gE} - N\bar{x}_E}{\sum_g N_g \bar{x}_{gE}}. \tag{A2.13}$$

They proved the relationship that:

$$I^A = I_W^A + I_B^A - I_W^A \times I_B^A. \tag{A2.14}$$

The problem with this type of decomposition is that it is difficult to define the $\bar{x}_{gE}$, the equally-distributed-equivalent-income of subgroup g separately. This is because welfare and inequality of a particular group also depend on other groups. This fact was also recognized by the authors.[52]

The welfare measures of inequality rely totally on the choice of individual utility function. This is precisely a measure to calculate the loss of welfare caused by improper distribution.[53] Meade (1976) called this welfare loss a 'distributional waste' and demonstrated that a measure of distributional waste is not a measure of inequality in the fundamental sense. Actually it is a measure of inefficiency or a measure of loss of utility from a less than optimal distribution of the available income. Moreover, although Atkinson's measure is subgroup consistent,[54] it is not additively decomposable. Also this measure cannot provide interpretable decomposition into various factor components of income. Therefore this measure, despite its wide use in the literature, is not very appropriate as an instrument of policy evaluation.

Notes

1 See Aristotle's *Politics* and Plato's *Republic*. Dover (1974) provides an excellent discussion of this thought.
2 For a different view on the justification of the claim of fundamental equality see Popper (1962) and Nielsen (1985).
3 See http://www3.grips.ac.jp/~kanemoto/UrbExt/A1Equal.pdf [accessed 24 April 2013].
4 A central postulate of social welfare philosophy has been called *asset egalitarianism* by Arrow (1973). According to this assumption, all the assets of a society including personal labour, skills and ability are in some sense the common wealth of humanity available for use in maximizing social welfare. In particular, redistributive policies that take the product of some individuals and give it to others are just, if they raise social welfare.
5 It is assumed that the means of both the distributions are same.
6 Bistochastic matrix: a matrix $\mathbf{Q}$ of order N is said to be bistochastic or doubly stochastic if its coefficient q_{ij} satisfies the following condition:

$$q_{ij} \geq 0 \quad \text{for all } i, j; \qquad \sum_{j=1}^{n} q_{ij} = 1 \quad \text{for all } i; \qquad \sum_{i=1}^{n} q_{ij} = 1 \quad \text{for all } j.$$

Permutation Matrix: If the bistochastic matrix has only one coefficient in each row equal to 1 and only one coefficient in each column equal to 1, such a matrix is called permutation matrix. To give an example of a permutation matrix:

$$\mathbf{P} = \begin{pmatrix} 0 & 0 & 1 & 0 \\ 1 & 0 & 0 & 0 \\ 0 & 0 & 0 & 1 \\ 0 & 1 & 0 & 0 \end{pmatrix}.$$

The income configuration $x = (x_1, x_2, x_3, x_4)$ when multiplied by $\mathbf{P}$ becomes $\mathbf{P}x = (x_3, x_1, x_4, x_2)$ that is, everything remaining the same the orders have changed.
7 Schur convexity: If f is a numerical function defined in n dimensional Eucledian space, D^n, where f is Schur-convex (S-convex, in short) in D^n if for all x in D^n and all

bistochactic matrices $\mathbf{Q}$:

$$f(\mathbf{Q}x) \leq f(x).$$

If the inequality sign changes its direction the function f would be S-concave in D^n for all x in D^n and for all bistochactic matrix $\mathbf{Q}$. In a different way S-convexity can be defined (using the Ostrowsky theorem, Berge 1963) as follows: If f is a symmetric differentiable function in D^n for all $x = (x_1, x_2, \ldots, x_n)$ in D^n such that x_1 is not equal to x_2, then f is strictly S-convex for the following condition:

$$(x_2 - x_1)\left(\frac{df}{dx_2} - \frac{df}{dx_1}\right) > 0.$$

Note that S-convexity is a much milder condition than convexity or quasi-convexity. For a more detailed discussion see Marshall and Olkin (1979).

8 Amiel and Cowell (1992), in their questionnaire investigation method found that people responding in a different way than the expected Pigou–Dalton condition of transfer.
9 In the context of relative deprivation, Podder (1996) also assumed the violation of the transfer principle. In his words,

> when a transfer of dollar takes place from a rich to a poor person, relative deprivation of the society as a whole may increase. This is a clear violation of the Pigou–Dalton condition which is considered the single most important feature of any relative inequality measure. The violation of the condition in our case clearly implies that when inequality increases relative deprivation may decrease or vice versa. The phenomenon can be visualised in the following example. Suppose there are six income units in ascending order and a transfer takes place from the third unit to the fifth unit. This will lead to an increase in relative deprivation of the third and the fourth units but a decrease in relative deprivation of the first, second and the fifth units. The net effect of the transfer then will depend on the magnitudes of the losses and gains. It is the net effect that determines if relative deprivation of the whole society will increase or decrease. The violation of the Pigou–Dalton condition is more likely when a progressive transfer takes place at the top end of the distribution (p. 365).

10 Kolm (1996) provides several examples of increasing returns in proximity.
11 This is Dalton's principle of 'proportionate addition to population'. Foster (1985) calls it 'population homogeneity'. Dasgupta *et al.* (1973) called it 'symmetry of population'.
12 'The simplest example is provided by the extreme case of increasing returns to proximity, which only discriminates between strict inequality and equality (and does not discriminate among different inequalities in pair)' (Kolm, 1996, p. 314–15).
13 The implicit assumption here is that the total income is the same.
14 A intermediate judgement provided by Eichhorn (1988) can be given by $I(x + \beta[\delta x + (1-\delta)e] = I(x)$ for all $0 < \delta < 1$ and $I(x + \beta[\delta x + (1-\delta)e] \geq 0$. Clearly, when $\delta = 1$ it reduces to a relative measure and when $\delta = 0$ it reduces to an absolute measure. This is different from Kolm's 'centrist', see Bossert and Pfingsten (1989).
15 Equation (2.8) presents a general case, however, for our study we will assume, $w(x_i, x_j) = 1$.
16
$$V = \frac{\sum(x_i - \bar{x})^2}{N}.$$

17 Pyatt (1976) considers a different interpretation of Gini coefficient. He considers a game in which for each individual he selects an income x at random from all possible values of income. If the chosen income is greater than the actual income of the individual, she/he can retain the new income, otherwise she/he would keep her/his actual income.

Clearly, all will gain from participating in the game except the richest person, and she/he will retain the actual income. Thus for a particular individual the expected gain will be $\frac{1}{N}\sum_{i=1}^{N}\max(0, x_j - x_i)$ for all i, summing up this for all individuals i and making it mean invariant by dividing the whole by the mean a version of Gini coefficient can be obtained. Broome (1989), using a different interpretation, reached the same formula, and argued that everyone in the society has the same claim for income. He suggested that an individual has a sense of unfairness if she/he finds her/his income is lower than others. According to Broome (1989) this unfairness could be called as the particular individual's complaint the extent of which could be measured by the difference between the higher income and the ith person's income. Thus the ith person's total complaint can be represented as $\sum_j \max(0, x_j - x_i)$. Therefore by calculating the overall complaints for all individuals the Gini coefficient can be derived.

18 To Pfahler (1987), graphical representation is one of the 'additional descriptive properties' of an inequality measure.

19 When total incomes are arranged in ascending order, a plot of the cumulative proportion of income against the cumulative proportion of the income earners gives the Lorenz curve of total income.

20 The premises of Yitzhaki and Hey and Lambert are, however, quite different.

21 However, Podder (1996) has shown a non-linear (and non-monotonic) relationship between the relative deprivation index and the Gini coefficient.

22 If an income vector is $y = ce + x$ it can be proved that $G_y = \bar{x}_x/(\bar{x}_x + c)G_x$, which means it is not an absolute measure of inequality. And if we define $z = cx$ it can be proved that $G_z = G_x$.

23 Using Ostrowsky theorem.

24 See Anand (1983, p. 317) for such proof.

25 Also see Atkinson (1970).

26 It was shown by Newbery (1970) that the Gini coefficient could not rank distributions in the same way as any additive social welfare function does. Even in the class of non-additive social welfare functions, a (strictly) concave welfare function is incompatible with the Gini ranking (Dasgupta *et al.* 1973). However, these criticisms are not very convincing. Additivity of the social welfare function is not a very acceptable property. It requires that the relative distributional weights on any two persons' income be entirely independent of another persons' income. In a sensational analysis of Hamada's (1973) axiomatization of additivity, Sen (1973a) has shown that two income distributions, differing broadly in their interpersonal comparisons from an intuitive point of view, may be ranked as 'equally unequal' as a consequence of this assumption. The Gini coefficient satisfies S-convexity which is sufficient to ensure the Pigou–Dalton condition of transfer. However, the Gini coefficient does not satisfy the transfer sensitivity property.

27 If total income x has two components x_1 and x_2 and if C is the coefficient of Variation (CV) for total income and C_1 and C_2 are the CV for the components x_1 and x_2 respectively, let λ be the proportion of the first component and let ρ be the correlation coefficient of x_1 and x_2; then,

$$C^2 = \lambda^2 C_1^2 + (1-\lambda)^2 C_2^2 + 2\lambda(1-\lambda)C_1 C_2 \rho.$$

Clearly, as the number of components increases the formula becomes complicated. Furthermore, in this case it will fail to identify the influence the changes in the distribution of one particular component independently for changes in each component's share.

28 If the cumulative proportion of income from source g is plotted against the cumulative proportion of individuals when they are arranged in ascending order of *total* income, there is a concentration curve of source g. Thus it is similar to the Lorenz curve (which

is drawn for total income). It is important to note that unlike the Lorenz curve, the concentration curve may lie above the egalitarian line. This happens when income from a specific source, such as government benefits, accrue mainly to the poor section of society. Like the Gini coefficient a concentration, the coefficient is one minus twice the area under the egalitarian line and the concentration curve.

29 See Podder (1996).

30 Khan *et al.* (1993) and Khan and Riskin (2001), for example, among many others.

31 For different disaggregation methods of the Gini coefficient, see Pyatt *et al.* (1980), Fei *et al.* (1978), Silber (1989).

32 See Shorrocks (1984) for more general results of decomposable inequality indices, also known as generalized entropy, the Theil index is a special case of this measure. Further results of decomposable indices can be found in Bourguignon (1979) and Shorrocks (1980), who consider alternative definitions of decomposability, and Cowell and Kuga (1981).

33 Love and Wolfson (1976) suggest an alternative way. According to their analysis it is possible to construct the within-group term by re-scaling group distributions to remove between-group inequality, and then it is possible to define the between-group term by eliminating the within-group component from the total inequality. However, this process may generate ambiguous results for the case when within-group inequality is very high.

34 Note here that the weights do not add up to unity like squared coefficient of variation.

35 To give an example where an income vector of $\{2, 4, 6, 8, 10\}$ is regrouped into $\{2, 4, 10\}$ and $\{6, 8\}$, the Gini coefficient for the total group would be 0.267. The Gini coefficient for the first group can be calculated as 0.333 and that for the second group would be 0.071. The between-group Gini can be calculated using the formula $G_B = (n_1 n_2 |\bar{x}_1 - \bar{x}_2|)/(N^2 \bar{x})$ as 0.066. In this case $G_W = \sum_{g=1}^{2} (n_g/N)(n_g \bar{x}_g)/(N\bar{x})G_g = 0.108$. Thus the residual is 0.148. Now the same income vector is grouped as $\{2, 4, 6\}$ and $\{8, 10\}$ $G_1 = 0.222$ and $G_2 = 0.111$. Therefore $G_W = 0.067$ and $G_B = 0.20$. Thus here, because of the absence of the overlapping term $G = G_W + G_B$.

36 Another type of controversy arises as to whether the residual terms are to be treated as a part of the between group component or as a part of the within group component. Paglin (1975, 1977) raises this issue as a continuum debate in the literature of inequality. However, this is beyond the scope of this study.

37 As the within group term measures the deprivation when individuals compare their income only to people in the same subgroup, and as the between group term is the average deprivation when inequality within group is assumed to be zero and individual compares their income to all other groups except their own.

38 Foster and Sen (1997) tried to explain the same criterion with the example $z = \{1, 3, 8, 8\}$, $z' = \{2, 2, 7, 9\}$ and $y = \{a, a\}$ – an equal distribution. 'Subgroup consistency would require the direction of change in overall inequality in going from $(1, 3, 8, 8, a, a)$ to $(2, 2, 7, 9, a, a)$ to be independent of the level of a. Indeed every generalized entropy measure exhibits this independence, with measures in the range $a > 2$ consistently ranking $(2, 2, 7, 9, a, a)$ above $(1, 3, 8, a, a)$ in inequality terms and measures with $a < 2$ consistently rendering the contrary argument' (p. 160). But the Gini coefficient exhibits the opposite pattern 'the distributional change is *inequality reducing* for the case $a = 2$, when we move from $(1, 2, 2, 3, 8, 8)$ to $(2, 2, 2, 2, 7, 9)$ and *inequality enhancing* for the case $a = 8$ when we move from $(1, 3, 8, 8, 8, 8)$ to $(2, 2, 7, 8, 8, 9)$. In determining the overall effect of a distributional change, the Gini index, like many other Lorenz consistent indices, takes more into account than just the incomes of the affected parties' (p. 160–1).

39 The Gini coefficient can also be interpreted in terms of weighted transfers from rich to poor to get an equal distribution. Thus the Gini coefficient does not only depend on the

amount of transfer, it also depends on the distribution of people in between where the transfer was performed.

40 Podder (1993a) demonstrated a new method of Gini decomposition to eliminate the effect of the overlapping term. The method is applicable only on micro data of individual income/consumption.

41 The concentration can be calculated using various algorithms. Silber (1989) devised a way in terms of matrix and vectors which is useful for grouped data. A simple formula recently derived by Milanvac (1997) as: $C_g = (1/\sqrt{3}) \times CV_g \times$ correlation (R_x, g), where CV_g is the coefficient of variation of source g and R_x is the income earner's rank according to total income.

42 For example, growth in period 3 is measured from 1976 to 1980 and is regressed on explanatory variables measured during period 2 (1971–5). Since yearly growth rates incorporate short-run disturbances, growth is averaged over 5-year periods. This reduces yearly serial correlation from business cycles.

43 Mehran (1975, 1976), Pyatt (1976, 1987), Donaldson and Weymark (1980), Weymark (1981), Nygard and Sandstrom (1982) also attempted to generalize the Gini coefficient.

44 That means the characteristics of W are known.

45 Dalton's inequality measure was computed by Aigner and Heins (1967) using three different functional forms of the utility function for the 1960 family income distributions in 50 states and in the District of Columbia and the United States. The ranking of the distribution, irrespective of the functional form of the utility function, is similar.

46 However, Sen (1973a) argued that the ordering of D is not affected by any positive linear transformations.

47 See also Kolm (1966).

48 Known as 'equally distributed equivalent level of income'.

49 There is a different type of normative approach to the comparison of inequality for which the underlying utility functions need not be precisely defined. Only some broad restrictions are required to be imposed. A measure can be given by the Atkinson's index such that the resulting inequality comparison can claim to satisfy a much wider range of value judgements. This is known as the principle of Lorenz ranking, propounded by Atkinson. For a given total income, Atkinson defined greater equality as higher social welfare. Assuming a utilitarian social welfare function, he showed that if it is at least known that the individual utility function is strictly concave then a distribution will have higher welfare (hence higher equality) if its Lorenz curve lies completely inside the Lorenz curve of another distribution with the same total income.

50 Even if additive, separable and homothetic social welfare function is assumed.

51 Atkinson's index is of great importance to the decision-maker in the problem of trade-off between efficiency and equity. With a known value of ε, the value of $\bar{x}_g$ is also known. Then the decision-maker using his/her value judgement can easily determine which is worth: an increase in income or reduction of inequality of the society.

52 Cowell (1995) showed that Atkinson's index is a non-linear transformation of the generalized entropy measure and in the light of that he proved:

$$I^A = 1 - [(1 - I_B^A)^{1-\varepsilon} + (1 - I_W^A)^{1-\varepsilon} - 1]^{\frac{1}{1-\varepsilon}}$$

In his numerical example of regional inequality of China the between group and within group components do not sum to total inequality. A formula of this type has interpretational problems as well.

53 Actually A or I^A equals 0.2 implies that incomes being equally distributed only 80 per cent of the total income is required to achieve the same level of welfare.

54 To show this Cowell (1995) took two distributions $z = \{60, 70, 80\}$ and $y = \{30, 30, 130\}$ which have changed to $z' = \{60, 60, 90\}$ and $y' = \{10, 60, 120\}$ due to some transfer.

Thus the combined income vector will be $x = \{60, 70, 80, 30, 30, 130\}$ before transfer and $x' = \{60, 60, 90, 10, 60, 120\}$ after transfer. Due to change in distribution from z to z' Atkinson's measure of inequality increased from 0.007 to 0.019 and that increased from 0.228 to 0.343 for a change in distribution from y to y'. An overall measure of the index is 0.125 for the distribution x and 0.198 for the distribution x' (the result is for the value of $\varepsilon = 1$, this is true for other values of ε).

3   Income inequality
       trends in Singapore

In November 1954 the People's Action Party (PAP), a coalition of moderate democratic socialists and left-wing communists, was formed in Singapore. Initially the party manifesto had the objective of alleviating 'unjust inequalities of wealth and opportunity'; however, in 1961 the left-wingers left the PAP. The new party manifesto (issued in 1982) reflects a shift from ideology to practicality. The objective of abolishing unequal distribution of wealth and opportunity was revised to 'the creation of a dynamic, disciplined and self-reliant society in which rewards are "in accord with each Singaporean's performance and contribution to the society" and the creation of equal opportunities to all Singaporeans' (Chee, 1989 p. 74). The shift in ideology resulted in spectacular achievements in the economic and social development of Singapore. The issue of income inequality in Singapore has been addressed extensively in the literature.[1] This chapter provides recent trends in income inequality in further detail.

Overall income inequality: 1984–2011

The Gini coefficent and the Theil index are presented in Table 3.1.

Ignoring minor changes in the indices, the following summary can be considered (see Figure 3.1). Over the period 1984 to 2011, the Gini increased from 0.470 to 0.529, while the Theil index increased from 0.446 to 0.530. However, it is notable that in the 1980s and 1990s inequality was quite stable; in fact, Singapore had high inequality in 1984. Due to high wage costs and competition from developing countries, in the 1980s Singapore lost its comparative advantage in labour-intensive industries. At that time the government decided on economic restructuring, and moved towards skill- and technology-intensive industries. Both the manufacturing and services sectors were actively promoted. As these required skilled workers, those with the requisite qualifications were well paid, and those without remained stagnant. Therefore, throughout 1984, income inequality was relatively high.

Since then inequality has decreased due to two major changes in labour market conditions: a substantial increase in the female labour participation rate;[2] and a lessening of the unemployment rate fuelled by a buoyant economy. Government regulation of wages through the National Wage Council (NWC) also assisted in

Table 3.1 Gini coefficient and Theil index for earnings, 1984–2011

Year	Gini coefficient	Theil index	Year	Gini coefficient	Theil index
1984	0.47	0.446			
1985	0.464	0.429	1998	0.471	0.413
1986	0.458	0.418	1999	0.476	0.427
1987	0.462	0.423	2001	0.473	0.453
1988	0.463	0.425	2002	0.472	0.456
1989	0.471	0.434	2003	0.486	0.484
1990	0.467	0.424	2004	0.488	0.488
1991	0.471	0.417	2006	0.509	0.518
1992	0.475	0.417	2007	0.516	0.526
1993	0.474	0.449	2008	0.525	0.533
1994	0.474	0.443	2009	0.519	0.523
1996	0.473	0.423	2010	0.525	0.53
1997	0.469	0.416	2011	0.529	0.53

Source: Computed from various LFS, Government of Singapore.

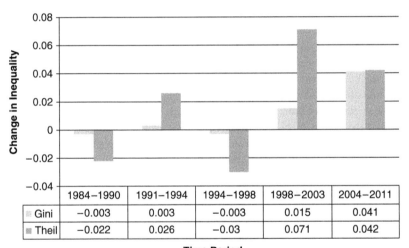

Time Period	1984–1990	1991–1994	1994–1998	1998–2003	2004–2011
Gini	−0.003	0.003	−0.003	0.015	0.041
Theil	−0.022	0.026	−0.03	0.071	0.042

Figure 3.1 Changes in income inequality in Singapore.

Source: Table 3.1 of this chapter.

decreasing the gap between rich and poor. The NWC often recommended a fixed quantum plus a percentage wage increase. The fixed sum component was crucial because it formed a larger percentage of an unskilled worker's wage than that for a skilled worker, and was thus crucial in increasing unskilled workers' earnings by a larger percentage.[3]

During the period 1991–7, the Gini was around 0.473, while the Theil index showed some fluctuations: starting at 0.417 in 1991, it reached a peak in 1993

(0.449); then continued to decrease to 0.416 by 1998. The Gini reached a maximum of 0.475 in 1992. During 1991 to 1994 the Theil index increased from 0.417 to 0.443. This increasing trend is attributable to the stretching of wage levels at both ends; Singapore exercised supply regulation on foreign workers. The recruitment of foreign labour covered two groups: low-skilled manual workers, and skilled professionals. The induction of unskilled foreign workers had segmented the labour market with a high degree of wage dispersion across sectors. There was also an active policy of recruiting professional skilled labour to meet demand for intensifying competition and globalisation. The recruitment of foreign professionals had necessitated raising wages to world-supply price levels. The high wages that the expatriate professionals received, coupled with low wages paid to unskilled foreign workers underlie the very high income inequality in Singapore (Rao *et al.*, 2003).

During the period 1994 to 1998, with the financial crisis changing the whole economic scenario in South East Asia, Singapore experienced a fall in the Gini from 0.474 to 0.471 and in the Theil from 0.443 to 0.413. Although the crisis did not affect Singapore severely, there was a decrease in inflow of foreign unskilled workers at the lower end of the income ladder, and at the higher income bracket not many people were hired. This led to a decrease in income inequality.

Throughout the 1997–8 crisis period, inequality decreased despite an increase in unemployment. With the economic downturn from the regional economic crisis, in June 1998 the overall non-seasonally adjusted unemployment rate in Singapore rose to 3.2 per cent compared to 2.4 per cent in June 1997. It was evidenced that unemployment rates for diploma- and degree-holders were higher compared to their secondary-educated counterparts, as proportionately more would have entered the labour market to search for jobs. The unemployment rate for workers aged below 30 also tended to be high as a large proportion of these workers included new entrants to the labour market. The turnover rate also was usually high among younger workers. Lower unemployment among older workers (aged around 50 and over, see LFS, 1998) was because of their lower turnover and higher probability of dropping out from the labour force completely when they left their jobs, often due to retrenchment or business closures, and ceased to be counted as unemployed. Thus due to increased unemployment, inequality in age groups below 30 and for people with below-secondary education, had increased. However, because of relatively smaller income shares in the total workforce for these subgroups, the effect on total inequality was eclipsed (see more in Mukhopadhaya and Rao, 2002).

As Singapore's economy recovered from the crisis, income inequality started to grow. In an effort to retain foreign talents, Singapore continued to pay high wages to skilled foreign workers, and as a result inequality continued to increase. During the period 1998 to 2003 the Gini increased from 0.471 to 0.486, and the Theil increased from 0.427 to 0.484. South East Asian economies at this period were badly hit by the severe acute respiratory syndrome (SARS) and businesses were affected as a result. Furthermore, growth in the IT sector was hampered due to a lack of global demand during this period. This generated loss of jobs

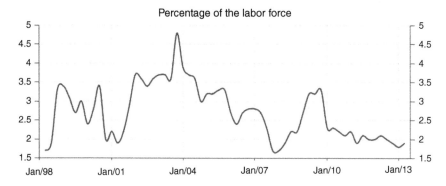

Figure 3.2 Unemployment rate.

(see Figure 3.2), and consequently income inequality increased. Note that at this time unemployment rates were higher both in the better educated cohort and in the low income groups: thus inequality increased unlike in 1998.

During 2007–8, the global financial crisis affected Singapore heavily once again. Thus global shocks did not allow Singapore to experience a lower rate of income inequality. The increasing trend of inequality in income continued, and the Gini coefficient reached 0.529 in 2011, while the Theil reached 0.530. Note that the rate of growth in Theil (see Figure 3.1) in the period 2004–recent is much lower than that in 1999–2004. Increase in inequality in the 2000s is a global phenomenon and Singapore is no exception. However, a lower increase in the recent period is once again because of the recessionary effect on the economy resulting from the global financial crisis.

Income inequality decomposed in age subgroups

From 1984 to 2011, the proportion of the labour force in the 15–24 age group declined by 79 per cent, while the proportion aged over 40 years rose by 119 per cent (see Table 3.2). There was a drastic drop in the labour force participation rates for the under-25 age group, as relatively more individuals started pursuing tertiary education. The age premium, for the age group 40–45 relative to the age group 25–29 declined from around 62 per cent during 1984, to 58 per cent during 2011. Such were the changes behind the narrowing of the within-age inequality. The decline in the age premium, evidenced in Table 3.2, is because of an explicit/implicit flexi-wage system. Under such a system, income is based on productivity and not correlated with experience/age.

The between-age income inequality pattern in Singapore from 1984 to 2011, measured in terms of Theil, is provided in Table 3.3. Between 1984 and 1994, there was a decline in between-age inequality from 0.069 to 0.048. During 1994–2004 between-age inequality increased to 0.061 and dropped once again to 0.053

Table 3.2 Population shares and relative mean incomes of various age groups, 1984–2011

Age groups	1984	1994	2004	2011
Population shares				
15–24	0.305	0.172	0.117	0.065
25–29	0.188	0.161	0.134	0.105
30–34	0.145	0.161	0.145	0.124
35–39	0.100	0.154	0.135	0.133
40–44	0.081	0.127	0.141	0.128
45–54	0.113	0.152	0.227	0.257
55 and above	0.067	0.073	0.099	0.188
Relative mean income				
15–24	0.511	0.465	0.333	0.412
25–29	0.915	0.814	0.764	0.811
30–34	1.297	1.056	1.112	1.098
35–39	1.510	1.253	1.296	1.292
40–44	1.482	1.283	1.259	1.291
45–54	1.292	1.270	1.115	1.064
55 and above	1.000	0.945	0.906	0.748

Source: Computed from various LFS, Singapore.

Table 3.3 Decomposition of the Theil index by age

Year	Theil index	Between-group inequality	Within-group inequality	Between-group contribution (%)	Within-group contribution (%)
1984	0.446	0.069	0.375	15.58	84.42
1994	0.443	0.048	0.395	10.88	89.12
2004	0.488	0.061	0.427	12.64	87.36
2011	0.530	0.053	0.477	9.89	90.11

in 2011, while within-age inequality increased continuously from 0.375 in 1984 to 0.477 in 2011.

The between-age Theil index is based on the disparities in the mean incomes among the different age groups. A narrowing of that disparity means erosion of the age premium in earnings, as evidenced in Table 3.3. To assist in an analysis of the increases in contribution of within-age inequality in more detail we present Table 3.4.

Table 3.4 indicates that as age increases, the within-age group Gini and Theil also increase. This shows the presence of heterogeneous skills among higher (older) age groups. Mukhopadhaya (2004b) also confirms the upward movement of the total within- group inequality and shows that the average annual change is positive only for the age groups 15–24 and 55 and over.

Figure 3.3 explains the age-education distribution in Singapore. It can be observed that this distribution is quite unequal and this is the reason for the high inequality within age groups.

Table 3.4 Inequality in individual age groups, 1984–2011

Year	15–24	25–29	30–34	35–39	40–44	45–54	55 and over
Gini coefficient							
1984	0.275	0.367	0.447	0.489	0.508	0.499	0.512
1994	0.335	0.340	0.412	0.472	0.495	0.516	0.534
2004	0.423	0.380	0.417	0.449	0.472	0.483	0.486
2011	0.362	0.343	0.415	0.460	0.511	0.561	0.569
Theil index							
1984	0.145	0.266	0.384	0.441	0.471	0.473	0.549
1994	0.226	0.328	0.426	0.462	0.500	0.578	0.443
2004	0.353	0.303	0.352	0.401	0.447	0.480	0.584
2011	0.243	0.237	0.326	0.384	0.473	0.589	0.713

Source: Computed from various LFS, Singapore.

Note that with the expansion of educational opportunities, all age groups encountered better-educated entrants over time. However, for the age group 50+, less-educated people dominate, although this has decreased in the very recent period (this is also reflected in the individual age group inequality presented in Table 3.4). For the age group below 20, the left tail was stretched by the shift of the median to the right (also reflected by an increase in inequality in Table 3.4). In the 20–29 age group, the increase in post-secondary educated people has been spectacular. However, for the age groups 30–39 and 40–49 this increase is more prominent for tertiary-educated people, and the distribution continues to be quite unequal. This explains the within-age diversity of income.

To further demonstrate the observation that the contribution of within-age inequality is relatively very high we present Table 3.5, which demonstrates the age-occupation diversity of 2011. It can be seen that the disparity (measured in terms of standard deviation) within age groups on average is 3.3 times higher than that measured for the occupational groups (for different ages, which indicates to between-age inequality). This also demonstrates that within occupational groups, disparity is quite high and that may be because of the diverse age groups in the same occupation. In the next section we will analyse the disparity in occupation in further details.

Income inequality decomposed in occupation subgroups

In Table 3.2 we observed the changing age composition of the Singaporean labour force. Table 3.6 shows the relevant figures for the occupational structure of the labour force for the period 1984–2011. The two groups 'Managers' and 'Professionals' need a relatively higher degree of skilled labour, as opposed to the groups classified as 'Sales and service workers', 'Production and related workers', 'Transport equipment operators and labourers'. In the 1970s, 'Production and related workers', together with 'Sales and related workers' and 'Clerical workers' made up the three largest groups. However, economic restructuring in the early 1980s

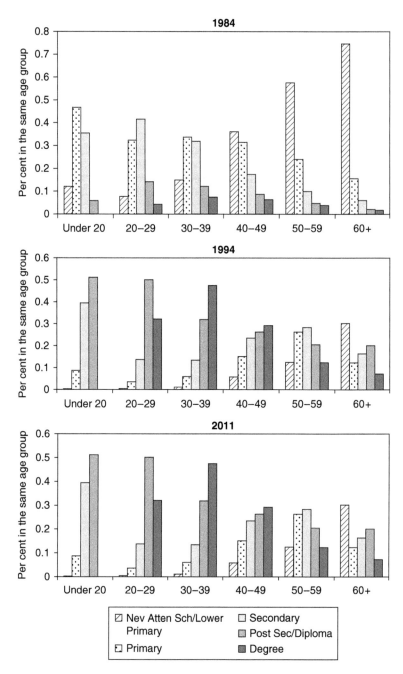

Figure 3.3 Age and education distribution, 1984, 1994 and 2011.

Source: Derived from LFS, Singapore: 1984, 1994, 2011.

Table 3.5 Median monthly gross wages in 2011 of various age and occupation groups

Occupation	25–29 years	30–39 years	40–49 years	50–59 years	Average for the occupation group	Standard deviation for the occupation group
Managers	3,926	6,000	8,000	8,200	6,531.5	1,732.88
Professionals	3,551	4,540	5,500	5,876	4,866.75	902.43
Associate professionals and technicians	2,700	3,188	3,420	3,423	3,182.75	294.57
Clerical support workers	1,950	2,172	2,343	2,342	2,201.75	161.16
Service and sales workers	2,396	2,644	2,596	1,867	2,375.75	308.10
Craftsman and related trades workers	1,943	2,530	2,699	2,894	2,516.5	355.28
Plants and machine operators and assemblers	2,262	2,237	2,284	2,085	2,217	78.00
Cleaners, labourers and related workers	1,416	1,450	1,334	1,200	1,350	96.32
Average for the age group	2,518	3,095.13	3,522	3,485.88		491.09[a]
Standard deviation for the age group		793.00	1,385.30	2,037.77	2,219.43	1,608.87[b]

Source: Computed from the MOM (2011, *Report of Wages in Singapore*).

Notes

[a] Average of standard deviations for occupation groups (indicates between group inequality).

[b] Average of standard deviations for age groups (that indicates within group inequality).

boosted the demand for professionals, managers and technicians. This increase was also due to the expansion of financial and business services as well as the commerce sectors. The employment share of managers and professionals increased from 16.4 per cent in 1984 to 53.4 per cent in 2011 (see Table 3.6).

This is attributable to the rise in educational attainment of the workforce. The share of the clerical workers remained relatively unchanged (with a moderate decrease) over the years. One reason is the relatively steady pool of secondary and post-secondary workforce. The pool of service workers experienced a drastic drop of 11.1 per cent from 1984 to 1994 due to a reduced pool of workers with below secondary education levels. The share of production and related workers also declined in this period. The reasons for this are both the reduction of Singaporean below secondary education, and the influx of foreign workers into these jobs.

Table 3.6 also reveals that the relative mean income of all jobs decreased over time. The wage premium of 'Professionals' over 'Clerical and related workers' in 1984 was almost 2.78, and that decreased to 2.10 in 2011. Note, too, that there was a 67 per cent decrease in relative mean income of 'Managers' and 42 per cent

Table 3.6 Population shares and relative mean incomes of various occupation groups, 1984–2011

Occupational groups	1984	1994	2004	2011
Population shares				
Professional	0.103	0.218	0.294	0.353
Managers	0.061	0.109	0.131	0.183
Clerical and related workers	0.168	0.148	0.131	0.126
Service workers, shop and market sales workers	0.237	0.126	0.110	0.127
Production workers, equipment operators and labourers	0.379	0.357	0.293	0.196
Relative mean income				
Professional	2.083	1.521	1.467	1.194
Managers	3.273	2.616	2.101	1.961
Clerical and related workers	0.749	0.688	0.674	0.569
Service workers, shop and market sales workers	0.796	0.605	0.570	0.456
Production workers, equipment operators and labourers	0.647	0.513	0.404	0.399

Source: Computed from various LFS, Singapore.

decrease in the relative mean income of 'Professionals'. As the Singapore government and companies do not reduce the wages of highly skilled professionals (even during recession periods, see Mukhopadhaya, 2004a) this decrease in relative mean income of skilled people is a direct manifestation of the presence of people with diversified skill levels in the same occupation group. Table 3.5 demonstrates this fact that in the two top high-earning groups the standard deviations are maximum. On the contrary in the period 1984 to 2011, the relative mean income for production workers decreased by 38 per cent. These occupational groups (which consist of less-educated people) experienced wage decreases; this can be linked with changing educational profiles and the needs of the economy over the period. Primarily, those occupational groups with a better-educated labour force obtained a declining mean income over the years because of the new workforce, the members of which are progressively more educated. Second, as the economy advanced, there was a reduced demand for manual workers who were usually less educated. As a result, these non-professional occupational groups have experienced wage declines, and this has been compounded by the fact that there was an influx of foreign workers. Because of lower wages, (and as at that relatively low wage the foreign workers were ready to work), the overall wage level of manual workers (including the locals) decreased over time.

Between-occupational inequality levels (Table 3.7) shows an upward trend between 1984 and 1994, it then stabilized until 2004, and once again increased after that. Between 1984 and 1994, the within-occupational inequality, as measured by the Theil index, decreased from 0.256 to 0.228. This shows a strong resemblance to trends in within-educational activity, thus illustrating that the education-occupation linkage is clear (discussed further in Chapter 4).

Table 3.7 Decomposition of the Theil index by occupation

Year	Theil index	Between-group inequality	Within-group inequality	Between-group contribution (per cent)	Within-group contribution (per cent)
1984	0.446	0.190	0.256	42.60	57.40
1994	0.443	0.216	0.228	48.76	51.47
2004	0.488	0.216	0.272	44.33	55.67
2011	0.530	0.238	0.292	44.93	55.07

Source: Computed from various LFS, Singapore.

Table 3.8 Inequality in individual occupational groups, 1984–2011

Year	Professionals	Managers	Clerical and related workers	Service workers, shop and market sales workers	Production workers, equipment operators and labourers
Gini coefficient					
1984	0.412	0.354	0.264	0.435	0.294
1994	0.413	0.374	0.206	0.303	0.307
2004	0.381	0.367	0.250	0.326	0.385
2011	0.406	0.404	0.344	0.384	0.375
Theil index					
1984	0.300	0.220	0.131	0.387	0.174
1994	0.292	0.270	0.079	0.172	0.164
2004	0.270	0.273	0.135	0.231	0.302
2011	0.311	0.295	0.186	0.282	0.267

Source: Computed from various LFS, Singapore.

The rise in between-occupational inequality can be attributed to a widening income share between the extreme occupational groups. The shortage of skilled labour has allowed the two most highly paid occupations – professional and managerial – to maintain their position relative to the other groups. On the other hand, the presence of cheap foreign workers has resulted in the relative stagnation of wages for workers in unskilled and semi-skilled occupations.[4]

The reduction in the contribution of within-occupational inequality is due to a reduction in individual group inequality for professionals and service people (Table 3.8). This implies that if between-occupational disparities had been kept in check, the overall level of income inequality may have gone down. The between-occupational inequality increase was due to the selective immigration policy referred to earlier. Immigration policy is not governed by income inequality considerations. The need to preserve international competitiveness may well mean that workers from both the upper and lower ends of the income scale will be attracted to Singapore. Thus, international competitiveness and rapid economic growth are not compatible with the objective of lowering the income inequality.

Table 3.8 presents the inequality of each occupational group. It is observed that in general the highest income inequality is for the occupational groups 'Professionals' and 'Managers'. Service workers also contribute highly in the national inequality. Most service and sales workers have a pay structure that comprises a fixed component and a variable component (sometimes called 'commission'). This variable component depends much on the individual's ability to provide a service and on the type of the service the individual is providing, which is why a wide

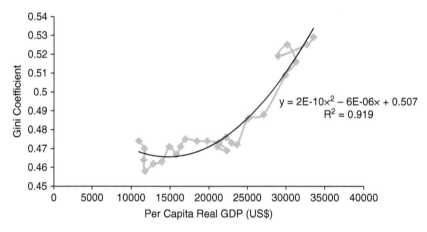

Figure 3.4 Relationship between inequality and growth in Singapore, 1983–2011.

Note: Per capita real GDP data is collected from *World Development Indicator* (2013).

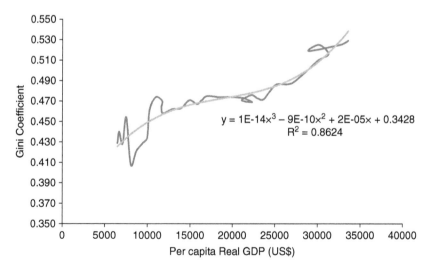

Figure 3.5 Relationship between inequality and growth in Singapore, 1974–2011.

Table 3.9 Gini coefficient: Singapore compared with other countries

Singapore	Hong Kong	Taiwan	Thailand	Malaysia	Indonesia	Japan	South Korea
1980s							
0.459 (average of 1980s)	39.4 (1980) 44.6 (1981) 42.2 (1986)	27.7 (1980) 28.0 (1981) 28.3 (1982) 28.7 (1983) 28.6 (1984) 29.0 (1985) 29.5 (1986) 29.6 (1987) 30.1 (1988) 30.1 (1989)	45.2 (1981)[a] 47.8 (1986) 43.8 (1988)[a]	48.6 (1984)[a] 47.0 (1987)[a] 46.2 (1989)[a]	31.0 (1980) 33.0 (1981) 30.5 (1984)[a] 29.3 (1987)[a]	33.4 (1980) 34.2 (1981) 35.7 (1982) 35.0 (1985)	29.0 (1988)
1990s							
0.472 (average of 1990s)	43.4 (1991) 43.4 (1996)[a]	30.9 (1990) 30.6 (1991) 31.1 (1992) 31.4 (1993) 31.7 (1994) 31.5 (1995) 31.5 (1996) 31.7 (1997) 32.0 (1998) 31.9 (1999)	43.6 (1990) 45.5 (1992) 44.0 (1994) 43.7 (1996) 43.0 (1998) 45.3 (1999)	47.7 (1992)[a] 48.5 (1995)[a] 49.2 (1997)[a]	29.2 (1990)[a] 29.3 (1993)[a] 31.3 (1996)[a] 29.0 (1999)[a]	35.0 (1990) 31.1 (1992) 24.9 (1993)[a] 30.3 (1997)	34.7 (1992) 31.5 (1993) 32.6 (1995) 32.6 (1996) 31.6 (1997) 36.9 (1998)
2000s							
0.504 (average of 2000)	52.5 (2001)[b] 53.3 (2006)[b]	32.0 (2000) 34.5 (2001) 34.1 (2002) 33.9 (2003)	42.9 (2000) 42.7 (2001) 42.0 (2002) 42.4 (2006)[a] 40.5 (2008)[a] 40.0 (2009)[a]	37.9 (2004)[a] 46.0 (2007)[a] 46.2 (2009)[a]	29.7 (2002)[a] 34.0 (2005)[a]		35.8 (2000)[c] 31.6 (2004) 31.0 (2010)[c]

Source: WIID, 2008 unless otherwise specified. Singapore Ginis are author's calculation from various LFSs.

Notes

[a] World Development Indicators 2013; [b] Half-yearly Economic Report 2012, Hong Kong Economy.

[c] CIA World Factbook.

variation is likely to be observed in this occupational group. On the other hand, 'Clerical and related workers' have little variation in their incomes. They usually have the same level of educational attainment and their pay is standardized across industries. Thus this group tends to have the smallest degree of income inequality over the relevant years.

Does growth and inequality follow any pattern in Singapore?

Figure 3.4 traces the relationship between growth and inequality in Singapore for the period 1983–2011. The fitted polynomial shows that the relationship resembles a truncated U, which means that for at least some years in Singapore in the 1980s as the economy was growing, inequality decreased. However, after 1987, inequality increased as the economy experienced high growth rates.

We noted in the previous chapter that Kuznets hypothesized an *inverted U-relationship* between per capita income and inequality. He reasoned that in the early stages of economic growth, inequality increases due to growth in income being often centred in some sections of the economy or the regions in the country. As the entire economy modernizes, increases in welfare spread across all sectors and regions. We failed to observe any such behaviour in the case of Singapore between 1983 and 2011. To examine this further by including the years before 1983, we present Figure 3.5 showing the relationship between inequality and per capita real GDP from 1974 to 2011. No such Kuznets-type pattern is observed here.

Singapore inequality compared

Table 3.9 presents Gini coefficients for some other countries in the region. This is to show that none of the other countries, except Taiwan, has compiled data on personal income distributions using the concept of earnings comparable to that employed in the Singapore LFS. The Taiwan Gini for individuals for all incomes (including property income) remained significantly lower than Singapore's Gini. If property incomes are included, the Singapore Gini would have been even higher.

The Income Inequality Database of WIDER indicates that Singapore's inequality is much higher than the Scandinavian and Benelux nations, Australia and the UK, while Singapore's inequality is lower than that of the USA (see Table 2.1).

Conclusion

This chapter provides a description of the trends in income inequality in Singapore over the period 1984 to 2011. In terms of Gini coefficients, the World Income Inequality Database (WIID) shows Singapore as ahead of Thailand, South Korea, Taiwan and Indonesia. This is a result of attracting talented and skilled workers by rewarding them handsomely in order to raise productivity, while at the same time allowing firms and households to employ workers at the lower end of the income ladder. It can also be observed that educational expansion has not lowered the level of income inequality.

The decomposition analysis has brought out some interesting facts. Within-age and within-occupation income disparities respectively contributed some 88 per cent and 55 per cent to the overall inequality. These between-occupational disparities have been high in overall inequality and this has been due to the impact of selective immigration policies and related factors.

We noted that over the years the within-age inequality had increased, while within-occupation inequality remained almost constant. Thus the increases in inequality are accounted for by the increase in within-age and between-occupational inequalities. The between-age inequality showed a reduction from the decrease in the age premium of income. Consequently, the drive to enhance educational opportunities in the country, along with increased numbers of better-educated entrants in the workforce, caused increases in the within-age groups disparity. Although, over time, and as a result of restructuring, the premium on salaries for better-educated workers decreased, income disparity remained quite high between skilled (educated) and un-skilled (less-educated) labourers. The selective immigration policy of the government of Singapore depresses the wage rate for some of the occupations related to construction etc., while professionals and managers attracted high salaries. Thus the between-occupation inequality also increases.

Appendix

Income inequality from the Household Expenditure Survey data

Table A3.1 presents the Gini of household incomes for various household sizes. Some government reports (published by Department of Statistics, Singapore, for

Table A3.1 Measurement of Gini from Household Expenditure Survey data

Household size	1982/3	1987/8	1992/3	1997/8	2002/3	2007/8
1	0.585	NA	NA	NA	0.471	0.541
2	0.700	0.705	0.688	0.574	0.595	0.686
3	0.749	0.777	0.751	0.685	0.712	0.712
4	0.754	0.819	0.775	0.737	0.726	0.661
5	0.778	0.839	0.763	0.745	0.729	0.618
6	0.779	0.840	0.739			
7	0.752	0.832	0.716			
8	0.740	0.837	0.564	0.673[b]	0.689[b]	0.575[b]
9	0.734	0.801	0.630			
10+	0.207	0.854	0.516			
Total: all sizes	0.463	0.402[a]	0.766	0.723	0.715	0.692

Source: Computed from the basic data in the respective Household Expenditure Surveys.
Notes
[a]Not household size adjusted.
[b]6 and above.
NA: Not available.

example, DOS, 2000 and DOS, 2005) use Household Expenditure Survey (HES) data to measure inequality in Singapore. It can be observed from Table A3.1 that overall Gini has increased from 0.463 in 1982/3 to 0.692 in 2007/8. We must warn the reader at this point that any fluctuation of Gini for the *total* sample from 1982/3 to 2008/9 has little significance because, in some cases, incomes were not household-size-adjusted (for lack of information); moreover, the changing income grouping provided by the reports affected the measurement of income inequality. In the early years after classifying the HES income data for household size, the sample size in each group was quite small and the results were not interpretable. For 2002/3 and 2007/8 data, a weighting factor is provided which makes the result more reliable. The estimates presented in Table A3.1 do not have much in the way of policy implications; the only conclusion that we may make here is that the Gini had increased since 1982/3.

Inequality calculated from Census of Population and General Household Surveys

Table A3.2 provides the values of Gini coefficients as reported by the *Singapore Census of Population*, 2000. The calculation excluded households with no income earners. These estimates are in the lower range compared to our calculations. Employing our methodology, our own calculations are also reported in the table.

Inequality calculated from income tax data

Gini coefficients are given in Table A3.3 for resident taxpayers. The Ginis are relatively low compared to the LFS. This is particularly due to the lower income groups not necessarily being in the taxpayer category and thus excluded. The trend of inequality as observed in the LFS is similar here. In 2011 (and the period

Table A3.2 Trend of Gini, 1990–2010

Year	1990	1995	1997	1998	1999	2000	2005	2010
Reported by *Singapore Census of Population*, 2000	0.44	0.44	0.44	0.45	0.47	0.48	—	—
Our calculation	0.468[a]	0.470[b]	—	—	—	0.483[c]	0.495[d]	0.542[e] (0.495)[f]

Notes
[a]Computed from *Census of Population*, 1990.
[b]Computed from *General Household Survey*, 1995.
[c]Computed from *Census of Population*, 2000.
[d]Computed from *General Household Survey*, 2005.
[e]Computed from *Census of Population*, 2010 (for total population and household size not adjusted).
[f]Computed from *Census of Population*, 2010 (household size not adjusted), 'No working people' are excluded.

Table A3.3 Trends in inequality in earnings, 1980–2011

Year	IRAS: Pre-tax Gini coefficient	IRAS: Post-tax Gini coefficient
1980	0.440	0.403
1990	0.470	0.443
2011	0.471	0.481

around, see Mukhopadhaya *et al.*, 2011) the value of post-tax Gini is higher than pre-tax, which demonstrates that tax in Singapore does not aim to redistribute income (at least in the recent period).

A note on the Singapore government's wage policy

In Singapore a periodic adjustment of labour costs through wage policy was used as an adjustment to achieve a near full-employment economy. In 1972 the government established the National Wages Council (NWC), a tripartite forum with representation from employers' federations, trade unions and the government. As a government advisory body, the Council recommends annual wage adjustments for the entire economy (this is non-binding but widely followed), and ensures orderly wage development so as to promote a sound economic environment. It assists in the development of incentive schemes to improve national productivity.

There is no minimum wage in Singapore.[5] This reflects the government's total faith on the operation of the market mechanism without any rigidity (which could have restricted business and increased unemployment). Also, for the wage determination of the blue-collar workers (almost 40 per cent of the total labour force) the influence of unions is stronger than NWC recommendations, but market forces have influenced the unions.

During 1973–9, actual wage increases followed NWC guidelines closely. In 1979 a 'wage correction policy' was introduced, when a 3-year high wage increase was recommended. It was designed to induce productivity of higher value-added operations, to reduce reliance on cheap unskilled foreign labour and to raise labour productivity. During 1980–4, actual wage increases exceeded recommended wages by 2.4 percentage points per year on average arising from very high labour demand. Moreover, for unionized workers the collective agreement lasted for 2–3 years with built-in wage increases. Thus despite a relatively low starting wage, as we have observed in this chapter, a huge inequality of income was institutionalized through longevity of employment and annual increases.

Mainly because of the high wage (the annual increase of wage and rise in mandatory Central Provident Fund (CPF) component), in 1985 Singapore experienced economic recession. To restrain wages, in mid-November 1986 the government instituted a 'flexi-wage policy', which became effective with the enactment of the Employment Amendment Act 1988. The flexi-wage system tries to overcome rigidities in wage structure and thus allows individual companies to adjust to rapidly changing economic conditions. The NWC recommended that up to 20 per cent of the total wage should be in the form of an annual variable component (AVC). The AVC represented an alternative way to adjust wages in the absence of government-instituted CPF cuts. The following features were also introduced in the wage determination process:

1 annual wage negotiations on the basis that total wage increase lagging behind productivity improvement;
2 adjustment of the variable wage component by means of a formula based on company productivity and/or profitability;
3 periodic review of salaries taking relevant factors into account; such a review was proposed to be made no more than once in 3-year intervals and should preferably coincide with the renewal of collective agreements;
4 individual performance to be taken into account for wage increases; and
5 sharing of relevant company information.

These policies aim to moderate wage increases through lower growth and higher productivity both at individual and at firm levels.

By 1998 the AVC was built up to 16 per cent of an employee's total wage on average. More than 90 per cent of unionized companies and 70 per cent of non-unionized companies have implemented some form of AVC. However, during the economic downturn at the time of the Asian economic crises in 1998, only 7 per cent of firms reduced wages under the flexible system, while 25 per cent froze wages and 40 per cent provided lower annual salary increases (Mukhopadhaya, 2004a).

Using AVC, a company was able to reduce wages by up to 16 per cent during the crisis. However, the reduction could only take place at the end of the year after negotiations between employees and employers. To increase the flexibility of the system, in 1999 NWC recommended an introduction of a monthly variable component (MVC) of 10 per cent of wages. The MVC would allow companies to adjust wage costs in a given month. It also recommended that a portion of the future wage increases be set aside each year as MVC, until total amounts reached 10 per cent. Therefore the new wage structure has 3 components: the basic wage (70 per cent), MVC (10 per cent) and AVC (20 per cent). NWC recommendations were accepted by the government on May 23, 2001. During that period NWC reported that 29 per cent of the unionized companies and 2.4 per cent of the non-unionized companies had instituted the MVC.

In 2002 the labour market was very weak due to the uncertain global environment; total employment fell by 40,900 and 19,100 workers were retrenched. While the total wage increased by 1.1 per cent in 2001, it came to a standstill in 2002. Basic wages of all employees rose by only 1.8 per cent. This increase was offset by a 15 per cent reduction in the variable component to 1.77 month of basic wage in 2002.

In early 2003 severe acute respiratory syndrome (SARS) hurt the viability of business and job prospects in various companies in Singapore. Employment fell by 9,400 during the first quarter and 4,200 workers were retrenched. On 15 April, 2003 the NWC recommended

1   implementation of a shorter working week;
2   temporary lay-offs; and
3   arrangements for workers to take leave or undergo skills training and upgrading provided by the Ministry of Manpower (MOM) and other agencies as temporary cost-cutting measures.

In view of the impact of SARS on the economy, the NWC recommended that companies directly affected may implement appropriate wage cuts to survive the economic downturn and to save jobs. If the wage structure of firms was not in line with current market conditions, they were asked to restructure their current wage system. Thus, the NWC emphasized on the conversion of the fixed- and seniority-based pay to productivity and profit sharing bonuses by transferring more than 2 per cent from the basic wage into the MVC. Companies that were not directly affected by SARS were asked to follow the same path. The demise of the seniority-based wage system was also recommended by the Economic Review Committee (ERC) and endorsed by the government. The NWC strongly urged companies and unions to speed up wage restructuring to narrow the wage maximum/minimum ratio to an average 1.5 or less. It also recommended implementation of measures for employees, whose salaries exceeded the maximum point in the desirable salary ratio, for example by reducing or freezing the maximum wage scales. These recommendations were to apply for a period for one year, subject to review by the NWC.

The global financial crisis hit Singapore once again in 2008–9. Singapore's economic growth slowed to 1.1 per cent in 2008; significantly lower than the 7.8 per cent growth in 2007. In particular, the fourth quarter of 2008 contracted by 4.2 per cent on a year-on-year basis. The total employment growth of 221,600 in 2008 was also lower than the growth of 234,900 in 2007. With the economy weakening towards the end of the year, the seasonally adjusted unemployment rate rose to 2.5 per cent (overall) and 3.6 per cent (resident) in December 2008; up from 2.3 per cent and 3.4 per cent respectively in September 2008. Redundancies also hit a high of 9,410 workers in the fourth quarter of 2008, making up more than half of the 16,880 redundancies over the whole of 2008. Along with this employment drop, overall labour productivity declined sharply from −0.8 per cent in 2007 to −7.8 per cent in 2008 due to slower GDP growth and strong employment gains in the first half of 2008 (see Table A3.4). This was the second year that labour productivity had contracted. With the economic downturn and increased business costs, wage increases granted were more restrained. Nominal total wages rose by 4.2 per cent in 2008, (2007 experienced a rise of 5.9 per cent). This was the result of a basic wage gain of 4.4 per cent (compared to 4.3 per cent in 2007) and a 2.1 per cent decline in the bonus payout of 2.31 months in 2008 (compared to 2.36 months in 2007).

Overall unit labour cost increased for the fourth straight year, by 9.6 per cent in 2008, which was higher than the 5.2 per cent increase in 2007, largely reflecting the contraction in productivity in 2008.

Table A3.4 Changes in real wage and productivity

Year	1994	1999	2001	2002	2003	2004	2005	2006	2007	2008
Real total wage change	5.4	2.8	0.1	0.4	1.0	1.9	3.8	3.5	3.8	−2.3
Productivity growth	6.8	7.7	5.7	5.6	5.0	7.5	2.8	1.6	−0.8	−7.8

Source: MOM Survey on Annual Wage Changes and DOS (Labour Productivity).[6]

As a result of this downturn the NWC recommended in 2009–10 to cut costs, save jobs and enhance competitiveness. However, the NWC also indicated that companies which performed well should reward their workers with moderate wage increases, in the form of variable payments. It was advised that companies with excess workers should take measures such as implementing a shorter work week, temporary layoffs, no paid leave, and other work arrangements as alternatives to retrenchments. The selective wage cut and increases demonstrate the trend of inequality in income that we observed in this chapter.

However, since the last NWC guidelines were released in January 2009, the government announced a $20.5 billion Resilience Package to help reduce costs and save jobs. The package includes the Jobs Credit Scheme, Workfare Income Supplement (WIS) Special Payment to help low-wage workers, and various tax concessions. The Managing Excess Manpower (MEM) Guidelines have been updated, and the Skills Programme for Upgrading and Resilience (SPUR) has also been enhanced to help more professionals, managers, executives and technicians (PMETs). These measures certainly restrict the increase in inequality, which may have increased more if these measures had not been implemented.

Furthermore, the NWC encouraged companies to make use of components of the flexible wage system, MVC, to manage their total wage costs. The MOM 2008 Survey on Annual Wage Changes indicates that companies with MVC in their wage structure are better able to gain employees' acceptance of a wage cut if it has to be implemented, compared to companies without MVC. To encourage more companies to implement MVC, the NWC endorsed the recommendation in the MEM guidelines that companies could implement a cut in basic wages by introducing it as a reduction in MVC, and therefore allow these companies the opportunity to introduce MVC and make their wages more flexible.

As Singapore's economy recovered throughout 2010–11, the NWC recommended wage increases through built-in and variable payments. It is worth noting that from 1 September 2011, employers' Central Provident Fund (CPF) contribution rate increased by 0.5 percentage points, and the CPF salary ceiling was raised from $4,500 to $5,000 per month. The NWC recommended that in granting wage increases, companies pay greater attention to low-wage workers. For example, companies could include a dollar quantum for built-in wage increases and/or variable payments. However, no specific guideline was provided. The Council also encouraged the tripartite partners to reach out to lower-wage workers, including contract and casual workers, to help them contribute to their CPF and be eligible for the Workfare Income Supplement (WIS). Companies and workers were also encouraged to tap into the Workfare Training Support (WTS) scheme to help workers upgrade their skills so that they can move into better jobs with higher pay and improved career prospects. In particular, the NWC noted that from 1 January 2012, employers were required to re-employ workers beyond the minimum retirement age of 62.

Companies were also encouraged to put in place proper performance appraisal systems. Employees were also asked to be flexible in working out re-employment arrangements with their employers, to be open to training and skills upgrading, and be prepared to make adjustments to their wages and benefits if necessary. Despite the evidence of re-employment of older workers the recent changes in the wage structure in Singapore aim to replace the seniority-based wage system to one

Table A3.5 Singapore: levy rates and quotas for foreign workers (as at 1 July 2012)

Sector	Dependency ceiling[a]	Category	Monthly rates
Manufacturing	Up to 25% of the total workforce	Skilled	$230
		Unskilled	$330
	Between 25% and 50% of the total workforce	Skilled	$330
		Unskilled	$430
	Between 50% and 60% of the total workforce	Skilled	$500
		Unskilled	
Construction	1 full-time local worker to 7 foreign workers	Higher skilled and on MYE	$280
		Basic skilled and on MYE	$400
		Higher skilled, experienced and exempted from MYE	$550
		Basic skilled, experienced and exempted from MYE	$650
Marine	1 full-time local worker to 5 foreign workers	Skilled	$230
		Unskilled	$330
Process	1 full-time local worker to 7 foreign workers	Skilled	$230
		Unskilled	$330
		Experienced and exempted from MYE	$500
Service	Up to 15% of the total workforce	Skilled	$270
		Unskilled	$370
	Between 15% and 25% of the total workforce	Skilled	$380
		Unskilled	$480
	Between 25% and 45% of the total workforce	Skilled	$550
		Unskilled	

Source: MOM (2013a).

Notes
MYE: Man-year entitlements.

[a] It is believed that there are also informal unpublished quotas on foreign workers from particular countries in particular sectors. These may change from time to time. This information however is not provided to the public by the authorities.

that is performance based. These changes are not abrupt; rather they were planned long ago at the time of restructuring in the mid-1980s.

Wages and unskilled labour and the non-Singaporean workforce

The NWC recommendation is not applicable to the foreign labour and unskilled workforce in Singapore. The persistent high demand for labour forced Singapore's government to import labour from Malaysia, Thailand, Indonesia, the Philippines and the Indian subcontinent, which created pressure on wages offered to unskilled local workers. The number of foreign workers rose from 210,000 in 1990 to 360,000 in 1995, 590,000 in 2001 and 1,088,600 in 2010 (about 870,000 of whom were unskilled). Thus in 2010, 27.7 per cent of Singapore's workforce consisted of foreign unskilled labour, while 7.0 per cent was foreign skilled labour.[7] With a view to not disturbing the local employment situation by the influx of foreign labour, the Singapore Government set a maximum ratio of foreign domestic workers in certain sectors. However, companies in the construction sector bypass the quota, satisfying the requirement only by employing *skilled local* workers.

The government of Singapore has imposed a monthly levy to be paid by employers for each foreign worker (see Table A3.5). This levy increases the cost of employing foreign workers and thus creates a disincentive to replace Singaporean workers. The levy amount is approximately the sum required to pay a local worker. The amount of this levy varies for sectors and skill levels. The foreign workers levy works as a minimum wage for local unskilled workers. Although theoretically the levy creates disincentives to employ foreign workers, employers find it cost-effective to hire foreigners so as to avoid the mandatory contribution to the CPF.

Notes

1 See, for example, Pang (1975), Rao and Ramakrishnan (1980), Islam and Kirkpatrick (1986), Rao (1990, 1996), Mukhopadhaya *et al.* (2011), Shantakumar and Mukhopadhaya (2008, 2002), Mukhopadhaya and Chung (2007), Mukhopadhaya (2005, 2004a, b, 2001a, b, 2003a, b), Mukhopadhaya and Rao (2002), Mukhopadhaya and Shantakumar (2009), Rao *et al.* (2003).
2 Analysis of the increase in female labour force participation in Singapore can be found in Mukhopadhaya (2001a). See also Mukhopadhaya (2001b).
3 See Appendix of this chapter.
4 Note that the increase of between-group inequality is quite not revealed from Table 3.6. This is because in Table 3.6 we did not present the miscellaneous group 'other'.
5 Orthodox economic theory shows that minimum wage generates risk of higher unemployment of marginal/inexperienced workers. This is the reason expressed by the Singapore government for not creating any minimum wage law to avoid the danger of companies departing Singapore for lack of competitiveness in the existence of minimum wage laws.
6 See further at http://www.mom.gov.sg/newsroom/Pages/PressReleasesDetail.aspx?listid=54 [accessed 29 October 2013].
7 http://www.migrationinformation.org/feature/print.cfm?ID=887 [accessed 29 October 2013]; *Report on Wages in Singapore*, 2011.

4 Educational development and income inequality

At the time of independence most Singaporeans were illiterate and only the rich were educated. Thus education was seen as one of the major reasons for the large disparity in income in the late 1950s and early 1960s. This lack of skill in the population impeded the growth prospects for the country as well. Therefore immediately after its independence the government of Singapore concentrated heavily on the development of education with the intent to generate a pool of skilled workers. With rapid expansion of education, universal primary education was attained in 1965 and universal lower secondary education was attained by the early 1970s. During the 1970s Singapore realized the necessity for it to become a high-skilled economy because of growing competition from other Asian countries for low-skilled labour-intensive industries, and that this could be achieved through education. However, it was not until 1979 that a new education system was introduced in an effort to improve the quality of education, particularly with the aim to produce a more technically skilled workforce to achieve this new economic goal.

Singapore introduced an education system based on ability ('streaming') to enable all students to reach their full potential, while accepting the fact that not everyone can grow at the same pace. More time was allowed to complete different stages of schooling; the multiple pathways to high schools were:

1 academic high schools to prepare students for university;
2 polytechnic high schools offering advanced occupational and technical training, and that could also lead students to university; and
3 technical institutes offering occupational and technical training to cater for the lowest fifth of students.

As a result, the drop-out rate declined and the quality of students was enhanced (as reflected in the Trends in International Mathematics and Science Study (TIMSS) results). Since 1992 Singapore has invested significantly in the Institute for Technical Education (ITE) to produce students with high quality technical and vocational education. This effort was made to sustain a continuous supply of technically equipped graduates to the new foreign companies (with sophisticated technical base) in Singapore.

Essentially the education system that was followed in Singapore was efficiency-driven. This was more pronounced when Singapore started placing emphasis on the growth of its global knowledge economy after the Asian financial crisis. Recently in Singapore a new educational vision was created to develop creative thinking skills, lifelong learning passion and nationalistic commitment in the young ('Thinking Schools, Learning Nation'). Streaming at the elementary level of education has been replaced by subject matter banding. This has created more opportunities for students to move between streams at the secondary levels and beyond. This is expected to benefit those who bloom late. The effect of these new changes may take some time to be reflected in terms of earnings etc.

Inequality and education

Between 1984 and 2011, the educational level of the labour force shifted upwards due to an increasing number of better educated entrants. The proportion of the workforce with below primary education decreased from 20.3 per cent in 1984 to 15.1 per cent in 1994 to 7.4 per cent in 2011 (see Table 4.1). On the other hand, the proportion of the labour force with secondary and higher education almost increased from 47.2 per cent to 55.9 per cent to 78 per cent in the same period.

Decomposition of the Theil index by level of educational attainment is presented in Table 4.2. This pattern was due to a shift away from the low value-added activities and towards the higher value-added skills- and technology-intensive sectors in the early 1980s. This restructuring of the economy shifted educational wage differentials in favour of professional and other skilled workers (Mukhopadhaya, 2003a), resulting in higher inequality levels between educational groups. However, the upward shift in the educational composition of the workforce, together with the recession in 1985/86, brought these skill premiums down in the mid-1980s. The decomposition results show that the contribution of within-group inequality is almost double of that of between-group inequality.[1] While the total inequality measured by the Theil index increased by 15.84 per cent during 1984 to 2011, the within-group inequality increased by 23.38 per cent and the between-group inequality rose by 11.30 per cent during the same period.[2]

The rapid increase in within-group inequality in education can be explained in light of the figures provided in Table 4.1. The increase in within-group inequality is the result of an increase in population share in the higher earning groups (that is, for the groups where educational attainments are higher) and due to the income disparity within the same educational groups (and not between educational groups). Table 4.1 shows that while in 1984 the tertiary educated earned 3.7 times more on average than the mean income for the whole population, in 2011 they earned only 1.7 times more (as a result the between-group inequality did not increase); and only 5 per cent of the workforce in 1984 had tertiary education, while in 2011 more than 29 per cent of the labour force were tertiary educated.

Table 4.1 Population share, relative mean income and inequality within various educational groups, 1984–2011

	1984			1994			2004			2011		
	Pop. share	Relative mean income	Theil index	Pop. share	Relative mean income	Theil index	Pop. share	Relative mean income	Theil index	Pop. share	Relative mean income	Theil index
Never attended school/lower primary	0.203	0.068	0.285	0.151	0.521	0.260	0.136	0.379	0.331	0.074	0.351	0.377
Primary/lower secondary	0.322	0.655	0.235	0.289	0.640	0.210	0.181	0.572	0.316	0.145	0.474	0.382
Secondary	0.314	0.962	0.303	0.303	0.882	0.296	0.255	0.742	0.360	0.202	0.704	0.410
Post-secondary	0.108	1.535	0.375	0.111	1.251	0.444	0.114	0.999	0.420	0.109	0.730	0.411
Diploma	—	—	—	0.054	1.300	0.299	0.107	1.098	0.307	0.177	1.013	0.345
Tertiary	0.050	3.712	0.195	0.091	2.843	0.291	0.205	2.055	0.249	0.292	1.723	0.306

Source: Computed from LFS, Department of Statistics, Government of Singapore, various years.

Table 4.2 Decomposition of Theil index by educational attainment, 1984–2011

Year	Theil index	Between-group inequality	Within-group inequality	Between-group contribution (%)	Within-group contribution (%)
1984	0.446	0.168	0.278	37.67	62.33
1994	0.443	0.149	0.294	33.63	66.37
2004	0.488	0.180	0.308	36.95	63.05
2011	0.530	0.187	0.343	35.32	64.68

Source: Computed from LFS, Department of Statistics, Government of Singapore, various years.

Table 4.3 Median monthly gross wages of people aged 35–39 for various industry and occupational groups, June 2011 (in $)

Industry/occupational groups	Managers	Professionals	Associate professionals and technicians	Clerical support workers	Coefficient of variation (%)
Financial services	8,085	6,388	3,761	2,338	43.46
Info & communications	7,859	5,122	3,327	2,159	46.55
Professional services	7,599	5,504	3,481	2,600	40.26
Manufacturing	5,946	4,568	3,263	2,075	36.46
Transport & storage	5,500	4,494	3,330	2,208	31.80
Wholesale & retail trade	5,450	4,424	3,261	2,135	32.54
Community, social & personal	5,098	5,262	3,000	2,148	34.53
Construction	5,050	3,800	2,800	1,819	35.57
Admin & support services	4,800	4,300	2,834	2,130	30.66
Real estate & leasing	4,500	4,060	2,680	2,127	29.06
Accommodation & food services	3,615	3,541	2,566	1,877	24.87
Coefficient of variation (%)	24.18	16.86	11.31	9.23	

Source: Computed from *Report of Wages in Singapore*, 2011.

This observation may be further substantiated using the recent *Report on Wages* (MOM, 2011). Table 4.3 shows the disparity in median monthly gross wage at age level 35–39 in various industry groups for several occupations. If we assume that the managers and professionals are generally the tertiary-educated people, a wide divergence can be observed in these occupational groups as the types of degrees differ (that lead to the graduates being employed in different industries). A manager in the financial services earns more than twice the salary of a manager employed in accommodation and food services. The disparity of wages in this age group for managers is 24.18 per cent measured by coefficient of variation, while for the professionals the disparity is almost 16 per cent. Within the clerical and support workers category the disparity is much lower. The high disparity in income coupled with increasing population share within the same educational group cause the high inequality as a whole. It is worth noting that the inequality in specific tertiary education groups as reported in Table 4.1 does not show a high value of inequality because the calculations in Table 4.1 are made for all age groups. This shows that with increasing training and age premium (that reflects productivity), there is some moderation of inequality within the same educational group.

A note on education policy

To respond to the public debate of increasing income inequality, government officials in Singapore stressed that the increase in inequality is not a local phenomenon. It has been claimed that the income data does not include several in-kind opportunities, which actually are meant for the poorer section of society, such as education policies.

Human capital theory offers a possible explanation for the wage differentials observed in an economy (see Chapter 1). The theory was built on the application of the principle of equal net benefits. In the human capital model, each individual makes an investment decision on education (schooling and training). Education is assumed to increase the productivity of the worker and consequently the worker's income. An individual normally forgoes income while studying in school and spending money on books etc. A rational individual will therefore choose to invest in human capital as long as the rate of return on his or her investment is greater than the prevailing discount rate. Thus occupations that require a longer period of education/training have to provide a correspondingly higher level of income if they are to attract people. This theory, therefore, suggests that in order to avoid a concentration of income, widespread educational opportunities are to be advocated.[3]

In the early 1990s the Singapore government started focusing on equal educational opportunities. The term 'equal educational opportunity' may have many different meanings. For example, in Richards and Leonor (1981), several variants of the principle were cited as:

1 An equal amount of education to everyone.
2 Sufficient education to bring everyone to a given standard.
3 Sufficient education for everyone to reach his/her potential.
4 Continued education provided gains in learning per unit of teaching match an agreed norm.

The first definition suggests that equal educational opportunity only in the absolute sense of an equal amount of schooling, by no means guarantees similar results for everyone due to the interplay of factors such as innate abilities. The second definition builds on the first, as the given standard would usually mean the completion of certain number of years of education. The third definition requires a large amount of resources to be devoted to the education system, as human potential is largely undefined.[4] The fourth definition is similar to the previous one, apart from the added constraint of the agreed norm. As there is a trade-off between the equalization of educational inputs and the equalization of results (Richards and Leonor, 1981), an important issue is whether educational policies should seek to equalize inputs or results. The latter, however, is inefficient for the economy, as those who are more capable would be restrained by the development of those who are less capable. However, this does not mean that the government should be satisfied with providing equal educational resources. The ideal policy stand might be to provide everyone with an equal chance of attaining the same education path. Whether the results are being equalized is of secondary importance. The Singapore government's education policy relies on this philosophy.

The structure of a formal education system: with emphasis on meritocracy

Every child in Singapore is expected to undergo at least ten years of general education.[5] Currently, students receive six years of primary education and four–five years of secondary education. This is followed by two years of junior college, polytechnic or the ITE (polytechnic education lasts for three years leading to a diploma, whereas ITE education lasts for three years depending on the subjects chosen). At the primary level, students go through a four-year foundation course whereby basic literacy and numeracy skills are emphasized. Science is introduced from Primary 3, with civics and moral education, social studies, health, physical education, art and music as the other subjects taught in primary school. Streaming was a key feature of the Singapore education system and was designed to allow students to progress at their own pace from Primary 5 onwards. In 2008 streaming was replaced by subject-based banding. Under the current system at primary 4, on the basis of the results from a school-based examination, students are recommended for a subject combination. Four bands are recommended at this stage:

1   If the student passes all four subjects and performs very well in Mother Tongue Language he/she is banded in the top.
2   If a student passes all four subjects, he/she is recommended for the second band.
3   If he/she passes three subjects the student is recommended for the third band.
4   And all other students (who pass two subjects or fewer) are placed in the bottom band.

Banding at the lower primary level theoretically provides an opportunity to the late-bloomer to shine at some later stage, however, in practice there is little scope left for these people to crawl to the top. This meritocratic-based educational framework leads to high earning disparity in the future. At the end of Primary 6 all students sit for the Primary School Leaving Examination (PSLE). Based on the results of this examination, the top 60 per cent of students are admitted to a secondary express course, 25 per cent are put in normal academic courses, and the final 15 per cent go on to regular technical courses in secondary schools.

Students in the express course follow a four-year programme leading to a general certificate of education (GCE) O-level examination. While students in the normal academic course follow a four-year course to GCE N-level and may sit for O-levels in year 5. The normal technical programme prepares students for technical higher education, jobs or the post-secondary ITE after a four-year programme leading to the GCE-N level. Recently, more choice has been offered to students in secondary schools, with a wider range of subjects at O-level and elective modules. Students who have the ability to go to university may study in the integrated Programme Schools where they can skip O-levels. This arrangement allows them to engage in broader learning experiences that develop their leadership potential and capacity for creative thinking. Compared to the situation before 2008, there is now more horizontal mobility between courses, and students who bloom later may transfer between streams. The ratio among streams is further enhanced with students being able to follow subjects from different streams. Schools specializing in visual art, sports etc. are also available (there are also a small number of independent schools). This flexibility may reduce any possible income differential that may arise in the previous more stringent system.

Students may go for post-secondary education after ten years of general education. Post-secondary education may be obtained from junior colleges (31 per cent of students), polytechnics (43 per cent) and ITE (22 per cent). Academically-inclined students may take GCE A-level examinations during this time and may proceed to university. Alternatively, some students may take diploma courses (in technical or business subjects) at polytechnics. Many polytechnic graduates with good results may also go to university. Students with GCE O- or N-levels can take skills-based certificate courses in technical or vocational subjects at the ITE. Outstanding ITE graduates can also go to the polytechnics or universities. Around 25 per cent of students in Singapore go to local universities; many students also go to foreign universities in the UK, Australia and the USA particularly.

At present in Singapore there are four polytechnics: Singapore Polytechnic, Ngee Ann Polytechnic, Temasek Polytechnic and Nanyang Polytechnic. These polytechnics offer a wide range of courses at diploma and post-diploma levels. Singapore has six national universities: the National University of Singapore, Nanyang Technological University, Singapore Management University, Singapore University of Technology and Design, Singapore Institute of Technology and SIM University.[6] Figure 4.1 outlines the educational system of Singapore.

Government financial support

Given the important role that education plays in ensuring a fairer income distribution, the government has been keeping public schools, including universities, affordable and open to all school-aged children and youths who qualified according to meritocratic selection regardless of race, gender and class background.

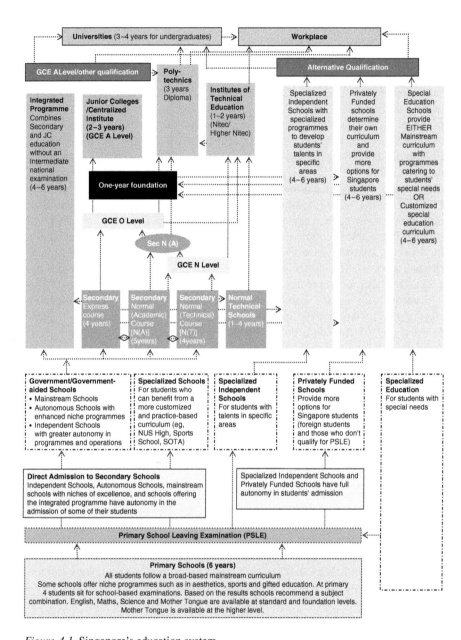

Figure 4.1 Singapore's education system.

Source: http://parents-in-education.moe.gov.sg/pie/slot/u1/About%20Singapore%20Schools/moe-corporate-brochure.pdf

Table 4.4 Government expenditures on education

Financial year	Real recurrent expenditure ($000s)	Real development expenditure ($000s)	Total real expenditure (recurrent + development) ($000s)
1997/8	3,865,791	1,272,493	5,138,284
1998/9	3,666,001	1,951,036	5,617,037
1999/00	3,769,530	1,852,563	5,622,093
2000/1	4,882,301	1,815,766	6,698,067
2001/2	5,392,176	1,666,279	7,058,456
2002/3	5,476,044	2,013,121	7,489,166
2003/4	5,646,092	1,375,868	7,021,959
2004/5	5,527,471	1,377,108	6,904,579
2005/6	5,769,136	959,046.5	6,728,183
2006/7	6,847,445	665,464.4	7,512,909
2007/8	7,280,714	796,183.5	8,076,897
2008/9	7,521,651	757,719.3	8,279,370
2009/10	7,837,909	847,147	8,685,056
2010/11	8,753,608	852,856	9,606,464
2011/12	9,005,524	966,509.2	9,972,033

Source: Computed from *Education Statistics Digest*, 2012, Ministry of Education, Singapore.

Note: Using CPI for Education 2009 = 100. The CPI data was obtained from *Statistical Highlights*, various issues.

In this regard the government emphasized an open boundary meritocracy. The principle differs from the kind of elitism proposed by Sir Stamford Raffles[7] in that it opens the doors of higher learning institutions to children from less privileged groups (Tan, 1986).

To ensure every child has the chance to receive the maximum amount of education, government policy is to allocate large subsidies, though not equally at all levels. Mukhopadhaya (2003a) observed that in the early 1990s, while there was a period of decrease in real operating expenditure, it started increasing again from 1994 onwards. Apart from the usual operating/recurrent expenditure, the government also allocates development expenditure on education. Mukhopadhaya (2003a) further observed that development expenditure on education increased in real terms from 1975 to 1985, followed by a drop in 1990 and 1995. It then rose steadily in the late 1990s. Summarily in that period there was almost a three-fold increase in education expenditure of government from 1980 to 1985, and a five-fold increase during 1990 to 1998. Table 4.4 shows the amount of government expenditure on education during financial years 1997/8 to 2011/12 in real terms. It can be seen from Table 4.4 and Figure 4.2 that while in this period real development expenditure dropped at an annual rate of 6 per cent, the real recurrent expenditure increased at almost the same rate. As recurrent expenditure on education is a much greater amount than that allocated for development, the total expenditure in real terms has increased by 4 per cent.

Such an increase in government expenditure meets any possible rise in household expenditure on education; especially for low-income groups (see

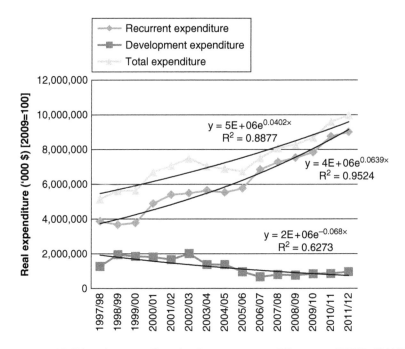

Figure 4.2 Education expenditure by the government of Singapore, 1997/8–2011/12.

Table 4.5 on household expenditure on education as a percentage of total expenditure). This is certainly equity enhancing.

Mukhopadhaya (2003a) showed that in 1998 government expenditure on education per student was about 1.6 times more for a secondary school student than a primary school student. Also, the cost of educating a polytechnic student was almost 1.9 times that of a secondary school student. The cost of educating a university student is twice as much as a polytechnic student. Table 4.6 describes the situation from 1998. It can be observed from the table that currently (2011/12) government expends 1.3 times more for a secondary school student compared to a primary school student, while costs incurred for a university student is three times more than that for a primary school student. It was noted previously that educational between-group inequality is not that major factor in income inequality in Singapore; results shown in Table 4.6 further emphasizes the fact that growth rates on government recurrent expenditure on primary school student is much higher than that for a student pursuing a higher level of education.

Educational Endowment Scheme

In 1993 the government started the Edusave Scheme to maximize educational opportunities for all Singaporean children. The Scheme rewards students who perform well or who make good progress in their academic and non-academic work,

Table 4.5 Household expenditure on education (% of total) and various expenditure groups: various years

Monthly expenditure groups 1987/8

Below $500	$500–$999	$1,000–$1,999	$2,000–$3,999	$4,000–$5,999	$6,000 and over
3.5	4.3	4.7	4.9	5.1	4.6

Monthly expenditure groups 1992/3

Below $500	$500–$999	$1,000–$1,499	$1,500–$1,999	$2,000–$2,499	$2,500–$2,999	$3,000–$3,999	$4,000–$4,999	$5,000–$5,999	$6,000–$6,999	$7,000 and over
3.0	3.2	4.5	5.4	5.4	6.3	6.0	5.6	6.8	6.1	5.7

Monthly expenditure groups 1997/8

Below $1,000	$1,000–$1,499	$1,500–$1,999	$2,000–$2,499	$2,500–$2,999	$3,000–$3,999	$4,000–$4,999	$5,000–$5,999	$6,000–$6,999	$7,000–$9,999	$10,000 and over
3.2	4.4	5.8	6.2	6.7	7.2	7.2	8.4	8.3	9.1	5.8

Monthly expenditure groups 2002/3

Below $1,000	$1,000–$1,499	$1,500–$1,999	$2,000–$2,499	$2,500–$2,999	$3,000–$3,999	$4,000–$4,999	$5,000–$5,999	$6,000–$6,999	$7,000–$9,999	$10,000 and over
1.3	3.5	4.9	6.5	7.7	7.3	7.6	7.9	9.5	9.7	9.1

Source: Computed from *Report on Household Expenditure Survey*, Singapore Department of Statistics, Various years.

Note: The latest *Household Expenditure Survey* (2007/8) reports expenses in a different format (in quintile groups), thus not comparable and we did not present here.

Table 4.6 Government real recurrent expenditure on education per student, ($) 1997/8–
2011/12

Financial year	Primary	Secondary	Polytechnic	University
1997/8	3,418	5,161	10,413	17,465
1998/9	3,250	5,176	9,426	14,560
1999/00	3,023	5,103	9,296	16,333
2000/1	3,581	5,826	10,897	17,562
2001/2	3,804	6,000	10,937	17,265
2002/3	4,012	6,372	11,116	16,217
2003/4	3,964	6,144	11,522	19,748
2004/5	3,972	6,384	11,883	19,566
2005/6	4,226	6,408	11,994	19,683
2006/7	4,647	6,841	13,037	20,232
2007/8	5,393	7,758	13,393	20,398
2008/9	5,430	7,597	13,560	19,783
2009/10	5,537	7,736	12,598	18,868
20010/11	6,444	8,763	14,156	20,068
2011/12	6,331	8,406	13,501	19,228
Growth rate (% per annum)	5.18	3.31	2.72	1.69

Source: Singapore, Ministry of Education, *Education Statistics Digest*, 2012.
Note: Figures are inflation-adjusted expenditure with 1999 = 100.

and provides students and schools with funds to pay for enrichment programmes
or to purchase additional resources. The Edusave Endowment Fund is built up
from government contributions. The fund is invested by the government and the
interest earned is used to finance the contributions, grants and awards given to
schools and students. The government contributed an initial capital sum of $1
billion to the fund in 1993. The capital sum reached the target of $5 billion in
August 1997. As at 31 March 2012, the Edusave Endowment Fund was $5.8
billion (Annual Report, Singapore Annual Report, EESS, 2011/12).

If the student is a Singapore citizen and is studying full-time in a government,
government-aided or independent school, junior college (JC), centralized institute
(CI), Institute of Technical Education (ITE) or special education school, he/she
can benefit from Edusave in three ways: the Pupils Fund; Grants; and Scholarships
and Awards.

Edusave Pupils Fund

A student is automatically given an Edusave account and receives a yearly contribution from the government's Edusave Pupils Fund. However, only the first,
second and third child were eligible for the Edusave account prior to 2004 and
only students between the age of 6 and 16 prior to 2009 were eligible for the
annual Edusave contributions. From 2009, the government contributes $200 and

$240 to the Edusave account of each eligible student at primary and secondary level respectively.

Edusave Grants

All primary and secondary schools, junior colleges, centralized institutes, Institutes of Technical Education and special education schools also receive annual Edusave grants. Schools use the grants to organize common enrichment programmes or purchase additional resources which benefit students.

Edusave Scholarships and Awards

Edusave Character Awards (ECHA)

The Edusave Character Award is to recognize students for demonstrating exemplary character and outstanding personal qualities through their behaviour and actions. The student is selected by his/her school for this award at the end of the year if he/she meets the criteria.

The value of the awards are: $200 for primary 1 to 3; $350 for primary 4 to 6; $500 for secondary 1 to 5; Pre-U 1 to 3; and Institute of Technical Education (ITE).

Edusave Scholarships (ES)

Students who are among the top 10 per cent of students in their level and stream in their school are eligible for the Edusave Scholarship for Secondary Schools. Recipients are selected by their schools for this scholarship based on overall school examination results for the year. The value of the award is $500.

Edusave Entrance Scholarships for Independent Schools (EESIS)

These scholarships are awarded to the top one-third of the total number of Secondary 1 students admitted to all independent schools, based on their PSLE results. Students with outstanding performance in the PSLE will be offered the award if they are admitted to an independent school. For students who are not in the Integrated Programme, the scholarship will be tenable for 4 years. For students in the Integrated Programme, the tenure of the scholarship will be 6 years. For students admitted to secondary 1 from 2008 onwards, the annual scholarship quantum is $2,400, or the annual school fees charged by the independent school less the annual amount of school and standard miscellaneous fees paid by students in government/government-aided secondary schools, whichever is lower, less any other subsidies provided by the Ministry of Education (MOE) or the school for Independent School fees.

Edusave (Independent Schools) Yearly Awards (E(IS)YA)

The Ministry offers these awards to students in independent schools who are not EESIS/ESIP holders. They are given to the top 5 per cent of each cohort by level in each independent school based on their overall school examination results for the year. The yearly awards cover the annual school fees charged by the independent school for that year less the annual amount of school and standard miscellaneous fees paid by students in government/government-aided secondary schools and any other subsidies provided by MOE or the school for Independent School fees.

Edusave Scholarships for Integrated Programme Schools (ESIP)

These scholarships are made available in schools offering the Integrated Programme (IP) that are (i) independent schools or (ii) charge additional fees known as 'Integrated Programme Miscellaneous Fees' (government/government-aided schools). Singaporean students in the IP at Secondary 3 who are not EESIS holders are selected for this scholarship on the basis of merit through an examination procedure. The tenure of the scholarship is up to the final year of the IP. For students admitted to Secondary 1 from 2008 onwards, for ESIP scholars in independent schools, the annual scholarship quantum is $2,400, or the annual school fees charged by the independent school less the annual amount of school and standard miscellaneous fees paid by students in government/government-aided secondary schools, whichever is lower, less any other subsidies provided by MOE or the school for Independent School fees. For ESIP in government/government-aided schools, the annual scholarship quantum is $2,400, or the annual amount of Integrated Programme Miscellaneous Fees charged by the school, whichever is lower, less any other subsidies provided by MOE or the school for Integrated Programme Miscellaneous Fees.

Edusave Awards for Achievement, Good Leadership and
Service (EAGLES)

Students who display good leadership, service to community and schools, or excellence in non-academic activities, are eligible for this award. It is given based on students' achievements in co-curricular activities and contributions to community services over a one-year period. The awards are given to a maximum of 10 per cent of Singaporean students in every school, from Primary 4 upwards. The recipients are selected by their schools for this award at the end of the year if they meet the criteria. The value of the award is $250 for Primary 4 to 6; $350 for Secondary 1 to 5; $400 for Pre-U 1 to 3; $500 for Institute of Technical Education (ITE).

Edusave Merit Bursary (EMB)

Students studying in either a primary or secondary school, Junior College/Centralized Institute or Institute of Technical Education, and not in receipt of any of the previously mentioned Edusave Scholarships, are eligible to apply for the Edusave Merit Bursary if they are within the top 25 per cent of each level and stream in their school.

The EMB is means tested. That is, if the gross monthly household income does not exceed $5,000, or per capita income does not exceed $1,250 (computed based on the gross monthly household income divided by the number of household members), the student is eligible to get this financial support. The value of this award for each level is $200 for Primary 1 to 3; $250 for Primary 4 to 6; $350 for Secondary 1 to 5; $400 for Junior Pre-U 1 to 3; $500 for Institute of Technical Education (ITE).

Good Progress Award (GPA)

Students who have made significant improvement in their academic performance are eligible for the Edusave Good Progress Award if they do not qualify for the Edusave scholarship or receive the Edusave Merit Bursary. The Good Progress Award is given based on the extent of a student's improvement in his/her school's overall examinations over the previous year. The awards are given to a maximum of 10 per cent of students in each level and stream in every school from Primary 2 onwards. Students in Primary 1 are excluded from the scheme as there is no basis for comparison. Recipients are selected by their schools for this award at the end of the year if they meet the criteria. The value of the awards are $100 for Primary 2 to 3; $150 for Primary 4 to 6; $200 for Secondary 1 to 5; $250 for Pre-U 1 to 3; $400 for Institute of Technical Education (ITE).

Is it equity enhancing?

The above summary (from the Ministry of Education information sheet: http://www.moe.gov.sg/initiatives/edusave/ [accessed 31 October 2013]) of the Singapore Edusave Scheme clearly indicates that the Singapore government is keen to develop the educational level and quality of the future workforce. The direction of government educational expenditure, which is increasing continuously, is quite clear from the above information. However, the scheme is based on supporting able students while not much provision is given to corrective justice. A *Straits Times* report (from Mukhopadhaya, 2003a) stated that 63 per cent of scholarship recipients stayed in Housing and Development Board (HDB) flats, which means that the scheme did not benefit only the rich and the middle-class Singaporeans. However, Mukhopadhaya (2003a) showed that most recipients of Edusave scholarships lived in HDB 5-room flats (24.9 per cent), HDB 4-room flats (22.0 per cent), terrace/semi-detached/detached house (21.5 per cent), and a smaller portion lived in HDB 1–3-room flats (16.1 per cent). In the absence of information of the income status of the scholarship recipients, housing status was linked with the income levels of the households (using the Report of Household Expenditure Surveys) in the Mukhopadhaya (2003a) study. It has been observed that 37 per cent of recipients had a monthly household income of $3,923; 21.5 per cent had a monthly household income of $9,694; and 16.1 per cent had a monthly household income between $1,638 and $2,382. Thus the study concluded that while the bright and poor were aided by the scheme, the rich and the middle class benefited more. It was noted that at least 29.5 per cent of the recipients came from well-to-do families, who could easily afford extra private tuition.[8] The poorer students who did not qualify for the scholarship can only depend on the Yearly Award to lessen the burden on their families, which means that they may have to forgo the private tuition that their better-off counterparts receive. Moreover, since the scholarship is tenable for four years, a poorer family could save around $5,000 or more over a four-year period, which was about the monthly income of the richer households. Mukhopadhaya (2003a) argued that the Yearly Awards scheme is better than the EESIS as the possible benefits accruing to wealthier households are limited to a year. It was suggested that the tenure of the scholarship should be reduced to only the first year and channel the rest of the resources to the Yearly Awards. The cap on the latter can then be raised from 5 per cent to higher, say, 25 per cent. This may increase in the possibility of students receiving the award and that may then further encourage the poorer students to do even better to lessen the family financial burden.

As both ESPS and ESSS are awarded on the basis of annual academic performance, subject to good conduct both are considered equitable, as there is a more even distribution of students of all backgrounds. Comparing ESSS with the Yearly Awards, it would be more equitable if the Yearly Awards in the independent schools were given to more than 5 per cent of the students because those students who go to the independent schools are usually the high achievers of the cohort of a particular year. Therefore, even those who did not score within the top 5 per cent would most likely be able to receive the ESSS awards if they had gone to a government or a government-aided school instead. The broadening of the Yearly Awards can thus be seen as a more accurate method of pegging the rewards to academic performance. The EMB and GPA both use merit and income level as the criteria, thus the scheme truly aims at providing a level playing field as it is targeted at students who are bright and relatively less well off.

The Education Endowment Scheme is on the whole, a well-thought-out scheme that attempts to provide an equal starting line for all students, especially the EMB and the GPA. The ESSS and EPSS and the Yearly Awards, on the other hand, seek to reward individuals who perform well, and are meritocratic in nature and generally not income biased. Although EESIS uses merit as a criterion, it can be seen that a considerable quantum has been used to help students from upper-class families. Therefore, this sub-scheme does not really serve to provide the same starting line for all students, but instead bring the students to a new starting line. Nevertheless, credit must still be given to the Edusave scheme for intending to equalize *opportunities* for all students.

Singapore in comparison on public expenditure on education

We have noted that Singapore has invested a substantial amount of money on education and the effect of this expenditure is evident on the development of its skilled workforce. In the next chapter we will discuss the effect of education on minimization of the gender wage gap. Table 4.7, however, shows that the Singapore government's expenditure on education is lower than other industrialized countries of similar national income. Furthermore, in comparison with neighbouring

Table 4.7 Public spending on education (per cent of GDP)

Year	Singapore	OECD	USA	UK	Australia	Malaysia	Thailand
1980	2.56	5.21	6.51	5.27	5.65	5.62	2.57
1981	2.59	5.17		5.51	5.40[a]	6.58	2.88
1982	3.28	5.38		5.45	5.47	6.91	3.27
1983	3.96	5.12		5.31	5.37		3.46
1988	3.67	4.77	4.85	4.54	4.92	5.60[c]	2.75
2000	3.38	4.96	4.90[b]	4.51	4.88	5.97	5.41
2001	3.02	5.24	5.67	4.63	4.93	7.48	5.02
2008	2.82	5.17	5.50	5.37	4.64	3.96	3.75
2009	3.28	5.60	5.43	5.60	5.12	5.97	4.13
2010	3.49					5.13	3.75
2011	3.20					4.50	
2012	3.30						

Source: WDI (2012).
Notes
[a] Marginson (1993).
[b] OECD (2012).
[c] UNESCO (2008).

Malaysia and Thailand, Singapore's spending on education as a percentage of GDP is low. This observation points to the fact that the Singapore government needs more structured focus on the education sector. Scholarship and bursary amounts must be increased and more money directed to enhance equity aspects while not ignoring ability. Recently the government has been more focused on spending based on needs. This is a welcome step in enhancing distributional fairness beyond income.

Conclusion

This chapter examined the trend of income inequality in Singapore at a dis-aggregated level of education. This decomposition analysis has shown that income disparities across educational groups have not been a major contributor to inequality.

The traditional views regarding the policy instruments of the government of Singapore changed from the 1990s. The growing economy of Singapore uses substantial amounts of its government budget on education. Instead of directing special attention to low-income groups, the government relied on ability-based policies. However, fairness is conceived with the primary objective to bring everyone to an equal footing. In this chapter we have seen that various merit scholarships and bursaries, which are aimed at the brightest students, are not aimed to reduce inequality. This is because the brightest students are those who have a better educational environment (and in several cases have parents who are better educated). Therefore the rich and middle class families, in several cases, become the beneficiaries of the scholarship schemes. Given this scenario, one can argue that the *favoured* ones are taking more than their share of the nation's resources.

This is compounded by the fact that the level of subsidization increases with the level of education and the same amount is given, regardless of socio-economic groups. Given that the level of education expenditure per student increases with the educational level this gives rise to the issue of equity in the distribution of educational resources. It has been observed that the education policy is 'elitist'. It may be argued that the existence of the Edusave scheme and the availability of financial assistance schemes will ameliorate the situation. However, a greater portion of GDP needs to be directed to educational development to effect real change.

Notes

1 It should be noted (see Table 4.1) that the disparity due to relative mean income (that is the disparity in wages/salaries earned at different education levels) has been reduced over time.
2 While the total inequality decreased in the period 1984–94, within-group inequality increased.
3 During the 1960s economists argued for investment in education that could contribute to growth and development, and could be a long-term method of equalizing incomes. However, later in the USA and the UK it was gradually revealed that there had been little or no reduction of income inequality after several years of educational expansion. For the USA, Bowles (1972) attributed the influence of social class and family background to the persistent income inequality, while research by Blaug *et al.* (1982) in the UK suggested that equalizing the distribution of schooling may help to equalize the distribution of income within the age group, even though it may make distribution of income more unequal among the population as a whole.
4 Maximizing an individual's potential may be subjected to measurement errors which, in turn, may lead to different educational paths for different individuals.
5 As yet there is no compulsory education.
6 The National University of Singapore and Nanyang Technological University each have more than 30,000 students and provide a wide range of undergraduate and post-graduate degree programmes including doctoral degrees. Both are also established research universities with thousands of research staff and graduate students. As of 2012, both universities are ranked among the Top 50 in the world.

A third university, Singapore Management University (SMU), opened in 2000, is home to more than 7,000 students and comprises six Schools offering undergraduate, graduate, and PhD programmes in Business Management, Accountancy, Economics, Information Systems Management, Law and the Social Sciences. The University has an Office of Research, a number of institutes and centres of excellence, and provides public and customized programmes for working professionals through its Office of Executive and Professional Education.

The fourth university, privately run SIM University (UniSIM), opened in 2005. The university currently admits only part-time students and offers part-time degree programmes to working adults. In 2012, the government granted UniSIM a national university status and plans are ongoing to expand the university by offering new full-time degree programmes.

Two other public institutions are also sponsored by the government: the Singapore University of Technology and Design and the Singapore Institute of Technology. Many private universities exist, including foreign universities which have established campuses in Singapore such as the Chicago Business School and Technische Universität München.

The James Cook University Singapore, University of Adelaide, Southern Cross University, University of New Brunswick, Queen Margaret University, Temple University, The

City University of New York, Baruch College, University of Nevada, Las Vegas, Aventis School of Management, Curtin University of Technology and University of Wales Institute, Cardiff have established offshore campuses in Singapore to provide local and foreign (in particular, Asian) students the opportunity to obtain a Western university education at a fraction of the cost it would take to study in Canada, the UK, the USA or Australia. University of New Brunswick College, Singapore, Queen Margaret University, Asia Campus, NYU Tisch School of the Arts, Asia began operations in Singapore between 2007 and 2008, with the Curtin University of Technology Singapore Campus and University of Wales Institute, Cardiff: Asia Campus joined them in 2008.

The government planned the fourth public university, Singapore University of Technology and Design (SUTD), to meet the rising demand for university education. It started its operations in April 2012. Its permanent campus at Changi will be ready by early 2015.

A fifth public institution Singapore Institute of Technology was established in 2009 and is intended to provide an upgrading pathway for polytechnic graduates.

7 When Sir Stamford Raffles first proposed to set up a native college in Singapore in 1823, he was thinking of providing higher education for sons of 'the higher order of native and others' and those of the Chinese who 'if not possesses of the advantage of birth, have raised themselves by their talents, to opulence and a respectable rank in society' (Tan, 1986, p.15).

8 Private tuition is a lucrative industry in Singapore, as many parents send their children for private tuition after school. A straw poll by *The Straits Times* (Toh, 2008) found that out of 100 students interviewed, only 3 students did not have any form of tuition. In 2010, the *Shin Min Daily News* estimated that there were around 540 tuition centres offering private tuition in Singapore ('540 tuition centres in Singapore – and growing', *AsiaOne*, 2010). Due to strong demand, tuition centres are able to charge high fees for their services; they had an annual turnover of $110.6 million in 2005.

5 Income differences

The gender dimension

Based on the *2012 Population Trends* report (DOS, 2012), Singapore's resident population was 3,818,200 of which about 50 per cent were female. The sex ratio has decreased from over 1,049 males per 1,000 females in 1970, to 970 males per 1,000 females in 2012. The recent *Population Trends* report reveals the predominance of women in the total resident population, which comprises citizens and permanent residents; if non-residents are counted, the total population could exceed 5 million. There were 1,241,300 women aged 30+ in 2012, compared to 1,172,700 men. Women over 30 years comprised 64.04 per cent of all women in Singapore.[1] There has been a substantial increase of the mean and median ages of females and males, largely from incipient declines in fertility: the annual growth rate of the population was 5.4 per cent in 1957, had fallen to 1.7 per cent by 1970 and, according to *2012 Population Trends*, the present population growth rate remains at 0.8 per cent. This decrease can be attributed to rapid economic growth, particularly in the industrial and service sectors; enhanced educational attainment, which increases female labour force participation rates; and the wider availability of education and better health.

It has been noted in earlier chapters that the Singapore economy relies on the market mechanism as a policy instrument. Singapore's wage policy, which is based on 'efficient' labour allocation, is the best example. Although in the initial phase of growth the policy emphasized labour absorption to ease unemployment, the mechanism has changed over time: wages and employment are largely determined by supply and demand conditions of the market; the public sector does not act as an employer of 'last resort'; and Singapore does not have any legal minimum wage. Therefore in the absence of any unemployment compensation, workers sometimes must take low-paying jobs, and this can diffuse useful skills throughout the economy. Unlike many other industrialized countries, Singapore's labour unions cannot unilaterally raise wages for their members[2] – this is one reason for a lack of labour unions, or where they do exist, the membership is limited and most are affiliated to the National Trade Union Congress (NTUC).[3] Perhaps this type of wage policy is the key factor behind high investment and that has led to a demand for better qualified labour.

To generate skilled and better qualified labour, the Singapore government has extended educational opportunity to everyone (note that the government did not discriminate based on gender), and has tried to ensure that its citizens achieve a minimum level of education. In the last two decades, real expenditure per student increased at an average annual rate of 5.18 per cent at the primary level and 3.31 per cent at the secondary level. Expansion of the post-secondary level started in the late 1970s. In 2010, 10.33 per cent of the total budget was spent on the development of education (WDI, 2012). As a result, the female resident population of Singapore has been progressing faster in terms of educational attainment than their male counterparts. The rate of increase in secondary-educated females has been spectacular.

It has been observed that at ages 40+, the increase in female educational attainment was not as pronounced (Mukhopadhaya, 2001a). In 2011 there was a large increase in female graduates from polytechnics.[4] Female enrolment in institutions of higher education has increased in the last two decades at a rate of 13 per cent per annum, whereas for males that figure is 9 per cent per annum. The increase in the female labour force participation rate is a clear indication of females' relatively higher rate of growth in educational attainment.

Education plays a major role in ensuring employability. Although this is a clear indication of the government's success in reducing inequality resulting from differences in education levels, the government's philosophy was never to provide special privileges to females *per se*. The Singapore government specifically emphasized equal educational opportunity, and sought to create this by providing equal inputs. As there is a trade-off between the equalization of educational inputs and the equalization of results, one important issue is whether educational policies should seek to equalize inputs or results. The latter is *inefficient* for the economy (in utilitarian sense), since those who are more capable would be restrained by the development of those who are less capable. To maintain its orthodoxy, the government aimed to provide equal educational resources. Thus, whether or not the results are equalized is of secondary importance.

In 1980, 93 per cent of women aged 30+ were or had been married (that is, currently married, divorced, separated, widowed) and by 2005 this figure had reduced to 87.2 per cent. Between 2001 and 2011, the proportion of females aged 30+ who were single increased: 56 per cent of females in that age group were single in 2011, up from 41 per cent in 2001. While in 1980 only 5 per cent of women remained single, in 2011 the figure rose to 25 per cent. Although there has been a reduction in widowhood due to increasing longevity of both sexes, there were 109,200 in 2005 (with the maximum at ages 70+) to 58,700 widows aged 50+ in 2011 (with the maximum at ages 80+).

In 2010, some 247,000 households (22 per cent) were headed by women, compared to 898,000 male-headed households. Twenty years earlier, 93,000 households had female heads (18 per cent) against 417,000 male-headed households. Even in 1990, 17 per cent of households were headed by women. Thus it can be seen that the proportion of women heading households has remained virtually unchanged.[5] That translates to some 80 per cent of all households being headed by males and this is by virtue of their incomes and traditional roles. This clearly implies that female heads have very little control over household resources as well as little equity in their homes, and the extent to which this is the case is more or less 20 per cent only. This also shows that the extent of intra-household inequality in Singapore remains very high and there has been virtually no change in this situation over two decades. In Singapore, joint ownership of housing by married couples is most common, with increasing incidence of rented and other forms of tenancy with age. At older ages many women are in dwellings that are not 'owned' but rented or provided for by others (family members) (Mukhopadhaya and Shantakumar, 2009).

Singapore laws do not make any distinction between sexes: women have equal rights to education and employment, are able to enter into contracts, institute law suits, buy, sell and/or transfer properties in their names (without requiring the consent of husband/father), and are able to take independent decisions on contraception, abortion, adoption and/or sterilization. According to the Women's Charter 1993 (first introduced in 1961 and amended many times), women enjoy equal rights with men after marriage. Thus, both husband and wife would share equal rights and responsibilities on household matters. Both parents have equal rights with respect to the custody of children. However, despite these laws and the Charter, the influence of traditional customs and attitudes is still prevalent in the society. Thus, although Singapore laws provide equal rights, policy-makers seem to retain a deep-rooted perception regarding women's traditional roles in the family. Thus even with the advent of equal opportunity in education, there remains a large *chasm* between males and females from both social and economic perspectives.

Educational attainment of women

As a result of the Singapore government's education development policies, the gender disparity in educational attainment has narrowed in the last two decades. Among those aged 25 years and over, the male–female ratio in the mean year of schooling has improved (the average number of years of schooling rose over the past decade, reaching 10.2 years in 2011) (DOS, 2012), and among the younger generations the male–female difference between mean years of schooling has completely evaporated.

It can be observed from Table 5.1 that the proportion of polytechnic and above graduates has increased among females over the last decade. In 2011, 30 per cent of females were university graduates (not shown in the table) up from 4.5 per cent in 1990. Those with polytechnic qualifications increased from 7.2 per cent in 1994 (2 per cent in 1984), to 18.4 per cent in 2011 when there were more tertiary-educated females (about 441,800) (the scenario has been reversed only a decade ago), due to the rapid expansion of Singapore's education facilities in the last three decades. The trend continued in the last decade, with female enrolment at the tertiary level as a ratio of the resident female population aged 18–22 increasing by 16 percentage points in the last two decades in polytechnic studies, and by 11 percentage points in university education. Female enrolment for polytechnics has continued to exceed that of the universities since the early 1990s due to the establishment of new polytechnics (Temasek in 1990, and Nanyang in 1992).

Table 5.1 Educational attainment by gender (working persons)

Educational attainment	1984	1994	2011	Growth: 1984–2011 (% per annum)	Growth: 1994–2011 (% per annum)
Females (%)					
Below secondary	46.41	41.99	19.8	−2.29	−3.52
Secondary	36.89	44.56	22.1	−1.60	−3.36
Upper secondary	12.07	16.10	10.0	−0.69	−2.53
Polytechnic +	4.5	20.68	48.0	38.67	8.81
Males (%)					
Below secondary	58.06	52.01	22.8	−2.43	−3.74
Secondary	25.62	33.14	18.7	−1.08	−2.90
Upper secondary	10.60	13.11	13.2	0.98	0.05
Polytechnic +	5.7	25.26	45.3	27.79	5.29

Note: Calculated from *Labour Force Survey*, 1984, 1994, 2011, Government of Singapore.

The last two decades also witnessed a significant shift of female tertiary students to technical subjects. According to the LFS (2011), 61 per cent of female undergraduates in local universities were in the arts and social sciences, business and accountancy/administration and science courses, compared to 40 per cent of males. In the last decade there was a 5 and 11 per cent point increase in the admission of females in engineering-related courses at the universities and polytechnics respectively. This enhanced female entry into male-dominated tertiary courses opens up the possibility of a higher proportion of women taking up professional and technical jobs.

It is evident from Figure 5.1 that in the age group 20–30 (and to some extent in ages 30–40), the female entrants in the labour market were better qualified than their male counterparts, but with increasing age there are more less-qualified female entrants. This indicates that constraints for re-entry into the labour market are strong for females at ages over 40 (even with higher education). This obviously has serious policy implications.

Trends in labour force participation rates

Since the industrialization programme in the late 1960s (besides few retrenchment cases due to uncompetitiveness and economic recession), workers have been absorbed at a very high rate, and career opportunities were opened up for Singapore women at all sectors. As many of the younger men had to spend time in National Service, there was an acute labour shortage and a floodgate of employment opportunities opened up for women. The improvement in women's educational profile during the last three decades is also reflected in the female labour force participation rate (LFPR) (see Figure 5.2). Furthermore, encouragement from the government and some legislative protection has worked positively

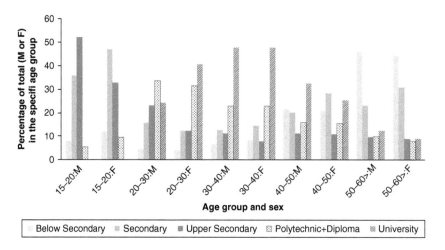

Figure 5.1 Age-sex-specific entrants by educational attainment, 2011.

Source: Computed from LFS (2011), Ministry of Manpower, Singapore.

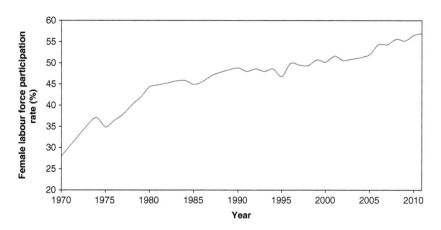

Figure 5.2 Female LFPR, 1970–2011.

Source: *Singapore Yearbook of Manpower Statistics,* 2012, Singapore Department of Statistics.

for women. With falling fertility rates women became less restricted to child bearing and rearing responsibilities.

The female LFPR increased from 28.2 per cent in 1970 to 47 per cent in 1987, and to 57 per cent in 2011 (the growth rate was less rapid in the 1990s due to the recession). The increase in female LFPR was most significant at the prime working ages of 25–54. It is worth noting that the LFPR for females falls short by a significant amount compared to that of males (not shown in Figure 5.2).

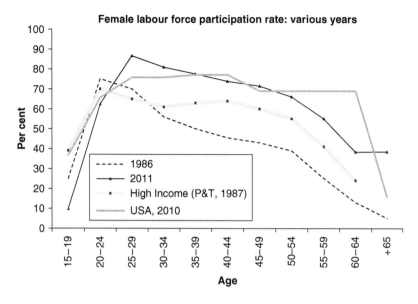

Figure 5.3 Female labour force participation rate: various years.

Source: *Report of Labour Force Survey*, 1987, 2012, Singapore, Ministry of Manpower; Psacharopoulos and Tzannatos (1989), *The 2012 Statistical Abstract*, US Bureau of Labor Statistics.

In Singapore (like all other Asian countries) men are traditionally the bread-winners of their families and many women remain economically inactive or withdrawn from the labour market because of childcare and other household activities. The LFS (2011) indicates that 221,000 women in the age group 25–54 were economically inactive and 43 per cent were engaged in homemaking, while 29.4 per cent were devoted to child caring. The overall LFPR of married women in 2011 was much lower than that of married men (59.9 per cent compared with 84.7 per cent). For single women, their economic participation was almost the same as single men (60 per cent compared with 61 per cent). Although singlehood status among women is increasing, 60 per cent of working women are still married (this figure has remained stable for the last decade), and as they have a tendency to withdraw from the labour force, it has a negative implication for economic welfare and growth.

Figure 5.3 shows the age-specific LFPR for women. With better educational development over the period, the LFPR for females in the prime working ages of 25–54 years trended upwards, from 45.8 per cent in 1986 to 75.7 per cent in 2011. Psacharopoulos and Tzannatos (1989) examined the female LFPR of various countries and provided an average age-specific LFPR figure for countries with various development statuses. Figure 5.3 compares their observation for high-income countries. For the age group over 35, Singapore's achievement was worse (for year 1986) compared to the average for high-income countries (of 1980).

Although in the recent period (2011) there has been a substantial increase in the LFPR, it is still far below that of the USA in age groups above 35 years.[6]

The LFS (2011) found that the most common reasons holding women back from joining the workforce were:

1 children and household responsibilities (42.1 per cent);
2 schooling/attending courses/training (30 per cent);
3 poor health/disability/old age (20 per cent); and
4 retirement (13 per cent).

It is true that rapid industrialization and the drive for structural change may lead to obsolescence of some skills and withdrawal from the labour market by women, so government support was extended for vocational training. Moreover, even with such training the take-home pay may not be sufficient to maintain childcare costs and a lack of affordable childcare and after school care facilities may constitute another problem for Singaporean women.

Provision of childcare and day care facilities has been addressed only recently. Otherwise government emphasizes on family values: tax concession and housing loan facilities are provided if married couples live near their parents, assuming that retired parents (or in-laws) will take care of small and school-going children and that will open the way for mothers to re-enter the workforce. At least two problems are apparent from this arrangement. First, it is difficult for the mother to re-start a highly responsible job. And thus she has to accept a low-paying job where responsibility/commitment is relatively low. The second problem is much wider. In the last two decades females who entered the workforce (with better education) may have had domestic help from their parents and in-laws whose education levels were either low, or in many cases not commensurate with present expectations. However, this arrangement will not be sufficient when the present workforce retires and without much delay their tertiary-educated daughters enter the workforce. This is because, with higher income and education, there are continuous shifts of perceptions regarding family and individuality/self dependency. The better-educated women (and men as well) who have finished working life would prefer to enjoy retired life differently from their own parents or in-laws. Therefore, alternative domestic arrangements to support re-entry into the workforce by females become a necessity.

Another contradiction of the policy (the policy to create of equal opportunity for everyone) emerged in the mid-1980s when the then Prime Minister Lee Kuan Yew advised graduate females to start families. He was concerned about the drop in marriage rates (among better-educated females) and lower fertility rates among Chinese women (particularly with higher education). Quah (1993) observed that there was a tendency for delayed marriage among Singaporean women as they wanted to have higher education levels and better jobs in order to be economically secure. The Singapore government argued that women must lower their expectations. Financial incentives in terms of tax relief were introduced to encourage educated women to have more children. In 1987 a few changes in family planning programmes were introduced to discourage women/men from undergoing sterilization, and women with less education were encouraged to stay at home with their children full time.[7] Thus it can be observed that the functions of the Singapore government has expanded beyond special purpose development agencies (such as family planning, education, health planning) to involving itself in the daily lives of Singaporeans. The logic behind the 'graduate mother' policy was that the women should delegate their responsibilities as mothers only if the country needs their labour (Goldberg, 1987). This implies clear gender discrimination at least in terms of creation of jobs for the citizens.

Changes in occupational patterns

With increasing levels of education and a growing demand for better-skilled workers, a higher proportion of females are in professional and technical jobs (see Table 5.2). While only 11.8 per cent of these jobs were held by women in 1984, the figure went up to 36.5 per cent in three decades. This trend is true for women in all age groups. There has also been an increase in managerial and administrative occupations. Although women have upgraded their occupational profile, there are still proportionately more men than women in administrative and managerial occupations; however, the proportion of females in professional and technical occupations was just above that of males in 2011 (LFS, 2011).

Data on occupational levels and sex from LFS (2011) suggests that certain occupations are still the domain of either men or women despite changes in economic

Table 5.2 Changes in occupational distribution by gender, 1986–2011

Occupational group	1984	1994	2004	2011	Change 1984–94 (%)	Change 1994–2004 (%)	Change 2004–11 (%)
Female (%)							
Administrative and managerial	3.00	4.87	10.90	13.70	+1.87	+6.03	+2.80
Professional and technical	11.4	21.73	33.10	36.50	+10.33	+11.37	+3.40
Clerical	31.68	27.82	25.80	21.60	−3.86	−2.02	−4.20
Sales and services	25.61	12.86	13.80	15.60	−12.75	0.94	+1.80
Production and related	28.00	32.47	16.30	12.50	+4.47	−16.17	−3.80
Male (%)							
Administrative and managerial	7.81	10.94	18.10	21.00	+3.13	+7.16	+2.90
Professional and technical	9.76	21.84	31.6	32.7	+12.08	+9.76	+1.10
Clerical	8.62	14.83	5.40	4.90	6.21	−9.43	−0.50
Sales and services	22.70	12.63	10.80	17.90	−10.07	−1.83	+7.10
Production and related	43.60	35.67	27.7	17.30	−7.93	−7.97	−10.40

Source: Computed from LFS (1984), LFS (1994), LFS (2004), LFS (2011).

structure and manpower composition over the years. Females comprised more than 70 per cent of the workforce in occupations such as managers and administrators, secondary and pre-university teachers, administrative clerks and assemblers, and service workers. In contrast, males made up 76.5 per cent of younger workers in occupations like computing professions, managers and administrators, technicians, architects and engineers. This observation follows directly from the fact that male and female tertiary students specialize in different fields of study. Furthermore, gender preferences and aptitudes are revealed from this observation; males tend to be more suited to manual jobs, while females prefer other types of non-manual work. Moreover, in the Singapore situation, females often look for a more flexible nature of work (e.g., teaching) to balance multiple tasks at the workplace and home.

Following the classification by MOM (2011), Figure 5.4 presents the number and share of female employment in various occupations.

It can be observed that over the period 1984 to 2011, the number of women workers in male-dominated occupations increased and their share increased from about 10 to 20 per cent. The most notable rise was observed among corporate managers (18 to 36 per cent) and legislators and senior officials (20 to 51.1 per cent). The recent rise in the category 'stationary plant and related operators' should be considered with caution: it could be due to recent definitional change at the 2-digit sub-major occupational group levels. There has been an increase in the number of females in IT and engineering jobs (attributed to availability of desk-bound engineering jobs), although the share of females holding such jobs increased only marginally (due to a similar increase in the absolute number of males in the same job). During this period the number and share of female machine operators and assemblers declined during 1994–2004 – this can be attributed to economic restructuring that shifted lower value-added manufacturing jobs to less-costly destinations. As we previously mentioned, the major increase in female share is observed in the 'teaching, associate and professional' category. The change in the share of females in customer service is less significant; however, the decrease in share in cleaning and related groups is significant. This pattern is a clear indication of higher educational attainment of females and slow but gradual shift towards higher paid jobs (see also Table 5.3).

Gender wage differentials

Gender variation in average incomes

Educational attainment, rapid growth and industrialization have increased female participation in the labour force, however, a survey in March 2008 revealed that substantial wage differences still exist between males and females.[8] We will explore the trend in gender wage differences using *Censuses* 1990 and 2000, *General Household Survey* 2005 and LFS, 2011 data.

It can be noted from Table 5.4 that the real income of women in general, increased over the period 1990 to 2011 more than their male counterparts; however, the increase is mostly concentrated in the age group 25–29, while in

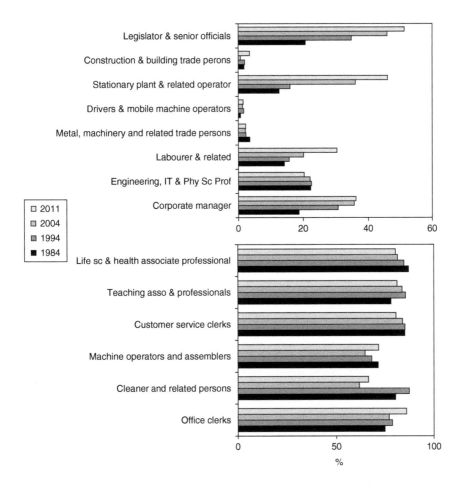

Figure 5.4 Share of female employment in various occupations, 1984–2011.
Source: Computed from LFS (1984), LFS (1994), LFS (2004), LFS (2011).

other age groups males mostly enjoyed a better increase. An examination of various LFSs shows that over a 21-year period those with incomes below $1,500 per month had proportionately declined for both sexes. These arise for the younger working cohorts who receive lower incomes, as well as those older workers (past 30 years) who might have entered higher income brackets. A substantial increase in women's incomes beyond $1,500 is noted, especially in the income bracket $1,500 to below $3,000. This is clearly due to better educational attainment which can be ascertained from the qualification-sex segregated data (Figure 5.1). For working people, women generally still earn lower incomes than men: this is despite higher income growth rates for women than men.

Table 5.3 Females aged fifteen years and over as a share of total by occupation (%)

Occupation	2001	2006	2011
Managers and administrators	30.1	35.7	36.1
Working proprietors	14.8	20.2	25.8
Professionals	41.0	39.6	43.2
Associate professionals and technicians	45.4	46.8	49.0
Clerical support workers	78.0	77.9	77.5
Service and sales workers	45.4	48.6	52.4
Craftspeople and related trades workers	8.0	9.2	8.3
Plant and machine operators and assemblers	26.2	22.9	17.0
Cleaners, labourers and related workers	49.2	50.2	56.8
Others	2.6	1.6	2.0

Source: Computed from LFS (2001, 2006, 2011).

Table 5.4 Average real monthly incomes ($) of working persons by age groups and gender, 1990, 2000, 2005 and 2011 (1990 = 100)

Age group	1990		2000		2005		2011		Change per annum 1990–2011	
	Male	Female	Male	Female	Male	Female	Male	Female	Male	Female
20–24	847	842	1,125	1,632	1,120	1,608	1,517	1,750	31.90	43.24
25–29	1,355	1,136	2,345	2,205	2,442	2,339	2,708	2,917	64.43	84.81
30–34	1,716	1,334	2,751	2,376	3,208	2,796	3,988	3,467	108.19	101.57
35–39	1,910	1,392	2,627	2,300	3,471	2,781	3,988	3,467	98.95	98.81
40–44	1,990	1,466	2,490	2,140	3,297	2,624	3,733	3,000	83.00	73.05
45–49	1,902	1,453	2,372	1,923	3,037	2,349	3,733	3,000	87.19	73.67
50–54	1,777	1,410	2,248	1,866	2,879	2,135	2,600	2,100	39.19	32.86
55–59	1,586	1,255	2,034	1,710	2,589	1,987	2,600	2,100	48.29	40.24
60–64	1,376	1,138	1,735	1,262	2,139	1,366	1,800	1,208	20.19	3.33
65–69	1,349	1,131	1,442	1,012	NA	NA	1,800	1,208	21.48	3.67
70+	1,461	1,037	1,361	1,006	NA	NA	1,800	1,208	16.14	8.14
Total	1,618	1,186	2,851	2,264	2,833	2,374	3,000	2,708	65.81	72.48

Source: Computed from *Census of Population,* 1990, LFS (2011), *Census of Population,* 1990, and GHS (2005), LFS (2011).

If women continue to attain better qualifications, the income gap may narrow but this is uncertain because of the influx of foreign skills (mainly for men). In 2011 the average real income for women was $2,708 per month compared to $3,000 for men, whereas it was $1,186 and $1,618 respectively in 1990. The higher rate of growth of women's income than for their male counterparts creates an illusion of equality between incomes, however, that is not true as women started from a lower base in the past – thus incremental points favour women. The largest increments were in ages below 30–39. Although age is a proxy determinant of wage level, since higher educational attainments/increments are tied to age, the better income increments for women are best explained by qualifications attained *per se* rather than age itself. The higher rates of increase in incomes for younger women are observed, as they would be expected to possess better qualifications than those in ages 40+. It is also apparent that women aged 40+ have not fared as well, since they may be less educationally endowed than their younger counterparts. The ages 60+ registered lower growth rates in mean incomes; and declining by age 65+. This reveals that older workers (especially women) are worse off in the employment market only because of lower commensurate qualifications against demand.

Table 5.5 shows the gender wage gap by education level and the rate of growth of income for different educational levels. In general, income levels increased for each educational attainment for both sexes during 1990–2011. As most workers in Singapore are wage earners, the better-qualified earn a higher income. Age as a proxy of experience may play a part in differentiating incomes even for the same qualifications, however, examination of that is not possible due to lack of data. Ignoring the age effect (though it is an important determinant), males always (for all the years and qualifications) earn higher incomes than females with identical qualifications. Secondary-educated females in 1990 earned 37 per cent less than their male counterparts, this reduced to 10 per cent by 2011, and still the differential may be explained by the rigidity of the market through discrimination, affecting female workers without a steady career path, and which may arise from disruption in work life.

Although the Women's Charter guarantees equal pay at the entry point, market segmentation reduces women's incomes and there is no compensation for time lost. Their value at home and contribution to family life are not factored into a free-labour market. It is noted in Table 5.5 that in the 21-year period shown, the differential decreased substantially to the 11 per cent level by 2011. Except for primary or lower level of education, the male–female income gap has reduced. However, for the tertiary education groups (polytechnic and university) an average of over 30 per cent premium to male wages over female wages remains constant. One plausible explanation is that the higher qualified women may be younger entrants as compared to men, and experience (through age) may show up this disparity. That means, even with the presence of equal treatment at entry, the market attracts male workers in the longer run.

The *Report on Wages in Singapore 2011* (MOM, 2011) highlights that females in Singapore earn less than males. Although the wage gap was narrower in white-collar occupations (clerical support, professional, associate professionals and technicians, and service and sales occupations) for females in the age group 35–39, the difference is wider in blue-collar occupations. This could reflect the different jobs males and females hold within the occupational group, for example, within the group of plant and machine operators, since females tend to concentrate in occupations such as electronic equipment/component assemblers which typically pay less than the male-dominated crane and hoist operators and lorry drivers. It was also noticed that the gender wage gap widened with age.

Table 5.5 Average real monthly incomes ($) of working persons by educational attainment groups and gender, 1990, 2000, 2005 and 2011 (1990 = 100)

Educational qualification	1990			2000			2005			2011		
	Male	Female	Male/Female	Male	Female	Male/Female	Male	Female	Male/Female	Male	Female	Male/Female
No qualification	984	867	1.13	1,444	963	1.5	1,373	894	1.54	1,500	975	1.54
Primary	1,001	792	1.26	1,649	1,098	1.5	1,600	1,044	1.53	1,600	1,138	1.41
Lower secondary	1,233	826	1.49	1,891	1,347	1.4	1,854	1,375	1.35	1,938	1,307	1.48
Secondary	1,670	1,220	1.37	2,385	1,950	1.22	2,361	1,985	1.19	2,383	2,167	1.10
Upper secondary	2,203	1,508	1.46	2,581	2,317	1.11	2,509	2,338	1.07	2,383	2,167	1.10
Polytechnic	2,479	1,828	1.36	3,158	2,452	1.29	3,163	2,459	1.29	3,500	2,917	1.20
Other diploma	NA	NA	NA	3,978	2,898	1.37	3,861	2,917	1.32	NA	NA	NA
University	4,237	3,083	1.37	5,797	4,156	1.39	5,780	4,373	1.32	6,196	4,652	1.33
Total	1,618	1,186	1.36	2,851	2,264	1.26	2,833	2,374	1.19	3,000	2,708	1.11

Source: Computed from *Census of Population* 1990, 2000 and *General Household Survey*, 2005, LFS (2011), Government of Singapore.

Note: 1990 and 2000, 2005, 2011 classifications differ (1990 Polytechnic includes other Diploma). NA: Data not available.

Table 5.6 Distribution of monthly income of women by marital status, 1990, 2000 and 2005

Monthly income ($ pm)	1990 (%)			2000 (%)			2005 (%)		
	Single	Married	Widowed/divorced/ separated	Single	Married	Widowed/divorced/ separated	Single	Married	Widowed/divorced/ separated
<500	23.6	0.8	7.5	1.1	2.4	4.5	3.1	3.4	4.0
500—<1,000	40.7	39.8	51.1	7.3	12.0	24.0	11.8	12.6	10.7
1,000—<1,500	19.4	25.2	27.4	19.8	17.7	26.1	14.9	15.0	12.6
1,500—<2,000	7.8	11.2	6.5	20.4	15.4	14.6	13.9	12.6	15.6
≥2,000	8.5	15.8	7.5	51.4	52.5	30.8	56.2	56.4	57.1
≥5,000	0.6	1.7	0.8	5.4	11.3	5.8	14.2	15.6	24.4

Source: Computed from *Census of Population*, 1990, 2000 and *General Household Survey*, Government of Singapore.

Further evidence may be adduced to support women's loss of income and compensation in the labour market (Table 5.6). Compared to 1990, women's incomes had improved tremendously by 2005. Among single women in 1990, 23.6 per cent earned below $500 per month, but this decreased to 3.1 per cent in 2005. In fact 56 per cent of single women earned $2,000 per month or more in 2005, compared to just 8.5 per cent a decade and half earlier. For married women the respective figures are 56.4 and 15.8 per cent. For the whole population in 1990, 74 per cent were single women who earned less than $500. By 2005 lower income groups registered a decline of single women workers (partly from reduced birth cohorts, partly by changing marital status and even educational attainment), compensated by a substantial increase of married women in lower incomes, as also for the widowed/divorced/separated. At the higher income scale, there is virtually no change in the marital status distribution but some 27 per cent of singles are in the $5,000+ grouping. Indirectly it may be deduced that women, on account of their marital status, may fare less well in the labour market and earn lower incomes. This is all the more acute for women with lower educational attainment. Some better qualified women (increasingly so) are likely to remain single to pursue a career track to compensate for the cost of their education. It is all the more certain that married women face some obstacles in securing high-salaried jobs. Average incomes of single women increased by a rate of 10 per cent per annum between 1990 and 2005, while that of married women increased at a rate of 7 per cent per annum. The difference is indicative of higher educational attainment and flexibility in choice of work by single women.

Average incomes by occupational status (see GHS, 2005) also confirm women's lower income levels relative to men's. For example, female employees in 2005 earned $768 less than their male counterparts on average. The 'own account workers' among women earned $560 less and the income difference of the employees was $600 on average (that table is not presented here).

In general, women do earn lower incomes than men, whatever their background. As fewer women may be found in highly-qualified jobs, their incomes are unlikely to increase or equal men's incomes. Over the last two decades women have improved their income levels, as attested by their higher incremental growth than for men. Women had previously started lower and this growth is not necessarily spectacular. For married women workers, their educational attainments do position them with some advantage if they improved their qualification levels. When familial responsibilities escalate, their incremental income growth is uncertain. Single women who were educated may fare better. Given the fact that more men than women work, it is clear that a majority of women would rather be attached to the family than be competitive in the labour market; this is the most plausible reason for the wide gaps in average income levels of the sexes.

Disparities in income would translate to lower Central Provident Fund (CPF) savings for old age for working women. For non-working women, there is no social security except what is shared with spouses. Some compensatory mechanism must address the gaps and labour market inequalities. More will be discussed on these social security arrangements in the next chapter.

Income differentials from other perspectives

It is obvious that the better-educated will earn higher incomes, at least in the wage sector. Table 5.7 indicates that for females the monthly average income for associate professional and technician jobs is 17 per cent lower than for their male counterparts and 7 per cent lower at the senior official and administrative levels. These differentials, even at the highest occupational categories, where qualifications should be similar or identical, may only be explained by age, career path and level of family responsibilities by sexes. Even after entering at the same scales, similar-qualified females in these high-level occupations may possibly lag through service and career opportunities, especially when women's dual roles are to be realized. Women, perhaps, accept these disparities in the short run, but in the long run, may be discouraged from striving harder in the labour market.

For average incomes, it is clear that there are wider variations at the skilled/highly paid categories. Thus the gap is quite large at the professional, associate professional and the technician levels as well. The disparity lessened (but was not eliminated) for clerical, sales and service workers perhaps because qualifications and skills background are more homogeneous than otherwise between the sexes. For the production sectors, such disparities continue depending on the

Table 5.7 Gender difference in average income by occupation, duration of job and number of hours worked

Occupation group	Earnings differential in $ (male/ female)	Duration of present job (years)	Earnings differential in $ (male/ female)	No of hours worked per week	Earnings differential in $ (male/ female)
Senior officials, administrators and managers	1,746	<1	491	<30	576
Professional & associate professionals	1,523	1	436	30–34	1,151
Technicians	843	2–3	593	35–39	1,124
Clerical	73	4–5	808	40–44	477
Sales and services	426	6–10	777	45–49	562
Production				50–54	826
Craftspeople	649	11–15	817	55–59	889
Operators	609	≥15	529	60–64	1,045
Labourers	261	Total	696	65+	985
				Total	615

Source: Computed from *Census of Population,* 2000, Government of Singapore.

requirements of the job. Here, more females than males are under-qualified, so receive a lower wage.

We now offer some explanation of the differential. Duration of present job is a proxy for experience and age for an economically active person. Less than one year in the present job translates to a $491 wage difference between the sexes: some difference is likely due to the two and half years of National Service for men; however, the huge gap is not explained by this factor alone. Our observation is comparable to the empirical study by Lee and Pow (1999).[9] The *1991 Graduate Employment Survey* revealed that male graduates earned $506 more in median gross monthly income than their female counterparts – and the maximum gap was in public sector jobs. It is argued by the employers that it is women's choice of degree (arts, social science, business and accountancy) that often results in low paying jobs compared to men (mainly engineering) and this is the reason behind this wage-gap. However, the findings of the *Graduate Survey* show those male graduates with an honours degree in the Social Sciences earned $540 more than female counterparts in the public service, and $457 more in statutory boards.[10, 11] Table 5.7 indicates that increasing years of experience translate into higher incomes for both sexes, but disparities remain even at a high level. Thus we can say that the career ladder for women is slower to climb than for men. A similar conclusion is found in the study by Arasu and Ooi (1984): women require 8 to 10 years to reach senior management positions, while men average 5 years. While there are 425,500 female graduates (diploma plus degree) compared to 509,100 men (53 per cent of the total) in the labour market in 2011 (LFS, 2011), men made up 64 per cent of all administrators and managers in 2011 – which clearly indicates the presence of non-economic constraints on women's upward mobility.

Average incomes by number of hours worked per week can also be indicative of income disparities. Although incomes generally increase according to increasing workweek, the observation is not universal. The maximum income difference is observed at the 30–34 hour and 35–39 hour workweeks. The workweek norm of 40–49 hours is the national average and the disparity correlates with overall income levels.

Income inequality within and between genders

Table 5.8 presents the inequality decomposition between genders. The estimates in the table have an interesting tale to tell. During 1984 to 2011, for ages 15–24, the Theil index for males increased by 76 per cent, while for females the Theil remained almost constant. The effect of education is indicative for males but not for females. Low-skilled male workers in the 15–24 age group are attracted to the workforce and perhaps they accept much lower wages. This could be the reason for the huge increase in the between male and female inequality from 0.003 to 0.028.

Mostly for all years the Theil for females increases as age increases. The spread of educational development has taken some time – thus only a few people in the higher age groups realized the benefit of higher education. This also reveals that

Table 5.8 Inequality in the Singapore labour force by gender for age, education, occupation and industry, 1984, 1994 and 2011

Groups	1984				1994				2011			
	Male Theil	Female Theil	Total Theil	Between-group contribution of Theil (%)	Male Theil	Female Theil	Total Theil	Between-group contribution of Theil (%)	Male Theil	Female Theil	Total Theil	Between-group contribution of Theil (%)
Age												
15–24	0.17	0.11	0.15	1.95	0.28	0.16	0.23	3.39	0.30	0.13	0.24	11.66
25–29	0.24	0.27	0.27	2.81	0.30	0.36	0.33	2.22	0.26	0.19	0.24	2.13
30–34	0.35	0.38	0.38	4.01	0.40	0.44	0.43	3.52	0.33	0.28	0.33	1.56
35–39	0.42	0.37	0.44	7.08	0.43	0.49	0.46	3.91	0.37	0.34	0.38	2.61
40–44	0.43	0.48	0.47	6.04	0.43	0.52	0.50	6.9	0.43	0.44	0.47	3.07
45–54	0.44	0.43	0.47	6.61	0.51	0.61	0.57	6.57	0.55	0.51	0.59	3.96
55 & over	0.52	0.51	0.55	4.80	0.42	0.44	0.44	5.06	0.69	0.59	0.71	4.44
Education												
No formal qualification/ lower primary	0.30	0.20	0.29	5.22	0.22	0.22	0.26	15.16	0.35	0.26	0.38	14.16
Primary	0.25	0.15	0.24	2.79	0.18	0.18	0.21	11.9	0.34	0.28	0.38	10.31
Lower secondary/ secondary	0.34	0.21	0.30	3.40	0.31	0.25	0.30	5.35	0.44	0.32	0.41	1.61
Upper secondary	0.40	0.27	0.38	3.76	0.46	0.38	0.44	2.87	0.48	0.28	0.41	0.19
Polytechnic diploma	—	—	—	17.74	0.34	0.21	0.30	2.47	0.39	0.20	0.35	3.01
Degree	0.18	0.23	0.20	4.00	0.32	0.18	0.29	9.52	0.28	0.25	0.31	5.75

Continued

Table 5.8 Continued

Age group	1984				1994				2011			
	Male Theil	Female Theil	Total Theil	Between-group contribution of Theil (%)	Male Theil	Female Theil	Total Theil	Between-group contribution of Theil (%)	Male Theil	Female Theil	Total Theil	Between-group contribution of Theil (%)
Industry												
Manufacturing	0.37	0.20	0.39	10.81	0.38	0.32	0.41	10.81	0.28	0.35	0.32	6.75
Construction	0.35	0.20	0.34	0.08	0.35	0.24	0.33	0.08	0.24	0.17	0.23	1.04
Commerce	0.41	0.27	0.4	6.82	0.4	0.33	0.41	6.82	0.36	0.35	0.36	0.64
Transport, storage & communication	0.31	0.20	0.29	0.41	0.36	0.22	0.33	0.41	0.37	0.25	0.37	9.29
Financial & insurance services, real estate, rental & leasing services	0.43	0.32	0.43	5.01	0.39	0.32	0.38	5.01	0.32	0.30	0.32	3.59
Community, social & personal services	0.54	0.41	0.50	3.30	0.55	0.51	0.55	3.30	0.31	0.29	0.31	3.33
Occupation												
Managers	0.20	0.21	0.22	4.86	0.26	0.29	0.27	1.09	0.30	0.23	0.30	0.77
Professionals	0.29	0.30	0.30	5.68	0.30	0.26	0.29	2.24	0.31	0.24	0.31	3.14
Clerical workers	0.14	0.12	0.13	2.8	0.09	0.07	0.08	0.01	0.16	0.16	0.19	0.26
Service workers, shop & market sales workers	0.36	0.25	0.39	14.43	0.15	0.20	0.17	6.58	0.27	0.24	0.28	6.29
Production workers, equipment operators & labourers	0.16	0.10	0.17	12.78	0.11	0.17	0.16	25.63	0.23	0.20	0.27	13.72
Total	0.42	0.33	0.45		0.36	0.35	0.44		0.42	0.49	0.53	

Source: Computed from LFS (1984), LFS (1994), LFS (2011).

the vocational or re-entry training was ineffective in enhancing wage rates and only few highly educated women continue receiving high wages. The between male and female inequality was quite pronounced in the 1980s for the age group 35–39 when the educational difference between males and females was quite substantial. However, with further educational development there was a clear decrease of these inequalities in this age group. Nevertheless inequality is persistently high at higher ages between the genders. As educational development has a gestation period, we expect that within a few more years even at the higher ages the between male and female inequality will be reduced further, if the subsidiary facilities (such as childcare, part-time and flexible job opportunities) follow with education.

During the period 1984 to 2011 the educational level of the labour force (both male and female) shifted upwards due to better-educated entrants. While in the 1980s the male–female inequality for polytechnic graduates was quite high (almost 18 per cent of the total), it has come down substantially to only 3 per cent of the total. We have seen previously that for the two-decade period under consideration there was a phenomenal increase in female polytechnic graduates. The within-female inequality for most groups went up over time.

This is because job opportunities that require better-educated workers were open to women, and within the same group a wide variation of experience can be observed. Furthermore, quite a number of females with extra training had managed to earn a higher income than their younger colleagues. For between the sexes, for university degree-holders, inequality is generally higher than for other educational groups. This is indicative of income differences within same education groups. We have seen that in Singapore women often prefer degrees that lead to jobs that are less remunerative than the degrees males prefer. Some effort is required by the government to find ways to generate equity among this group.

In the industry groupings, the decrease in between-group inequality of commerce is also an effect of education. The between-group inequality in transport and storage is quite high. Note that in this group female within-group inequality is relatively low compared to male or total inequality. The female share of employment in this group is also not very high. Perhaps all these women are employed at a low level of income and as some males in this group may earn high income (male inequality is high) the between-group inequality is high.

At the occupational level, female inequality is lowest for clerical jobs. Over the two decades examined, an increase in female share in employment is observed among professional jobs. Between-group inequality, although lower, remains high (considering high share of employment). At the occupational level not much change in within-female inequality is observed. This is likely because similar levels of education are needed for the same occupation group. Here we see that age does not play a big role within the same sex grouping. If there is any income difference in the same occupation between male and female, the gender bias factor is responsible.

Total inequality between women increased over the years due to the huge remuneration gap between the skilled and unskilled. Low paid foreign workers depress local unskilled wages, and some women still have non-commensurate skills and are thus earning a very low wage. This is true for the male workers as well – but the bulk do not suffer from this problem because their family responsibility is much lower (if not negligible) than their female counterparts. Thus even with higher skills, some women have to accept low-paid jobs to maintain flexibility between home and work. At the other end of the income ladder at the highest income group only a few women (compared to their male counterparts) make an entry. This dispersion generates a high level of inequality among women workers in the labour market and this has increased over the years.

Gender bias in earnings and policies of the government of Singapore

The Singapore government has total faith in the operation of the market mechanism without any rigidity (which could have restricted business and increased unemployment). The determination of wages in Singapore is based on productivity. We noticed in this chapter that women are on the losing side because of their familial responsibilities, and when the policy-makers in the country mandate wage determination based on productivity, it is not unnatural that women will earn a lower wage on average. There is no minimum wage in Singapore, however, for the wage determination of blue-collar workers the influence of unions is stronger than NWC recommendations (note that market forces have influenced unions). Despite higher educational attainment, Singapore has proportionately fewer females in blue-collar jobs.

In higher education, for subjects like arts, social sciences, accounting and business where females are concentrated and in related jobs, the rate of productivity growth is slower than in construction and engineering. Thus the sex bias in the wage differential is in-built in the wage system of Singapore. An empirical survey by Lee and Pow (1999) also shows that both private and public sectors tend to recruit women for operational level jobs rather than supervisory or managerial positions. Classified advertisements for positions such as production operators, secretaries, receptionists and general clerks often include an additional job specification inviting females only. Advertisements for general managers or chief executive appointments specify male candidates only; women still have difficulty in accessing male-dominated jobs. Thus where there exists a genuine gender bias on specific jobs, the gender wage differential is explained.

The *Economic Review Committee* in 2003 recommended a stoppage of the seniority-based wage system in an effort to narrow the wage gap, and this move was endorsed by the government. However, the effect of this is not a boon for female workers who choose to leave the labour force temporarily to have children. If a woman wants to re-join the workforce after few years of homemaking, she has to start from scratch in a rapidly changing/growing economy (Singapore is too dependent on new technology – particularly IT – which changes so fast that within a few years, skills become obsolete). Lee and Pow (1999) observed that some women when returning to the labour force after beginning motherhood, are offered a job at a lower occupational level (and wage) and hardly any training is given for their career development.

As a policy prescription, women aged 40–59 who have higher education attainment levels may have to be motivated through continuing education and upgrading of skills to ensure their relevance in the present labour market. All the more, women below age 60 must be empowered through enrichment and skill enhancement programmes at state expense. Such an approach will boost labour participation rates for women. Sakellariou (2006) indicated that the vocational education system in Singapore has served women with secondary vocational qualification particularly well. They earn more, have higher labour force participation, experience higher employment rates associated with a narrower gender earning gap compared with women with general education. However, the case for women with polytechnic qualifications is quite different, and is where the gender wage gap is more pronounced.

Married women who are regarded as less productive/committed to work because of their family responsibilities are the unintended victims of Singapore's wage policies. They also encounter discriminatory practices in selection and recruitment. Single women may often be preferred over married; there is no constitutional right to protect against gender discrimination in employment (Balakrishnan, 1989). Thus to protect the rights of women, the government needs to take the initiative to enact a sex discrimination law which could provide a framework to deal with such incidences of bias.

The entitlement and assistance provided to mothers in the form of unpaid childcare leave and fully paid unrecorded leave to look after sick children under six years of age are available mostly in the public sector for civil servants. The provision of paternity leave is quite uncommon in Singapore, with the exception of some MNCs (which follow their parent countries' norm). This is a clear indication of Singapore society's non-recognition of men's role in parenting. Even in the public sector men get medical benefits for their spouse and children: women are deprived of such benefits except when the husband is unable to work. This is a clear indication that in the workplace women are not treated equally to men and there lies the fundamental cause of income differences.

Although flexi/part-time employment is one solution to the women's work–family conflict, many do not want to have this type of employment opportunity for lesser benefits, pay and job security. The NTUC in 1993 carried out three surveys to assess Singapore's flexible work arrangements. In one study it was found that 15 per cent of women aged 25–54 wanted flexible work arrangements. Another study found that only 2.3 per cent of female employees worked under flexi-time and such flexi-time arrangements offered lower wages and fewer benefits. The study observed that flexi-time work arrangements are quite unavailable in Singapore. As at June 2011 (LFS, 2011), only 14.1 per cent of employed people worked part-time, while 63.7 per cent of part-time workers were female. Mostly they were married (66.7 per cent), 32.8 per cent were aged 35–49, while 28.5 per cent were aged 50–59, with 60 per cent secondary- and above secondary-educated. They mainly took up jobs as technical and associate professionals

(17.4 per cent), clerical (15.2 per cent) and service and sales workers (27 per cent). In a productivity-based wage system, flexi-time and part-time work may not be a solution for women, although Western developed nations, through this system, find a solution to the problem of low female labour force participation rates at higher ages. The Singapore government needs to consider this aspect of female work participation in their labour-short economy.

The LFS (2011) shows that out of 153,600 potential entrants, 98,300 were female; of these 37.4 per cent were between 30 and 49 years of age and 50 per cent were married; 47.3 per cent of females had expressed the main reason for being economically inactive as family responsibilities like housework, children care, and care giving to families and relatives (only 1.8 per cent of males cited this reason). Of these women 30 per cent are secondary educated and 48.1 per cent are better educated. This clearly indicates that satisfactory childcare arrangements are a necessary condition to encourage mothers to enter or re-enter the workforce. However, the lack of quality childcare centres (at affordable prices, in the proximity of residence or work place) is one major problem in Singapore.

According to the recent *Statistics on Childcare Services* (Early Childhood and Development Agency, 2012), there were 1,044 childcare centres in Singapore (up from 690 in 2004), with a total enrolment of 77,091 children. These centres provide full-day and half-day care programmes for children aged 18 months to 7 years. Infant care centres are fewer and less pronounced (although increased to 309 by the end of March 2013, from 126 in 2008). The *Census 2010* reveals that there were 214,414 females with one child; 383,718 with two children; 221,939 with three children; and 163,298 females with four or more children. In the age group below 30, about 25,204 women have one child, and 12,144 women have two children. We can safely assume that all these women have all children of 7 years or below and that would require some 49,492 seats at childcare centres to entice mothers to re-enter the workforce. Over that, in the age group 30–34, some 34,974 women have two children and we expect that at least one of those is eligible for a place in a childcare centre.[12] These figures indicate the insufficiency of childcare places in Singapore.

In March 2013, the average monthly fee for a full-day childcare is $863, with $640 for half day. It can be seen from the *LFS 2011* that 50 per cent of females aged 15–24 earned less than $1,499 a month and 21.3 per cent of the total female workforce also earned less than $1,499. Thus there is a question of affordability of childcare costs. The government provides a nominal childcare subsidy ($150 per month, for licensed childcare centres). For the very low income group further assistance is also provided. However, the amount of subsidy and additional assistance may be insufficient to encourage women to re-join the labour force. The third problem is related to children at ages 7+ and their after-school care facilities. In a productivity-based economy and wage structure, women have to take responsibility for their school-going children (in the absence of proper structured after-school care facility) and thus relinquish a part of their incomes. Proper policy prescription in this regard is also warranted. Some measures were taken to reduce the cost of foreign maids for working families. By the end of 2010, there were

201,000 foreign maids in the country (MOM, 2013b). Tax relief is given to offset the cost of the government levy for working women. This is a welcome policy.

The inadequacy of the policies regarding women's labour market participation and the conflict between work and family constitute an open question in the Singapore context. A survey by the Ministry of Community Development (MCD, 2004) identified that the common practice of a 5.5 day working week is a constraint on employees' ability to achieve work–life balance. We have already seen that potential entrants to the labour market prefer part-time jobs; however, in a productivity-based system this work arrangement is not welcomed by companies.

Thus it is paradoxical to ask women to be productive workers while retaining their traditional role in the family (Lee *et al.*, 1999). The concept of family in the Singapore context is different from other nations that have acquired developed status. For most countries, through phases of development the structure of the family has turned to a 'nuclear' from a 'joint' family system. However, Singapore has a migrant history and this background has a direct bearing on social life structures in the country. Male workers who came to Singapore in the colonial period mostly left their families in their native land and after independence a family nucleus started in Singapore. The largest ethnic group, the Chinese, perceived life differently from their traditional Chinese culture. The family value that the government wanted to impose on the life of Singaporeans by asking males to be involved more in the workplace and females in homemaking is not a continuation of the traditional Asian culture and hence can lead to conflict. However, Singaporeans are quite conforming subjects of government policy and such a conflict is yet to be experienced. But with the advent of education, the singlehood status among educated women has been increasing. Lack of facilities continues to hamper the dual/multiple role in the family and, despite the government's ardent efforts, the fertility rate remains as not very encouraging. Furthermore with globalization, living costs in Singapore are increasingly forcing married couples to earn money for a decent living. In such a situation the disparity of incomes between the sexes may generate a social conflict in the near future.

Conclusion

In Singapore women have fared well through various facets of development: there are universal education opportunities, employment openings and potentially high earnings for both men and women. Market forces sideline equally qualified women from the workforce, as employers may concentrate on gender-based labour demand. Trade unions do not practice collective bargaining as in developed societies, and women employees often get a bad deal compared to their male counterparts. Added to this predicament, women's dual roles in the workforce and in the domestic sphere are an impediment to gaining better wages. Despite the government's constant admonition to employers to accord the same terms and leave conditions, employers tend to favour single women and those without families as effective employees. Familial responsibilities weaken women's bargaining position; not that they are able to voice their grievances. They have to accept what is on offer if they enter the labour market, but once they exit for family reasons, re-entry on the same conditions is no longer easy. This is true even of highly qualified female workers who may have to accept conditions pertaining to the role of supplementary income earners.

Notes

1 In 1970 more than half the females were below 20 years of age. Only 20 per cent were above 40.
2 A market based economic theory considers this type of wage increase is an efficiency loss as other members of the society are worse-off due to this increase.
3 In the labour market there is no segmentation between a small group of well-paid unionized workers and a large group of unemployed are destined to informal sector workers.
4 In 1987: 1,891 females; 1999: 6,530 females; 2006: 86,900 females; 2011: 169,600 females, while the corresponding figures for males are 4,545, 8,111, 128,100 and 209,300 respectively.
5 Note that female headships are prominent for lower priced housings in most cases. This can be explained by increasing widowhood and legacy from spouses.
6 LFPR for Singapore women is very close to those of the females of Hong Kong. Taiwan has lower participation rates than Singapore for younger women below 35 years and slightly higher rate for older women. Japan has markedly higher participation rates for older women in their 40s and 50s. Unlike Singapore (and Hong Kong and Taiwan) the female LFPR for Japan shows two distinct peaks, one in the 20–24 age group and the other in the 45–49 age group. These humps reflect the withdrawal of married Japanese women from the labour force upon marriage and their re-entry into the labour market when they are in their middle ages after their children have grown up (similar to the USA in Figure 5.3).
7 This certainly created jobs in the labour market – but not for educated women.
8 The male median wage was $57,935 and that for female $42,734. The maximum salary earned by males was for Managing Director ($218,064) and other high paying jobs are Business Development Manager ($122,555) and IT Manager ($97,942), while the female IT project manager received $85,734 on average and the maximum salary a female earned was $160,491 (as Project Manager, Banking). See http://www.payscale.com/research/SG/Country=Singapore/Salary/by_Gender http://www.payscale.com/research/SG/Gender=Male/Salary, http://www.payscale.com/research/SG/Gender=Female/Salary [all accessed 31 October 2013].
9 This survey cites four reasons behind the wage gap: paper qualification, level of competence, amount of working experience and perception of women as the second wage earner.
10 The statutory boards of the Singapore government are organizations that have been given autonomy to perform an operational function. They usually report to one specific ministry.
11 Women in Taiwan do not receive equal pay for work of equal value. However, Taiwan's labour laws prohibit gender wage discrimination for equal work of equal efficiency. Japan and Korea have similar clauses and employers can be fined for breaching this clause. Like Singapore, Hong Kong does not have equal pay for equal work rules. Like Singapore, both Hong Kong and Taiwan have no regulation offering women equal treatment in recruitment, hiring and promotion. However, firms in Japan and Korea are officially required to equalize opportunities in various aspects of employment.
12 Roughly from these, 85,000 childcare seats are necessary while the availability is only 77,000.

6 Inequality, older women and necessity for social security

In the previous chapter we observed the income differential between genders. Low incomes that are concentrated in certain groups (due to educational variations, family responsibilities etc.) may generate a lack of saving potential, which creates an aggravated inequality effect in old age. In this chapter we will discuss some such possibilities.

Singapore's aged population

In Singapore in 2012, there were 592,700 people aged 60+, representing an average annual growth rate of 5.6 per cent from 1990 (246,900). Corresponding figures for the 65+ age group are 378,700 in 2012, up from 164,100 in 1990; growing at 3.6 per cent annually (see Table 6.1).

In 2012 14.6 per cent of males were aged 60+, compared to 16.4 per cent of females. Over the period 1980–2012, females aged 60+ have been proportionately higher than males; though it is an expected phenomenon from differential longevities between the genders, the absolute increase is substantial for females (318,300 from 132,200 during 1990–2012). The number aged 65+ has certainly increased for both genders, but the number of female survivors has increased even more.

In Singapore there were 1,880,000 males of all ages compared to 1,938,000 females in 2012, which implies a sex ratio of 1,031 females to 1,000 males. The sex ratio of age groups 30+ for 2012 is summarized in Table 6.2.

In this chapter we discuss the income security of older generations, and so we focus on the ages of 30 upwards. It is important to note that more working females could also contribute to labour market segmentation by gender arising from their often lower commensurate skills, which would work to women's disadvantage especially when family responsibilities increase. The increasing sex ratio beyond 50 indicates the unavoidable process of increasing feminization in the older age groups.

Marital status

Table 6.3 presents the marital status distribution of women during 1980–2010. In 1980, 92.2 per cent of women aged 30+ were 'ever married' (that is,

Table 6.1 The aged population, 1980–2012

Year	Ages 60+ ('000)	% in population	Growth rate (%pa)	Ages 65+ ('000)	% in population	Growth rate (%pa)
Both sexes						
1980	170.4	7.5	—	111.9	4.9	—
1990	246.9	9.1	3.8	164.1	6.1	3.9
2000	348.7	10.7	3.5	237.6	7.3	3.8
2006	427.3	11.8	3.7	306.4	8.5	4.8
2012 (June)	592.7	15.5	5.6	378.7	9.9	3.6
Males						
1980	81.0	6.6	—	51.2	4.2	—
1990	114.7	8.4	3.5	73.8	5.4	3.7
2000	161.8	9.9	3.5	102.2	6.3	3.3
2006	196.2	10.9	3.5	136.9	7.7	5.6
2012 (June)	274.4	14.6	5.8	168.6	9.0	3.5
Females						
1980	89.4	7.6	—	62.7	5.3	—
1990	132.2	9.9	4.0	90.3	6.8	3.7
2000	187.0	11.5	3.5	128.9	7.9	3.6
2006	231.2	12.7	3.9	169.6	9.31	5.2
2012 (June)	318.3	16.4	5.5	210.1	10.8	3.6

Source: *Census of Population*, 1980, 1990, 2000, *Population Trends* 2006, and *Monthly Digest of Statistics Singapore April 2013*, Singapore Department of Statistics, Government of Singapore and author's computations.

Note: Per cent of respective population by sex.

Table 6.2 Sex ratio by age group, 2012

Age group	Sex ratio (males per 1,000 females)	Sex ratio (females per 1,000 males)	% of women in total female population
30–39	926	1,080	16.32
40–49	984	1,016	16.38
50–59	1,013	987	14.92
60–69	963	1,039	9.01
70–79	821	1,218	4.88
80+	583	1,717	2.53

Source: Computed from *Monthly Digest of Statistics Singapore April 2013*, Singapore Department of Statistics, Government of Singapore.

currently married, divorced, separated, widowed) and by 2010 it had reduced to 86.5 per cent. This may be explained by increasing singlehood status.

Ever-married women aged 30+ increased from 423,000 to 1,043,000 in the thirty-year period, with more women remaining married. Increases in singlehood status can also be seen in ages below 60, but certainly at ages below 40.[1] Despite

Table 6.3 Females by age group and marital status, 1980–2010

Age group — Ever-married women: Per cent

Age group	1980 M	1980 W+D	1980 Total	1990 M	1990 W+D	1990 Total	2000 M	2000 W+D	2000 Total	2005 M	2005 W+D	2005 Total	2010 M	2010 W+D	2010 Total
30–39	83.1	3.4	86.5	78.4	3.5	81.9	79.3	3.5	82.8	78.04	3.5	81.54	74.8	4.2	79.0
40–49	85.0	9.8	94.8	82.5	7.6	90.1	79.7	7.2	86.9	79.6	6.6	86.2	79.2	7.4	86.6
50–59	71.1	26.0	97.1	75.6	19.4	95.0	76.6	14.4	91.0	75.8	12.8	88.2	75.0	12.5	87.5
60–69	47.6	47.7	95.3	53.5	43.5	97.0	62.9	32.5	95.4	65.5	28.6	94.1	66.3	25.2	91.5
70–79	24.6	69.8	94.4	30.8	65.2	96.0	37.4	60.3	97.7	34.8	62.4	97.2	42.5	53.1	95.6
80+	11.2	83.7	94.9	15.4	79.5	94.9	17.5	80.2	97.7	NA	NA	NA	15.1	82.8	97.9
Average	72.3	19.9	92.2	71.6	17.2	88.8	72.8	15.3	88.1	72.3	14.9	87.2	70.3	16.2	86.5
No. ('000)	332	91	423	482	116	598	678	143	821	773	159	932	847	196	1,043

Source: Computed from *Census of Population*, 1980, 1990, 2000, 2010; and *General Household Survey*, 2005, Department of Statistics, Government of Singapore.

Notes
Ever married = M + W + D.
M = Married, W = Widowed, D = Divorced/Separated.
Row-wise add to 100% in each age group in each year. Singles are not shown.
NA: For 2005 source does not provide data for age group 80+.

Table 6.4 Widowhood in 2010

Age group	Number (000s)	Widowed (%)
50–59	18.6	11.8
60–69	36.6	23.2
70–79	52.6	33.4
80+	42.7	27.1

Source: Computed from *Census of Population,* 2010, Department of Statistics, Government of Singapore.

Table 6.5 Distribution of household dwellings by gender and headship, 1980–2010

Dwelling type	1980 (%)		1990 (%)		2000 (%)		2010 (%)	
	Males	Females	Males	Females	Males	Females	Males	Females
HDB/JTC:	65.8	63.3	85.1	82.2	87.7	89.3	81.7	84.7
1–2 rooms	19.3	27.2	6.7	15.6	3.9	10.1	3.5	8.4
3+ rooms	46.5	36.1	78.4	66.6	83.8	79.2	78.0	76.0
Other flats	2.3	0.8	1.7	1.1	0.9	0.8	NA	NA
Private flats/ condominiums	3.6	4.5	3.9	4.9	6.1	5.6	11.6	10.2
Landed properties	9.4	8.8	6.9	7.3	5.3	4.2	6.0	4.3
Rest	18.9	22.6	2.4	4.5	0.0	0.1	0.7	0.8
Total	100.0	100.0	100.0	100.0	100.0	100.0	100.0	100.0

Source: Computed from *Census of Population,* 1980, 1990, 2000, and 2010, Department of Statistics, Government of Singapore.

these proportionate changes of singles, the widowed and divorced/separated women cannot be ignored; they increased from 91,000 to 196,000 during 1980–2010. The distribution of widows for 2010 by age group is presented in Table 6.4.

There were some 150,400 widows aged 50+ in 2010, with the maximum in the age group 70+ (95,200 or 60.5 per cent of widows aged 70+). These magnitudes have been escalated in the last three decades as the life expectancy of women has increased.

For the old age security of women, the above trends underline the importance of adequate financial and other supports for widowed and divorced women primarily as there are very pertinent and high incidences of widowhood in the older age groups.

Housing and households

In the last two decades the proportion of women heading households has remained *unchanged*. That is, about 80 per cent of all households are headed by males by virtue of their incomes and traditional roles. The distribution of households (for all ages) by dwelling type and headship does not vary much between the sexes, as seen in Table 6.5.

Table 6.6 Tenancy status and dwelling type of 60+ female household heads, 2000

	No.	(%)
Tenancy status		
Owner (self + others)	99,230	87.2
Tenants (rented)	11,600	10.2
Others (provided by others)	2,920	2.6
Dwelling Type		
HDB 1–2-room flats	12,360	34.1[b]
HDB 3-room flats	40,220	24.6[b]
Other public flats[a]	46,780	20.2[b]
Rest (non HDB)	14,390	20.9[b]
Total	113,750	22.8[b]

Source: Computed from *Census*, 2000, Department of Statistics, Government of Singapore.
Notes
[a] Includes HDB 4+ room flats and public flats.
[b] % of population (females) within each dwelling type.
Similar information is not available from 2010 Census.

In the last thirty years the female headships have increased for HDB/JTC flats especially for 3+ room types, with a corresponding decline of 1–2-room flats.[2] Most probably, these lower-priced apartments would house singles, widowed and even divorced/separated older women, thus enhancing affordable shelter and living arrangements.

Information on females by headship and tenancy status for ages 40+ may provide clues on the home equity status of older women (Table 6.6).

The important statistic here is the *increasing* incidence with age of both rented and other forms of tenancy; some 12.8 per cent for ages 60+ compared to 7.9 per cent for ages 40–59. In the absence of detailed information, we assume that at older ages some women would be in dwellings that were not 'owned' but rented or provided for them. With increasing age, women-headed households increase, especially in the 60+ age group, whatever the dwelling type. For the lower-end of HDB housing (1–3 room flats), the increasing predominance of women heading the households can only be explained by increasing widowhood and legacy from spouses. For upper-end housing (larger public flats and non-HDB private homes, including condominiums and landed properties), the explanation may be found in the legacies of higher income families. For lower income families, including downgrading for some, more older women have home equity only through HDB dwellings. The latter constituted around 46 per cent for ages 60+, while it was 42 per cent for ages 40–59. Female household heads also increased from 11.8 to 22.8 per cent through the ages 40 to 60+, for all types of dwellings.

Educational attainment of women

In the previous chapter we discussed the increasing trend of educational attainment for women. Here we further extend the observation by analysing age-specific educational attainment between genders. Table 6.7 provides age–sex segregated data on educational attainment from 1990 for ages 40+. It can be observed that educational attainment between men and women in ages below 60 and 60+ differ considerably; while the period has witnessed increasing higher educational attainment for both genders, attainment rates for 'below secondary level' (which includes persons *without* any qualification at all) escalate with age, reaching substantially high levels in the older age groups. For ages 60+, 79.2 per cent of females had a 'below secondary' qualification in 2010, compared to 96.6 per cent in 1990. For males, 74.2 (in 2010) and 90.3 (in 1990) per cent were in this category, indicating that older people had lower levels of education, especially females. Attainment of polytechnic and university qualifications for ages 60+ was 0.4 per cent in 1990 for females, increasing to 5.2 per cent by 2010. Corresponding figures for males are 1.7 and 13.0 per cent.

Although education attainment levels have improved with cohort attrition (here 20 years), there is still a considerable number of females *without* a secondary education, which is a desired qualification for skilled workers in the Singapore economy.

Income inequality within older age groups

Table 6.8 presents Gini coefficients for older age groups calculated from the *General Household Survey*, 2005 (these Ginis must not be compared with the LFS Ginis that we presented in the previous chapters). For the older ages (60+), both sexes experienced higher Gini when compared to the national Gini, signalling greater heterogeneity in skills composition among older workers. Older people had less than commensurate educational attainments, while few (both genders) possess the requisite skills, and this is reflected in the higher Gini value.

For ages 65+, the situation differs from age 60+, suggesting that the age group 60–64 may comprise better-qualified persons (males more than females). Here, the combined Gini (of 0.478) is higher than for each gender Gini (male 0.469, female 0.476). This indicates that the within-gender inequality is also quite high for this age group. Women aged 65+ are even more heterogeneous in skills/income composition, resulting in this high Gini.

Most income differentials by age and gender may be explained through educational–occupational and skills attainment levels. The restructured economy of the 1990s required a technical and engineering bias to reduce labour-intensive manufacturing industries. Higher education as well as technical/vocational education attracted better remuneration, benefiting both men and women. Lower-qualified female workers were mainly employed in occupations that did not command premiums in the labour market, especially in production-related vocations and the services. These differences might have diminished through age, as older workers of both sexes had minimal or no qualifications, were generally not commensurate with market demand, and therefore depressing or keeping wages stagnant. Homogeneous skills at *both ends* of the educational scale tend to reduce income inequalities, but when the better-educated workers experience

Table 6.7 Educational attainment by gender, age group and level, 1990–2010

Educational attainment	1990 various ages (%)			2000 various ages (%)			2005 various ages (%)			2010 various ages (%)		
	40–49	50–59	60+	40–49	50–59	60+	40–49	50–59	60+	40–49	50–59	60+
Females:												
Below secondary	73.1	90.2	96.6	47.2	68.5	90.0	38.9	60.3	87.3	28.4	48.8	79.2
Secondary	18.8	6.0	—	31.0	18.5	—	30.6	23.7	6.4	28.4	28.7	11.9
Upper secondary	5.0	2.6	3.0	9.3	6.2	7.9	10.8	6.9	2.9	10.6	8.8	3.8
Polytechnic+	3.1	1.2	0.4	12.5	6.8	2.1	19.5	9.1	3.4	32.6	13.6	5.2
Males:												
Below secondary	62.7	79.2	90.3	41.7	54.8	76.8	35.7	49.5	74.2	25.9	43.4	64.5
Secondary	21.4	11.7	—	28.7	22.1	—	25.0	23.8	12.2	20.4	23.5	15.9
Upper secondary	6.6	4.2	8.0	9.2	8.5	16.8	10.0	9.4	4.6	11.5	10.2	6.6
Polytechnic[a]	9.3	4.9	1.7	20.4	14.6	6.4	29.3	17.3	9.1	42.2	23.0	13.0

Source: *Census*, 1990, 2000, 2010 Department of Statistics, Government of Singapore and *General Household Survey*, 2005, Department of Statistics, Government of Singapore.

Note
[a] Includes other diploma and university qualifications. Columns in panel will add to 100 per cent, subject to rounding errors.

Table 6.8 Inequality within older age groups and genders

Age group	Males	Females	Total
15+ (national)	0.498	0.480	0.495
60+	0.573	0.564	0.578
65+	0.570	0.579	0.581

Source: Computed from *General Household Survey*, 2005, Department of Statistics, Government of Singapore.

Table 6.9 Average number of hours worked by gender, various age groups

Age group	Average number of hours worked per week			
	Males	Females	Total	Δ (Males–Females)
15+	48.5	44.7	46.8	3.9
50–54	49.4	44.0	47.2	5.4
55–59	48.5	42.8	46.4	5.7
60–64	47.1	41.5	45.1	5.6
65–69	45.1	38.6	43.1	6.5
60+	45.3	39.4	43.4	5.9
65+	44.3	38.4	42.5	6.0
70+	43.6	38.1	42.0	5.5

Source: Computed from *Census*, 2010, Department of Statistics, Government of Singapore.

higher demand, the income gap will widen. With increasing age comes increasing inequality. This happens because of changing technology that results in changes in generic abilities, while existing technologies and corresponding skills become redundant.

Hours worked by older workers

The income distribution above was analysed using different workweek records. The older workers may not be able to contribute a full workweek and this may affect their incomes. Also, the market may not provide sufficient incentives and opportunities for older workers to contribute a full workweek, thereby depressing their incomes. Some older workers may actually prefer flexi-work arrangements, working part-time or in casual employment, or even on a piecework basis. These aspects are not captured in full by the *Census* enumeration, but the 'number of hours worked' within a week may be used as a *proxy* measure of the workweek expended. In this analysis, the cut-off for the standard workweek is taken as 40–44 hours. Table 6.9 provides distributions for workers aged 15+, 50+ and 60+ by gender.

At the national level, the average workweek recorded in the 2010 *Census* was nearly 46.8 hours. The age group 50–59 also recorded such levels, generally high for a near-aged or ageing working population. At these ages and beyond, the Singapore labour system may only encourage a productive labour force, as these

Table 6.10 Percentage of people with various average numbers of hours worked per week (various age groups by gender, 2010)

No. of hours worked per week	Age group (%)					
	15+	*50–54*	*55–59*	*60+*	*65+*	*70+*
Males						
Below 30	3.5	3.5	5.1	10.4	15.0	16.7
30–39	4.0	4.2	5.4	9.2	11.4	12.8
40–44	34.9	32.8	33.5	31.4	28.8	27.7
45–49	20.2	18.5	18.1	17.4	16.2	16.3
50+	37.4	41.0	37.9	31.6	28.7	26.6
Females						
Below 30	8.1	10.9	13.6	22.2	29.7	30.9
30–39	6.3	8.2	9.7	12.6	14.5	16.4
40–44	41.5	38.8	37.5	31.4	26.6	24.8
45–49	20.4	19.1	18.9	16.2	13.4	12.1
50+	23.7	23.0	20.2	17.6	15.9	15.8

Source: Computed from *Census*, 2010, Department of Statistics, Government of Singapore.

figures attest. At 60+, there is a slight decline in the workweek expended: 43.4 for 60+ age group and 42.5 hours for 65+. Gender-differentials arise for many reasons, as women must shoulder dual (even multiple) roles in society. In general, at the national level, males contribute a higher average workweek (48.5 hours) than women (44.7 hours), this perhaps is related to their respective roles and responsibilities. Such a differential may also affect incomes.

At ages 50–59, the near aged, this differential ranges about 5.4 to 5.7 hours per week. The differential increases to 5.9 to 6.0 hours at ages 60+ and 65+. Although these are minor differences, on a yearly basis it may add up in economic terms.[3]

The distribution of workers according to the workweek norm adopted here can be visualized further from the following reconstruction in Table 6.10.

Irrespective of age or gender, most of the working population expends an average workweek of 40–49 hours. At the national level, 55.1 per cent contribute within this norm, while 37.4 per cent work above 50 hours per week. By ages 50–59, this reduces slightly to 51.6 per cent, since more are working below 40 hours. At ages 60+, there is an increase in persons working below 40 hours, as would be expected of an ageing workforce: corresponding figures for males and females respectively are 19.6 and 34.8 per cent, and 10.5 and 35.8 per cent for ages 50–59. That is, at older ages, part-time or flexi work arrangements may be progressively preferred, and this is even truer for older females. By ages 60+, such preferences are high and this is acute for females (44.2, 47.3 per cent respectively for ages 65+ and 70+) compared to males (26.4 and 29.5 per cent). Despite reductions in workweek with age progression, those working beyond 50 hours remain more or less constant (for 60+; 31.6 per cent for males and 17.6 per cent for females, compared to the national figures of 37.4 and 23.7 hours). This could partly explain lower incomes for older women.

Health-related issues

Female mortality is generally lower than that for men and higher longevity is the norm for older women. By 2012, life expectancy at birth for females had reached 84.5 years when compared to males (79.9 years). Thus, the life span will *exceed* the life expectancy at birth. In 2012, the average life expectancy for both sexes taken together at age 65 was 20.2 *additional* years, which translates to an average life span of 85.2 years.[4]

For 2012, the life expectancy for females at age 60 was 26.3 years, and 22.6 years for males. By age 65, their respective life expectancies were 21.9 and 18.5 years. Potentially, males would live on average 83 years and females 86 years had they lived to 60. If they lived to 65, the life span would be 84 and 87 years respectively. Additional years of life imply longer retirement years from age 60 or 62. Longer retirement is an extra dependency burden on old age security, even more so for longer-living women. Available life-years may be translated into *productive* life or productive ageing, through work innovations and policies.

WHO (2004)[5] estimates for Singapore (for 2002) that 'health expectancy' would be 71.3 years for women, and 68.8 years for men, compared to 'life expectancy' of 81.7 and 77.4 years. Number of years lived in 'disability' would be 10.4 and 8.6 years respectively (or 12.7 and 11.1 per cent of life spans). This suggests a greater need for long-term care for women.

Importantly, public hospital admission rates for ages 50–59 in the last three decades have declined, especially for females, however, an increase at ages 60+ has been recorded. After age 70, there is a perceptible increase in hospital admissions for women, since feminization of ageing is correlated with increasing disability rates. Hospital patient statistics indicate an increasing incidence of degenerative diseases among the elderly, and increasingly of women.[6]

The proportionate share of *operating* expenditure by the Singapore government on health increased from 9.5 to 11.2 per cent of total *government operating expenditure* during 1970–2012. This has been accompanied by higher private health consumption expenditure on medical services (2.4 to 7.0 per cent) during 1970–2011. Both are correlated, underlying self-financing through Medisave, Medishield (both personally-financed) and Medifund (government aid for the absolute needy).

Necessity of social security and its current provision

The above scenario indicates that for a healthy economy the provision of social security is essential for everyone (irrespective of gender). However, women need more support because of their shorter working life, low income and longer life expectancy.[7]

In Singapore, healthcare, pension (social security arrangements) and housing are managed through the Central Provident Fund (CPF) scheme (Asher and Shantakumar, 1996; Asher and Nandy, 2011). This is a pro-family, defined contribution scheme where the individual's benefits are derived from total contributions accumulated *plus* the interest earned. This scheme has existed since 1955. A nomination scheme was introduced in 1957 to speed up payments to beneficiaries of deceased members. A law was passed in 1980 to revoke nominations upon marriage by making married members re-nominate aims to protect immediate members (e.g., spouse and children). Among CPF members with nominations, family members stand to inherit CPF savings in 98 per cent of cases, and among CPF members without nominations, CPF savings are distributed to next-of-kin under the law of intestacy in Singapore. As of 2011, the total membership of the CPF is 3.376 million; however, only 51.4 per cent are active members. An active member is one that has at least one contribution paid for him/her for the current or any of the previous three months. As the active members constitute 86 per cent of the total labour force,[8] we can safely say that labour force coverage of the CPF is almost universal.

Only gainful employment entitles a person to a CPF account, to which employers contribute a share. People with no income are excluded from the CPF system. As the CPF system is based on contributions from both employee and employer, a self-employed person does not get the benefits of a wage earner. However, self-employed people make contributions to their Medisave accounts to ensure that they have sufficient savings for their healthcare needs. The discipline of regular saving is especially relevant since, unlike employees, self-employed people do not receive regular Medisave contributions from employers. Therefore they set aside a portion of their income to build up Medisave savings in anticipation of their future healthcare needs, especially during old age when they have stopped working.

Current CPF contribution rates vary with age, and are subject to a wage ceiling (see Table 6.11). The rate from 2011 for a Singapore permanent resident private sector employee or a government non-pensionable employee aged 50 or less is 36 per cent of the wage (16 per cent by employers, 20 per cent by employees) with a stipulated maximum monthly contribution. People in the labour force who are over 50 are subject to lower rates of contribution. This is designed to partly de-link wages from seniority and to reduce the cost of hiring older workers (*CPF Board Annual Report*, various years). The contributions are channelled into three separate accounts: (i) Ordinary Account (approximately 65 per cent, decreasing with age, used for housing, pre-retirement investment and other purposes); (ii) Special Account (approximately 17–27 per cent, increasing with age until 55, reduces to zero for employees over 55); and (iii) Medisave Account (between 19 and 83 per cent, increasing with age, the balance in the Medisave Account can be used for health purposes only and any surplus after death is distributed among the beneficiaries). Although the Medisave Account ensures medical care after retirement, the health insurance scheme is inadequate, with more than one third not covered by the scheme. Also contributing to this narrow coverage, is the fact that it pays only a small proportion of a hospital bill, typically 25–40 per cent. Over the years, this share has declined, mainly through government legislation and NWC guidelines to address high operating expenses of businesses.

Concerns have been raised (e.g., Williamson *et al.*, 2012) about the minimum sum requirement of the CPF and its ability to provide sufficient protection against old-age destitution. Large 'leakages' for housing equity in the past, especially

Table 6.11 Central Provident Fund contribution rates, 2011 (effective September, 2011)

				Credited into		
Employee age (years)	Employer contribution (% of wage)	Employee contribution (% of wage)	Total contribution (% of wage)	Ordinary account (housing and others)	Special account (retirement)	Medisave account (health)
	Up to wage ceiling of $5,000	Up to wage ceiling of $5,000	Up to wage ceiling of $5,000	Share of contribution (%)	Share of contribution (%)	Share of contribution (%)
35 & below	16	20	36	64	17	19
35–45	16	20	36	58	19	22
45–50	16	20	36	53	22	25
50–55	12	18	30	43	27	30
55–60	9	12.5		53	4	42
60–65	6.5	7.5	14	25	7	68
Above 65	6.5	5	11.5	9	9	83

Source: CPF Annual Report, 2012.

Note: The information applies to employees with monthly wages above $1,500. Workers included are: (1) Private Sector; (2) Government Non-Pensionable employees; (3) Non-Pensionable Employees in Statutory Bodies & Aided Schools; (4) Singapore Permanent Resident employees from their third year onwards.

for public flats, have diminished total CPF savings for the average worker, and the higher contributory rates of the past have yet to be restored. During the late 1980s and 1990s about 70 per cent of the contributions were withdrawn annually. Such a high level of withdrawals for non-retirement purposes – especially for housing – adversely affected the accumulation of CPF balances, and suggests that the intention of the Singapore government with respect to CPF, at least until the last decade, was not to secure old-age earnings but rather an arrangement for asset holding. Studies by Hateley and Tan (2003) and McCarthy *et al.* (2002) show that average workers in Singapore are 'asset rich and cash poor' as housing values generally rise in real terms. However, if there is a depression in the housing market (as has happened in many countries including Singapore in the past), the retirement asset accumulation could be reduced substantially. If retirees do not have enough income or savings to live at a subsistence level, they would need to encash some of the value from their house.[9]

Other leakages for approved investments, shares, medical care and annuities further erode CPF savings. From 1987, CPF top-ups and voluntary contribution schemes allow cash or CPF savings to be used to top-up parents' and spouse's retirement accounts, and cash to supplement CPF savings of family members, subject to a cap to prevent tax shelters. The high CPF contributory rates have in the past reduced the potential for private savings unless the mandatory CPF is considered private savings. Over and above, despite government guarantees, the returns on the tax-exempt CPF contributions have been below expectations compared to other forms of long-term investment instruments. Those who do not work at all have no CPF savings; those with short work history (mostly women) have far smaller CPF balances, after paying for mortgages, insurance, healthcare, etc.

Current situation of CPF balance

Figure 6.1 depicts the gender variation of CPF balances over the last 26 years. In 1984 males had almost 40 per cent more in their CPF balance than did women, and in 2011 this difference had reduced to 17 per cent. This is an indication of higher female labour force participation with better education (and consequently wages). In the age group 40–50, men's average balance is only 13 per cent more while in the age group 60+, males hold almost 58 per cent more on average in CPF balances than their female counterparts. This aspect creates concerns about the robustness of Singapore's CPF system. Because of the average shorter working life of females, they have less accumulated balance at retirement, and to sustain a healthy after-retirement life they need extra state support.

Note that the balances referred to here are not total savings from aggregate contributions, but balances *remaining* after approved leakages for housing, medical care, insurance, shares and so forth. Members may be active or inactive. By age 55, the balances would be accumulative of interest, dividends, profits and other returns (when a second mortgage is taken, the previous partial withdrawal must be returned with prevailing interest), so as not to deplete CPF savings for old age. At age 55, most members would withdraw their balances after purchasing annuities as per legal provisions. Thus, by ages 55–59, the balances would have reached rock-bottom levels. Any balances in ages 55+ would reflect contributions

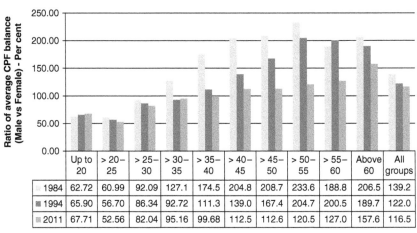

	Up to 20	> 20– 25	> 25– 30	> 30– 35	> 35– 40	> 40– 45	> 45– 50	> 50– 55	> 55– 60	Above 60	All groups
1984	62.72	60.99	92.09	127.1	174.5	204.8	208.7	233.6	188.8	206.5	139.2
1994	65.90	56.70	86.34	92.72	111.3	139.0	167.4	204.7	200.5	189.7	122.0
2011	67.71	52.56	82.04	95.16	99.68	112.5	112.6	120.5	127.0	157.6	116.5

Age groups

Figure 6.1 Gender variation in CPF balance at various ages, 1984–2011.

Source: Computed from *CPF Annual Report*, various years.

(at reduced rates) from work incomes, which may be less than for pre-retirement employment. These *caveats* have to be borne in mind when CPF balances are analysed. Also, substantial withdrawals from existing accounts (including future loan repayments to the Central Provident Fund Board (CPFB)) for housing would reduce balances, but this is considered as home equity for both males and females. With universal home equity, CPF savings may be large for high-income earners. CPF savings also replicate the income distribution from which contributions had been made.

About 42 per cent of female CPF members aged 30–49 'own' 56 per cent of their total CPF balances. Older females (aged 50+) account for only 38 per cent of the balances. Corresponding figures for males are 42 per cent and 51 per cent balances in ages 30–49; older males own 44 per cent. Only in ages up to below 40 are women's CPF balances expected to be equal or higher than those for men; beyond age 40, the disparity between the sexes widens to the advantage of employed men. By ages 50–55, just prior to withdrawal, men had $102,258 on average as compared to $84,821 on average for women (year 2012). These attest to the inequality of the sexes in terms of CPF savings for old age; if the withdrawn savings were intact on the death of the spouse, widowed women may benefit through adequate social security.[10]

From the above discussion we may conclude that the female workforce has not fared *justly* to eradicate past injustice. Labour market segmentation is a possible explanation for employer discrimination and hiring practices with respect to female labour. To this may be added the lower work participation levels of women and their lack of commensurate qualifications at older ages. A combination of factors would have worked against employed women, including their dual role which may inhibit them from seeking a full-time career. Thus, the lower average CPF savings of women as compared to men, and the existing gender disparity in CPF savings, are testimony of market imperfections that may discriminate against women employees.

The necessity of state support is further reinforced, as can be seen in Figure 6.2, which shows that older people, particularly females, are extremely dependant on the allowance from their children. Support from the state in its present form is not enough to sustain older people in Singapore.

Conclusion

In this chapter, we have found that the Singapore government needs to provide more support to older people and a greater commitment is necessary to treat the sexes equally. Because of longer female life expectancy and higher widowhood rates, social security provision by the government (particularly for housing and medical facilities) needs to be adequately safeguarded. Using headship of household as a proxy for intra-household inequality we observe a strong presence of intra-household inequality in Singapore. This implies a need for more individually-based social security provision. It is further observed that older women's earnings are always *lower* than those of their male counterparts,

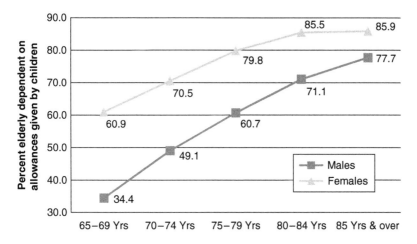

Figure 6.2 Elderly dependence on children for financial support.
Source: Computed from Singapore *Census of Population*, 2010.

and that is not because of a lesser workweek expended by women. This arises from the obsolescence of skills and the inability of older workers to re-skill themselves.

The current CPF system in Singapore is based on lifelong continual employment. In a globalized world with flexible labour markets that allow restructuring and reorganization of firms, the trend is to employ staff on a contractual and/or part-time basis. Continual re-skilling and job changes in interim unemployment and underemployment are quite common. The CPF scheme does not protect workers from non-employment (or structural unemployment). Thus, re-skilling at a fast pace becomes necessary to move to a higher paid job. Although the government has increased vocational training institutes over the years, it has not been able to target older women (and men) who were out of the workforce during their active life to help them re-adjust within the new world of work. The modern generation is less interested in being out of the workforce, thus creating a downward trend in the fertility rate. With this present trend, the medical provision for older people (particularly women) is largely financed from the children's CPF, and this is difficult to sustain in the long run.

Appendix

Holzmann *et al.*'s five-pillar pension system

The World Bank's (1994) *Averting the old-age crisis* study laid the foundation for pension policies and reforms in several countries around the globe. The study proposed a three-pillar pension system to achieve the goal of old-age security. The key features of each of the pillars are:

Pillar 1 is a mandatory, publicly managed, unfunded defined-benefit system with the goal of reducing poverty among the old;

Pillar 2 consists of a mandatory, privately managed, funded defined-contribution (savings) system; and

Pillar 3 comprises a voluntary, privately managed savings system.

The World Bank (1994) report advocated an increasing role for the second pillar as a means of providing financial security in old age through individual savings accounts. Since the publication of the report, pension reforms based on the second pillar have been implemented in Latin America and in the transition economies of the post-Soviet Union era of East and Central Europe. Gill *et al.* (2005) criticize the World Bank (1994) report for not paying attention to the application of a microeconomic framework of insurance and savings along with the primary policy objectives of old-age income security. Holzmann *et al.* (2005) extend the World Bank framework and propose an alternative five-pillar pension system to achieve the objective of ensuring universal old-age income security for all citizens. The five pillars (numbered 0 to 4) have the following key characteristics:

Pillar 0 is a universal or means-tested, publicly funded, basic (zero) pillar to overcome old-age poverty;

Pillar 1 consists of a mandatory, publicly managed, defined benefit or notional defined contribution system;

Pillar 2 comprises a mandatory, fully funded, occupational or personal defined benefit or defined contribution system;

Pillar 3 is supported by a voluntary, fully funded, occupational or personal defined benefit or defined contribution system; and

Pillar 4 is a non-financial pillar that encompasses family support and access to healthcare and housing.

Table 6A.1 summarizes the key characteristics of Holzmann *et al.*'s five-pillar pension system.

Holzmann *et al.*'s view incorporates several principles that are deemed essential to any successful reform: (i) all pension systems should have an element that provides basic income security and poverty alleviation across all income groups; (ii) prefunding for future pension commitments is advantageous both economically and politically; and (iii) in countries where prefunding has beneficial promises, a mandated and fully funded second pillar provides a useful benchmark against which the design of a reform may be evaluated. The framework states that the primary goal of a pension system should be to provide adequate, affordable, sustainable and robust retirement income while seeking to implement welfare-improving programmes in a manner appropriate to an individual country. The model emphasizes that the design of a pension system or its reform must explicitly recognize that pension benefits are claims against future economic output, and that

Table 6A.1 Summary characteristics of each pillar in the World Bank's three-pillar and Holzmann *et al*.'s five-pillar pension systems

	Zero pillar	First pillar	Second pillar	Third pillar	Fourth pillar
Objectives	Alleviate absolute poverty	Reduce relative poverty	Savings plus coinsurance – for efficiency and growth	Savings plus coinsurance	Family support, healthcare, housing
Predominant target group	Lifetime poor	Formal sector employees	Formal sector employees	Formal and informal sector employees	All citizens
Form of pension plan	Basic pension (universal or means tested)	Public pension plan	Occupational or personal pension/ savings plan	Occupational or personal pension/ savings plan	*Not applicable*
Participation	Universal or residual	Mandatory	Mandatory	Voluntary	Voluntary/Mandatory
Management	Public	Public	Private	Private	Private
Funded/Unfunded	Unfunded, budget or general revenues	Contributions, plus financial reserves	Funded	Funded	*Not applicable*
Benefits to individuals	Defined benefit	Defined benefit	(Various/flexible)	(Various/flexible)	*Non-monetary*
Contribution by individuals	Non-contributory	Notional defined contribution	Contributory (defined)	Contributory (flexible)	*Non-monetary*
Singapore CPF system	**Not satisfied**	**Partly satisfied**	**Satisfied**	**Satisfied**	**Satisfied**

Source: Summarized from Holzmann *et al*. (2005).

reforms should be designed and implemented in a manner that supports growth and development and diminishes distortion in the capital and labour market. The five-pillar pension system generates a variety of diversification gains. Retirees from the labour market are exposed to substantial risk under pure capitalized individual savings systems that translate stock savings into a flow of retirement income because of interest rate volatility or limited capacity to manage mortality risk. This happens because the private annuity markets are inefficient. The zero and first pillar arguments offset the risks of earnings volatility and employment dislocation that underlie voluntary employment-based pillars.

The social, economic and political impacts of the five-pillar pension system are discussed by Holzmann *et al.* (2005) for both developed and developing economies. Mature pension system economies operate a fully-funded pillar and outline the benefits of such an approach. Three particular positive impacts are identified in this system:

1 Increased output: the suggested mechanisms that determine the effects of funding on output are essentially threefold: through higher aggregate saving, through lower labour market distortions and through more efficient financial markets (see Bailliu and Reisen, 1997; López-Murphy and Musalem, 2004).

2 Labour market performance: to the extent that a funded system (or a funded pillar within a mixed system) links contributions more directly to benefits and thus leads to lower labour market distortions (including those emerging from financing the transition), positive output and even growth effects should emerge. Such effects on growth have been documented for Chile (Holzmann, 1997b), and recent empirical evidence claims growth effects in both OECD and emerging-market economies (Davis and Hu, 2004).

3 Increasing individual welfare: enhanced individual choice of retirement provisions and instruments under a scheme with funded pillar(s) is another potential benefit of funding that is important for at least a subset of the population. A partially-funded scheme should also provide a higher rate of return than an unfunded system (especially where there is no tax burden to fund transition costs, as in this scenario).

Another scenario is a transition toward a partially-funded five-pillar system starting from a fully developed and dominant unfunded pillar with comprehensive coverage. The critical cost value for the move toward funding is the implicit pension debt resulting from the current pension obligations to retirees and workers. The relevant definition of implicit debt (accrued-to-date liability) in mature pension systems amounts to 20–30 times the annual public pension expenditure (Holzmann, 1997a). Moving from an unfunded to a funded system makes the implicit pension debt explicit. To achieve the economic benefits requires the repayment of this debt (and hence a reversion of the initial income transfers toward the start-up generation). Debt repayments of this size create a major cost for current (and future) generations, and, despite the potential advantages, the net benefits of a major move toward funding may not be positive.

Holzmann *et al.* (2005) acknowledge that there is no universal 'best' system for all countries, and that the choice of one or more pillars would depend on the specific situation of a country. For example, most developed countries are likely to have both the resources and the institutions to manage the complex five-pillar system, whereas many less developed countries would be hard-pressed to build even one or two pillars of the pension system. Asher (2008) indicates that the World Bank's multi-pillar pension taxonomy may be used as a framework for considering pension reform but cannot be regarded as a blueprint. St. John and Willmore (2001) explain that New Zealand's success lies in ensuring stable and adequate retirement income for all citizens, moderating income inequality in retirement and protecting all elderly citizens from uncertainty during rapid economic change without conforming to the five-pillar pension system. In Mauritius, for example, the poverty rate among households with an older person would be 30 per cent were it not for a universal social pension that reduced the poverty level to 6 per cent (Willmore and Kidd, 2008). A shift towards Holzmann *et al.*'s zero pillar is evident in a number of Latin American countries. Recognizing the limitations of a single-pillar approach to retirement benefits, Chile has passed legislation strengthening the zero pillar to be financed from budgetary revenue (Kay and Sinha, 2008).

Examining Singapore's CPF system against the World Bank pillars

In light of Holzmann *et al.*'s five-pillar pension system, Singapore's old-age security system is rather weak since it lacks the first two – zero and first – basic, foundational pillars (see Table 6A.1 last row and Figure 6A.1). As CPF members in Singapore are allowed to withdraw part of their balances for expenditures like college education and home ownership, Holzmann *et al.*'s fourth pillar is satisfied. Although this flexibility often leads to reduction of funds available for retirement, it creates reciprocal filial responsibility for post-retirement care of the elderly by family members. The notional defined contribution criterion of Holzmann *et al.*'s (2005) first pillar is not used in Singapore. Their pillar one also assumes that a large proportion of contributions made to the CPF over the years would be available for annuity income during retirement, which is not the case in Singapore. However, a new CPF scheme started in 2009, LIFE (Lifelong Income For the Elderly), is mandatory at age 55 for those with \$40,000 or above in their CPF retirement account (CPF, 2011). Under this scheme workers become eligible for monthly pension payments for life based on the size of the balance at the time they become eligible to receive a pension. The total size of the annuity is \$380–\$1,090.[11] About 11.75 per cent of active CPF members over 60 would be eligible for this scheme as most members of the other groups do not have sufficient CPF cash balance to fulfil the scheme's criterion. Thus in summary, the Singapore CPF system lacks the basic zero and first pillars of Holzmann *et al.*'s pension system.

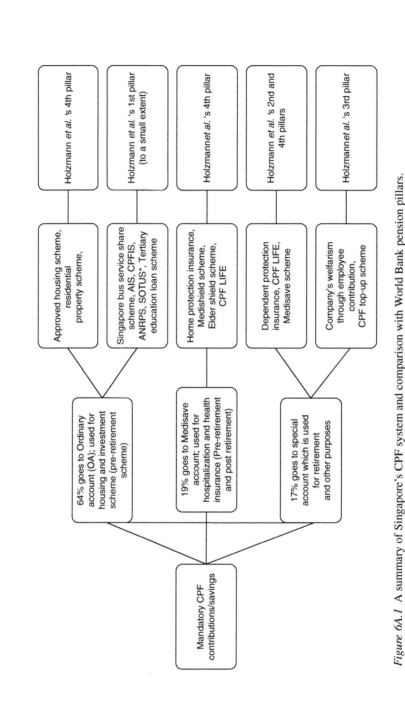

Figure 6A.1 A summary of Singapore's CPF system and comparison with World Bank pension pillars.

Notes

* AIS: Approved Investment Scheme; CPFIS: CPF Investment Scheme; ANRPS: Approved Non-Residential Properties Scheme; and
SOTUS: Share Ownership Top-Up Scheme.
Contribution proportions are given for age 35 or below. See Table 6.11 for the contribution for other age groups.

Notes

1 Singlehood incidence can be seen as 100 *minus* 'ever married'.

2 HDB and JCT are respectively, Housing Development Board and Jurong Town Council, both statutory entities, that have built and maintained public apartments and industry areas in Singapore.

3 In older age groups it is known that women have higher semi and full disability levels and these may hamper the workweek (Shantakumar, 1994a, b).

4 Detailed discussion will be found in Lee (1990), Mehta (1997), Koh (2001), Heng (2001), DOS (2002), MOH (2002), Mukhopadhaya and Shantakumar (2009).

5 See http://www.who.int/whr/2004/annex/country/sgp/en/index.html [accessed 31 October 2013].

6 In terms of higher proportion discharged and increases in hospital bed days (but length of stay may have declined).

7 In some other context, Elson (1991) argues that failure to provide basic social security generates cost escalation which could generate multiplier repercussions onto other important economic variables. In the male-breadwinner model, benefits are directed to men and their families while a modest means-tested sum is provided for women in the absence of men. Many Western countries (like Britain) follow this model. Other countries (e.g. France), however, follow the economic dependence of women was not assumed; and in the universal-breadwinner model, benefits are provided universally to adults who actively participated in the labour force (Sweden, for example).

Many social security policies treat the family unit as a whole (thus women are entitled as wives or mothers) to deal with inter-family inequality where intra-family inequality is vastly neglected (see Sen, 1990; Blumberg, 1988; Woolley, 1993; Phipps and Burton, 1994; Dwyer and Bruce, 1988; Haddad and Kanbur, 1990). Income-related benefits such as age pensions, although provided to an individual, are expected to provide for the family – thus women's access to this income is not assured. In a reform of the Canadian old age security system (Finance Canada, 1996), the basis of entitlement has changed from individual to joint income, with a promise of issuing a separate cheque to each spouse of half the amount. Some other countries (for example, Britain, Australia and New Zealand) provide individual entitlement to social security (healthcare). Although splitting of income-related pension credit helps married women, such splitting can never make up for the penalty women face due to labour market inequality and the penalty to earnings from unpaid and caring activities they are generally involved in Joshi and Davies (1992). There are further complexities in this family versus individual entitlement of social security benefits. Aslaksen and Koren's (1995) study on Norway indicates that under individualization of social security benefits, older women face greater loss of inherited income-related pension rights from spouses, which increases pension inequality among women. Nelson (1996) suggests an appropriate tax structure to tackle the problem of lone individual versus the nuclear family as the unit of policy analysis (see Cigno, 1994; Gustafsson *et al.*, 1995; Jones and Savage, 1995; Ontario Fair Tax Commission, 1992, 1993; Gordon, 1988; World Bank, 1992, 1993; Jarvis, 1995).

On the other hand, the state does not have unlimited amounts of resources: developed countries with advanced, established and extensive social security programmes have started considering imposition of eligibility to accommodate fiscal pressures. East European countries are examples (Goldberg, 1991; Duggan, 1992, 1995). Middle-income countries are also experiencing high fiscal pressure (Mesa-Lago, 1989). Low-income countries did not establish any extensive programme. Singapore (considered a highly human-capitalized developed country with per capita annual national income exceeding thirty thousand US dollars per annum) does not have any specific social security policy as such for older women (and neither for men).

8 See *Singapore Yearbook of Statistics* (DOS, 2011).

9 One alternative for the elderly home-owners is to purchase a 'reverse mortgage'. This is a method of dis-savings that enables the retired home-owner to convert some of the wealth embodied in his/her house into a lump sum payment or a steady stream of monthly income without relinquishing occupancy (see Bartel and Daly, 1980). This practice is in vogue in the USA, Europe (e.g., Britain and France), Canada, Australia and New Zealand. The Studio Apartment Project (SAP) for the elderly is another policy that the Singapore government has launched in 1998 to resolve the problem of 'cash poverty' for elderly Singaporeans. The owners of large Housing Development Board (HDB) flats who are 55 or older and have owned their property for at least 10 years are entitled to this scheme which enables them to move to a smaller home and encash the difference in the price between their old, larger home and the new, smaller home, and thus gain additional income. Analysis by Lim (2002) indicates that the take up rate by HDB home owners for the reverse mortgage scheme is lower than that for SAP. The reverse mortgage scheme is not very popular in Singapore, partly because only two financial organisations offer it. Thus the objective of translating the asset value of a house into an income stream for the elderly has not been fully realized in practice, forcing the poor elderly to continue to live with limited cash to meet their day-to-day needs or depend on their children for financial support.
10 For an illuminating analysis of this see Mukhopadhaya and Shantakumar (2009).
11 http://mycpf.cpf.gov.sg/CPF/Templates/SubPage_PrinterFriendly_Template.aspx? NRMODE=Published&NRORIGINALURL=%2FCPF%2FNews%2FNews-Release% 2FCOS_Speech-A-Simpler-CPFLIFE.ht&NRNODEGUID=%7B07D5676C-5ED3- 4336-9E4F-AC1AB64FBFA6%7D&NRCACHEHINT=Guest [accessed 1 November 2013].

7 Trend in equity and efficiency trade-off in Singapore

In the previous chapters we witnessed an upward trend of income inequality in Singapore. This increasing trend is no different from other developed and developing nations. Thus, Singapore's levels of inequality may not generate much attention, particularly as there is no abject poverty. The effectiveness of the economic management of Singapore in its quest for rapid economic growth and full employment has been a major concern, and therefore income disparity has not been a significant issue. We note that the selective immigration policy of the government, on the one hand, embraces skilled professionals, who receive high compensation, and on the other, low-skilled construction workers and foreign maids, who are paid very low wages. This can be seen as one reason for the high rate of inequality. Expansion of education is used as a strategy to slow down the high inequality rate, but that does not guarantee a reduction of inequality in the manner as it is practised.

Educational opportunities are expanding fast, with new institutions being established within Singapore, and also jointly with overseas universities that are seeking Singapore students with ever increasing enthusiasm. The government for its part, besides providing hefty general subsidies at all levels of education for all students, has also introduced many schemes to help students from low-income groups. There are clearly two major issues pertaining to educational opportunity. First, government financial assistance in terms of scholarships is not always linked to the economic circumstances of families; and second, the need to provide non-financial help to raise the educational standards of children from families with relatively less-educated parents (Mukhopadhaya, 2003a).

Furthermore, because the drive for fairness through education policies only started in 1975, a large proportion of Singaporeans did not get the benefits. According to the 2010 Census, about 40 per cent of people aged 60+ have had no formal education. In the absence of proper safety nets, these older people are in a destitute situation. Our analysis of the trend in inequality in the previous chapters (mostly based on LFS data) considered only the active labour force. If people aged 60 years and above are also considered, the inequality situation is worse. The government provides tax relief for dependant aged parents and in-laws. This is means-tested and the taxpayer is allowed $3,500 per year for each aged parent (or in-law) provided they reside with the taxpayer: however, such a constraint is extremely restrictive. In several cases, the housing policy might provide the aged person his or her own residence, however, many may still need financial help from their children.

Second only to Japan, Singapore has the fastest-growing ageing population in the world, which leads to a greatly increased demand for medical care. However, as an aspect of privatization during the 1980s, the government encouraged commercialization in an effort to increase efficiency and reduce unnecessary demand in the healthcare system. The main emphasis regarding healthcare is on individual and family responsibility (Asher, 1993). The Singapore government gives an assurance of affordable healthcare; however, the equity aspect is eclipsed by the ever-increasing emphasis on economic efficiency and financial accountability. In the early 1990s the government anticipated increasing costs of healthcare, and supplemented Medisave with private health insurance and the non-mandatory Medishield scheme. However, there seems some indifference as to whether people over 70 are able to finance their healthcare needs from their own resources (Asher, 1993), and with the Medishield scheme being non-mandatory, this is leaving a portion of Singaporeans uncovered. The NTUC's Managed Healthcare System (MHS) provides some support to the middle-income class by providing subsidized treatment, but the insurance premium is sometimes quite high and several diseases are not covered.

Having understood the above situation in Singapore, in this chapter we analyse the changing trends in Singapore's social welfare in terms of equity and efficiency.

Step 1: The Lorenz curve ranking

Bergson (1938) introduced the concept of the Social Welfare Function (SWF), which would depend on the amount of non-labour factors of production employed by each producing unit, the amount of labour supplied by each individual, and the amount of produced goods consumed by each individual. The SWF can then be seen as a real valued function defined on a set of alternative social states. Samuelson (1947) investigated various uses for which SWF can be utilized in welfare economics. The most general form of SWF is the Bergson–Samuelson, expressed as:

$$W = W(u_1(x_1), u_2(x_2), \dots, u_n(x_n)), \tag{7.1}$$

where $u_i(x_i)$ is the utility obtained by the person i for his/her income x_i. A priori, there is not much that can be said about the form of the SWF. Although the function may take any form, it is supposed to be increasing, unique up to the monotonic transformation and permutation symmetric in incomes.

Atkinson's (1970) seminal paper considered the ranking of social states with the same mean income on the basis of an additive separable SWF as[1]

$$W = \sum_i u_i(x_i). \tag{7.2}$$

Table 7.1 Trend of income inequality in Singapore, 1984, 1994 and 2011

Decile/year	Cumulative shares of income (%)		
	1984	*1994*	*2011*
Lowest	2.17	1.38	1.25
Second	4.34	4.21	3.42
Third	8.16	7.92	6.38
Fourth	12.33	12.85	10.10
Fifth	16.70	18.80	14.68
Sixth	22.54	24.80	20.63
Seventh	29.14	33.12	27.62
Eighth	38.16	43.40	36.83
Ninth	50.00	58.96	50.00
Top	100.00	100.00	100.00
Gini coefficient	0.470	0.474	0.529

Source: Computed from the LFS of 1984, 1994 and 2011.

The form of the utility function might also vary from person to person. However, Atkinson (1970) proved that with the minimum restriction of the concave utility function (that is, assuming diminishing marginal utility of income), it is possible to show that for a quite broad class of SWF, Lorenz curves can rank alternative social states. Thus Atkinson shows that if the Lorenz curve of one distribution lies north-east of another, the distribution of income corresponding to the first is said to be better than the latter.[2]

However, if the two Lorenz curves cross, it is always possible to find out different concave utility functions which can rank two social states differently (this criterion is still true when the higher/upper Lorenz curve has a higher mean income).

Table 7.1 shows that the Lorenz curve of 1994 is above the Lorenz curve of 2011 (see also Figure 7.1). However, the Lorenz curve of 1994 intersects that of 1984 from below at the fourth decile. Also we note that the Lorenz curve of 1984 is always above the Lorenz curve of 2011 up to the ninth decile point. We mentioned that the Lorenz curve allows for an unambiguous comparison of the regular distribution in the cases where the curves do not intersect. This requires that for all k, the share of the bottom k decile at time t is greater than that at time t^*. In such a situation the distribution at time t is Lorenz superior to that at time t^*.[3] From Table 7.1 and Figure 7.1, the first conclusion is that an unambiguous comparison regarding welfare ranking cannot be made except for 1994 and 2011, and 1984 and 2011 (though the Gini coefficient is increasing from 1984 to 2011). On the basis of the above Lorenz curves we may say that social welfare in Singapore during the years 1984 and 1994 was higher in comparison to 2011. However, since the per capita incomes of 1984 and 1994 are lower than 2011 we are unable to make a definite welfare judgement on the basis of Lorenz curves.

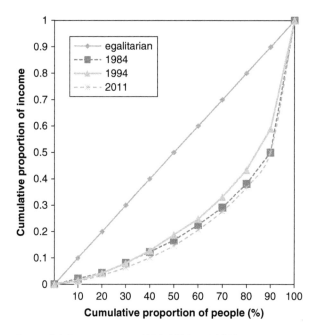

Figure 7.1 Lorenz curves, 1984, 1994 and 2011.

Step 2: The generalized Lorenz curve ranking

Atkinson's (1970) paper created a lot of excitement in the literature of inequality; however, it is observed that the dominance of Lorenz curves as a criterion for welfare comparison gives only a partial ordering of income distribution. This is because the Lorenz curves intersect (this was also the observation for our Singapore exercise). Moreover, Lorenz curves permit comparisons only when distributions have the same mean. In our case we are interested in examining welfare changes in Singapore over time, and it is important to notice also that mean incomes changed over time. Moreover, the Lorenz criterion has completely ignored the economic efficiency/growth aspect of a social welfare consideration. Shorrocks (1983b) extends Atkinson's formulation by introducing the concept of 'Generalized Lorenz Dominance'. Generalized Lorenz curves can be obtained by scaling the ordinary Lorenz curves up by the states' mean incomes. Thus if the Lorenz curve of a distribution is $L(p)$ and the mean income of the distribution is $\bar{x}$ then the generalized Lorenz curve of this distribution is given by $\bar{x}L(p)$. According to Shorrocks (1983b) if the generalized Lorenz curve of one state lies north-east of another, the social welfare corresponding to the first is said to be better than the latter.[4]

Thus, it demonstrates that the ranking of two income distributions with different means can only have an unambiguous welfare ranking if the generalized Lorenz curves do not intersect. Moreover, Shorrocks (1983b) demonstrates that even if

Table 7.2 Points of generalized Lorenz curves at different deciles, 1984, 1994 and 2011

Deciles/year	Cumulative income per capita ($)		
	1984	1994	2011
Lowest	31.23	31.58	53.69
Second	62.47	96.44	146.92
Third	117.38	181.19	274.00
Fourth	177.44	294.14	433.78
Fifth	240.35	430.20	630.77
Sixth	324.44	567.70	886.43
Seventh	419.42	758.18	1,186.50
Eighth	549.21	993.34	1,581.98
Ninth	719.60	1,349.45	2,147.91
Real mean income (2009 = 100)	1,439.20	2,288.86	4,295.82

Source: Computed from the LFS of 1984, 1994 and 2011.

ordinary Lorenz curves of two distributions intersect, the condition of Generalized Lorenz Dominance may still be satisfied.

As a next step in our analysis we have constructed the generalized Lorenz curves for three years. Using 2009 as the base year, the per capita monthly real income of Singaporeans was found to be $1,439.20, $2,288.86 and $4,295.82 respectively for the years 1984, 1994 and 2011. Real income has increased over time in Singapore. Table 7.2 presents the decile points of the generalized Lorenz curves for the different years.

Figure 7.2 represents the generalized Lorenz curves for different years. We observe that for Singapore the generalized Lorenz curves are increasing at a faster rate with time at the higher decile points. From both Table 7.2 and Figure 7.2 it may be noticed that the generalized Lorenz curve for the three years 1984, 1994 and 2011 do not intersect. This implies that in terms of Generalized Lorenz Dominance, 2011 was the best year for Singapore, 1994 ranks second, while 1984 ranks third.

Thus in our empirical analysis we find that the Generalized Lorenz Dominance criterion resolves the *intersection* of ordinary Lorenz curves, and provides complete social welfare ordering of Singapore for the years 1984, 1994 and 2011.

Step 3: Ranking using the Social Welfare Index: a social welfare function approach

An alternative approach for obtaining a complete ordering is the method of cardinal Social Welfare Function (SWF) that provides numerical values to all possible social states. We discussed in Chapter 2 that the Gini coefficient (G) is defined as twice the area between the Lorenz curve and the 45° egalitarian line, then $(1 - G)$ is twice the area below the Lorenz curve. In the same fashion a cardinalization of the generalized Lorenz curve can be done by finding the area below

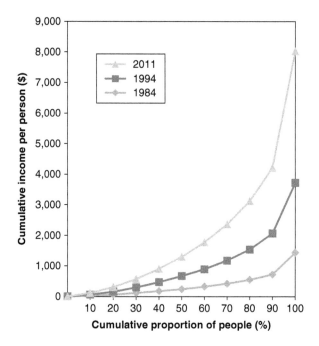

Figure 7.2 Generalized Lorenz curves, 1984, 1994 and 2011.

the generalized Lorenz curve

$$2 \int_0^1 \bar{x} L(p) \, dp = \bar{x}(1 - G),$$ (7.3)

and this could be denoted as a SWF.

Since the utilitarian SWF given by equation (7.1) depends only on individual utilities, which in turn depend on the consumption bundle or real income of each person, it does not allow for any externalities. While the level of utility of a person may depend on his or her consumption bundle or income, some disutility may be created due to inequity in the society as a whole. It is agreed that equity and efficiency are the twin concerns of a social decision-maker. Therefore, a common non-utilitarian form of the Bergson–Samuelson SWF may be written as

$$W = W(S, \theta)$$ (7.4)

where S stands for total income representing efficiency and $\theta = \theta \, (x_1, x_2, \ldots, x_n)$ denotes a measure of inequality representing inequity. A SWF of the above type must satisfy the condition

$$\frac{\partial W}{\partial S} > 0, \quad \text{and} \quad \frac{\partial W}{\partial \theta} < 0. \tag{7.5}$$

This would mean social welfare will increase with rising total income and will decrease with rising inequality. Obviously, the set of admissible SWFs satisfying these conditions is enormous. In order to narrow down the set, further restrictions are needed. These restrictions may be specified in terms of a number of axioms. On the basis of a set of four axioms, Sen (1974) arrived at a specific form of the Bergson–Samuelson class of SWFs which is

$$W = \bar{x}(1 - G). \tag{7.6}$$

Sen (1976) shows that this index, calculated from income distribution, is a sub-relation of social preference relation defined in the distribution of commodities.[5]

We will estimate, in this section, the SWF of equation (7.6) in order to examine the changes in social welfare in Singapore during the period 1984 to 2011.[6] Let us consider that both the arguments in SWF of equation (7.4) change over time. Then we can find out the total derivative of equation (7.4) with respect to time as

$$\frac{dW}{dt} = \frac{\partial W}{\partial S} \frac{dS}{dt} + \frac{\partial W}{\partial \theta} \frac{d\theta}{dt}. \tag{7.7}$$

Using equation (7.6) for the specific form of the SWF we get

$$\frac{dW}{dt} = (1 - G) \frac{d\bar{x}}{dt} - \bar{x} \frac{dG}{dt} \tag{7.8}$$

for approximation of the changes between two discrete points of time we can write

$$\Delta W \approx (1 - G)\Delta\bar{x} - \bar{x}\Delta G, \tag{7.9}$$

(where $\Delta W = W_t - W_{t-1}$, $\Delta\bar{x} = \bar{x}_t - \bar{x}_{t-1}$ and $\Delta G = G_t - G_{t-1}$).

We will now use equation (7.9) to study changes in social welfare in terms of changes in equity and efficiency over 1984 to 2011. Table 7.3 presents estimated values of the SWF and its arguments provided in equation (7.6).

The increase in inequality (quantified by the Gini coefficient) is not that prominent during the period 1984 to 1994. Real mean income[7] during this period in Singapore increased by 5.9 per cent on average per annum. Thus, for this period the increase in real income is the prime factor to determine the increase in social welfare. Social welfare, measured by SWF, shows an increasing movement throughout the whole period. During 1984 to 1994 welfare increased by 5.8 per cent (on average per annum), and during 1994 to 2011 welfare increased by 4.0 per cent per annum (on average) and in the whole period the average increase was 6.1 per cent per annum. Thus we observe that in terms of SWF ranking, the

Table 7.3 Mean income, Gini coefficient and social welfare in Singapore, 1984, 1994 and 2011

Year	Mean income[a]	Gini coefficient	Social welfare
1984	1,439.00	0.470	762.67
1994	2,288.86	0.474	1,203.94
2011	4,295.82	0.529	2,023.33

Note
[a] In constant 2009 prices.

Table 7.4 Change in welfare and its components in Singapore, 1984–2011

	1984–94	*1994–2011*
Welfare change	441.27	819.39
Mean change	849.86	2,006.96
Inequality change	−0.00	−0.06
Due to mean: $(1-G)\Delta\bar{x}$	448.73	1,000.47
Due to inequality: $\bar{x}\Delta G$	−7.46	−181.08

Note: Figures are rounded to two decimal places.

year 2011 was better than the other two years. Table 7.4 presents the measure of social welfare for Singapore attributed to the changes in equity and efficiency.

From Table 7.4 we can observe an increase in social welfare, despite an increase in inequality as the changes due to the mean at both the intervals are quite high. Singapore is one of the high performing 'miracle' countries, which maintained an average annual growth rate of 4.7 per cent (average annual GNP) during 1980–90, 8.9 per cent during 1990–5, 8.5 per cent during 1999–2007, and lately in 2011 the growth rate became 3.25 per cent (see Chapter 1). This growth rate (increase in efficiency) overshadowed any increase in inequality and as a whole social welfare increased.

Step 4: Equity–efficiency trade-off

For the Sen-SWF the rate of substitution between inequality and efficiency at a constant welfare level can be captured by the elasticity between equality (that is 1 minus the Gini) and the mean income

$$\frac{dG}{1-G}\frac{\bar{x}}{d\bar{x}}=1. \tag{7.10}$$

That means, in 1984 if the government wanted to have a growth policy, which would have increased mean income by 100 units, a deterioration of the Gini by 0.036 point would be admissible, while the welfare level remained constant. Note that in 1984 the Gini was 0.470 and the real mean income was $1,439.00. In contrast to 2011 when the country's real mean income was $4,295.82 and the Gini 0.529, for a policy of same growth rate (that is, to increase mean income by

100 units), a 1.096 point deterioration of Gini is admissible, while the welfare level remains the same. The point to note here is that, compared to 1984, in 2011 when the real average income was almost three times that of 1984, more importance should have been placed on preservation of equity. However, that did not happen in the above situation as the SWF is highly sensitive to mean income and less sensitive to inequality. Thus, in the case of inter-temporal comparison, this SWF will always be biased since Singapore's per capita income increased at a very high rate even at the cost of an adverse income distribution.

In addition, an underlying assumption in the Sen-SWF is the following

$$\frac{\partial W}{\partial x_i} > 0 \quad \text{for all } i. \tag{7.11}$$

This means that any addition to anyone's income, other things remaining the same, social welfare will increase. This assumption is called Paretianity (see Mukhopadhaya, 2003c, d). Thus, (to take an extreme case) if there is an increase in the income of the richest person (or section) of the society, welfare will increase. Note that *ceteris paribus*, an increase in the richest person's income will increase inequality as well as total income. But the increase in welfare due to the increase in total income must be greater than the decrease in welfare due to the increase in inequality. This means that equation (7.11) implies

$$\frac{\partial W}{\partial S}\frac{\partial S}{\partial x_i}dx_i + \frac{\partial W}{\partial \theta}\frac{\partial \theta}{\partial x_i}dx_i > 0 \tag{7.12}$$

this principle deals with the 'efficiency' aspect of the SWF. However, if the efficiency gain of the entire society is enjoyed by the richest person (or group) whether or not it is a welfare gain is subjective.

The Sen-SWF may be easily modified to make it more general and flexible. Such a class of generalized SWF can be presented as[8]

$$W = \bar{x}^\beta(1 - G), \quad 0 \le \beta \le 1. \tag{7.13}$$

This SWF with variable values of β has certain advantages over the Sen-SWF. If one wants to attach more importance to efficiency than equity she or he will choose a high value for β, that is near one, and on the contrary if she or he is an equity-lover, will set a low value for β.[9]

Let us now examine whether or not this SWF is Paretian. From equation (7.11) we know that the SWF is Paretian if

$$\frac{\partial}{\partial x_i}[\bar{x}^\beta(1 - G)] > 0 \tag{7.14}$$

which implies

$$\beta - \beta G + G > \frac{2i - n - 1}{n}, \quad \text{for } i = 1, \ldots, n.[10] \tag{7.15}$$

This expression is always true from the lowest income to the median income as the left hand side of the expression (7.15) is always positive. With knowledge of the existing level of inequality in a society, by varying the value of β, one can easily determine the direction of a change in social welfare when a person, above the median, gains some additional income (other things remaining the same). If the condition of Paretianity is satisfied for the richest person it will satisfy others, thus putting a maximum value for i in (7.15) we get

$$\beta + G - \beta G > \frac{n-1}{n}. \tag{7.16}$$

For a large n this can be written as

$$\beta + G - \beta G \geq 1 \tag{7.17}$$

which will never be satisfied for a value of β less than 1. Thus this SWF is Paretian for the highest possible value of β, in which case this SWF will become the Sen-SWF. It is obvious from condition (7.17) that if only the richest person or the richest group enjoys the fruit of growth, the welfare of the society will not increase as long as $\beta < 1$. This SWF might be criticized for its bias in favour of the poor. If there is a rise in income of the poorest whatever be the value of β and G (in the specified range, i.e., between 0 and 1), the welfare must increase. Thus, this SWF has some Rawlsian flavour. However, for a Rawlsian SWF if the richest person's income increases, social welfare remains unchanged; but for the modified SWF (with $\beta < 1$) with an increase in the income of the richest person, social welfare decreases. This class of SWF (with $\beta < 1$) is not Rawlsian, nor is it Paretian.

We now turn to an examination of the changes in social welfare in Singapore for various values of β.

Table 7.5 depicts the situation in social welfare in Singapore when we consider a more general SWF. When consideration of efficiency is negligible/low ($\beta = 0$ to 0.10), we observe a decrease in welfare particularly in the 1994–2011 period. When the value of $\beta = 0.50$ the change in welfare in both the time intervals (i.e., 1984–94 and 1994–2011) is almost the same. This clearly indicates that over-emphasis on efficiency depicts a rosy picture of Singapore which is not the reality. In previous chapters where we examined the education and gender dimensions of inequality we concluded similarly.

To consider the effect of growth on various sections of the society let us re-examine our findings in previous chapters.

Table 7.6 shows that incomes of the poorer deciles increased by the least amount, while a decrease in the mean income of the first decile is seen between 1984 and 1994. During 1994–2011 the top decile gets the maximum fruit of the growth. However, it is clear that growth does not accrue *totally* to the richest section of the society. But there should be concern that the richest 20 per cent of people are benefiting most from the economic growth in Singapore.

Table 7.5 Change in social welfare in Singapore at various degrees of trade-off between equity and efficiency

	$\beta = 0.00$	$\beta = 0.01$	$\beta = 0.05$	$\beta = 0.10$	$\beta = 0.50$	$\beta = 1.00$
1984	0.53	0.57	0.76	1.10	20.11	762.67
1994	0.53	0.57	0.77	1.14	25.16	1,203.94
2011	0.47	0.51	0.72	1.09	30.87	2,023.33
Change						
1984–94	0.00	0.00	0.01	0.04	5.06	441.27
1994–2011	−0.06	−0.06	−0.06	−0.05	5.71	819.39

Table 7.6 Increase in mean income of various decile groups

Decile	1984	1994	2011	Change: 1984–94	Change: 1994–2011
Lowest	376.81	353.83	608.40	−22.98	254.56
Second	376.81	726.68	1,056.33	349.87	329.65
Third	662.47	949.59	1,439.92	287.12	490.33
Fourth	724.64	1,265.44	1,810.45	540.80	545.01
Fifth	758.97	1,524.39	2,232.03	765.42	707.64
Sixth	1,014.49	1,540.59	2,896.95	526.09	1,356.36
Seventh	1,145.92	2,134.15	3,400.05	988.23	1,265.90
Eighth	1,565.89	2,634.82	4,481.11	1,068.94	1,846.29
Ninth	2,055.61	3,989.83	6,412.49	1,934.22	2,422.66
Top	8,681.61	10,525.22	24,337.73	1,843.61	13,812.51
Total	1,439.20	2,288.85	4,295.82	849.66	2,006.96

Source: Computed from the LFS of 1984, 1994, 2011.

Conclusion

This chapter has examined changes in social welfare in Singapore over the period 1984 to 2011. To find the change ranking based on Lorenz curve, the generalized Lorenz curve and cardinal Social Welfare Function are used. We find by Lorenz ranking that social welfare in Singapore during 1994 and 1984 is better than in 2011, and no unambiguous conclusion can be drawn on the welfare rankings of 1984 and 1994 as the Lorenz curves for these periods intersect. To solve this crossing problem (the mean incomes of these years are changing, which creates another problem) and to introduce the concept of efficiency in the social welfare construct, we analysed and applied the generalized Lorenz ranking method. We then found that this criterion ranks 2011 as the first, 1994 as the second and 1984 as the third. The ranking based on the Sen-SWF shows a continuous increase in social welfare in Singapore. It was also found that the increase in inequality is overshadowed by the increase in mean income.

Considering the limitations of the Sen-SWF, which is Paretian and which puts too much emphasis on efficiency aspect, we introduced a more general SWF which could be non-Paretian in special cases. With this SWF we found that when the emphasis on equity is very high, social welfare in Singapore is shown as decreasing.

Note that inequality and consequently social welfare are multi-dimensional phenomena. Thus a discussion of social welfare in terms of income alone is too restrictive. However, due to non-availability of relevant information it was not possible to extend our analyses to non-income items of inequality and social welfare.

Appendix

Proof of equation (7.15)

$$\frac{\partial W}{\partial x_i} = \frac{\partial}{\partial x_i}[\bar{x}^\beta(1-G)]$$

$$= \frac{\partial}{\partial x_i}\left[\left(\sum\frac{x_i}{n}\right)^\beta\left(1-\frac{\sum(2i-n-1)x_i}{n\sum x_i}\right)\right], \quad \text{as } G = \frac{\sum(2i-n-1)x_i}{n^2\bar{x}}$$

$$= \beta\bar{x}^{\beta-1}\frac{1}{n}[1-G]+\bar{x}^\beta\left[\frac{0-(2i-n-1)n^2\bar{x}+n\sum(2i-n-1)x_i}{(n\sum x_i)^2}\right]$$

$$= \frac{\frac{1}{n}\beta\bar{x}^{\beta-1}n^4\bar{x}^2(1-G)-n^2\bar{x}^{\beta+1}(2i-n-1)+\bar{x}^\beta n\sum(2i-n-1)x_i}{(n^2\bar{x})^2}$$

To satisfy Paretianity this expression has to be greater than zero – that means

$$\frac{1}{n}\beta\bar{x}^{\beta-1}n^4\bar{x}^2(1-G)+\bar{x}^\beta n\sum(2i-n-1)x_i > n^2\bar{x}^{\beta+1}(2i-n-1)$$

$$\Rightarrow n^3\beta\bar{x}^{\beta+1}(1-G)+\bar{x}^\beta n\sum(2i-n-1)x_i > n^2\bar{x}^{\beta+1}(2i-n-1)$$

$$\Rightarrow n\beta(1-G)+\frac{1}{n\bar{x}}\sum(2i-n-1)x_i > 2i-n-1$$

$$\Rightarrow \beta(1-G)+\frac{\sum(2i-n-1)x_i}{n^2\bar{x}} > \frac{2i-n-1}{n}$$

$$\Rightarrow \beta-\beta G+G > \frac{2i-n-1}{n}$$

for $i=1,\ldots,n$.

Notes

1 See also Kolm (1966).
2 Formally this can be written as: If $F_1(x)$ and $F_2(x)$ are two distributions with corresponding mass functions $f_1(x)$ and $f_2(x)$ respectively with the same mean income and if $L(p)$ is the Lorenz curve, then $L_{F_1}(p) \geq L_{F_2}(p)$ in the interval $0 \leq p \leq 1 \Leftrightarrow \sum u(x)f_1(x) \geq \sum u(x)f_2(x)$ for utility functions such that $u'(x) > 0$ and $u''(x) < 0$

Dasgupta *et al.* (1973) showed that the strict concavity can be relaxed to Schur-concavity.

3 Also for this comparison the errors surrounding the estimates of the distribution is another aspect to consider. Beach and Davidson (1983) and Bishop *et al.* (1989) considered the sampling variability and tried to indicate whether crossing of Lorenz curves (and generalized Lorenz curves, which will be discussed further below) were statistically significant or not. Other references can be found in the above-mentioned articles. However, our analyses do not follow this route.

4 Formally, if $F_1(x)$ and $F_2(x)$ are two distributions with corresponding mass functions $f_1(x)$ and $f_2(x)$ and mean incomes $\bar{x}_1$ and $\bar{x}_2$ respectively, then $\bar{x}_1 L_{F_1}(p) \geq \bar{x}_2 L_{F_2}(p)$ in the interval $0 \leq p \leq 1 \Leftrightarrow \sum u(x) f_1(x) \geq \sum u(x) f_2(x)$ for all strictly concave utility functions. See Kakwani (1984b).

5 Dagum (1990, 1993) arrived at the same SWF from a utilitarian premise. Alternatively Yitzhaki (1979, 1982) showed that this index could be based on relative deprivation. Sheshinski (1972) also arrived at this index from the Gini coefficient.

6 Kakwani (1986) analysed the Australian redistribution policy by adopting Sen's SWF. However, our approach is different as it makes comparison over time.

7 Mean incomes were computed from the same data set that is LFS. LFS considers people in the labour force only and we have already discussed in Chapter 1 that the mean income is lower than the National Accounts' estimates. Our intention in this chapter is to enumerate the change in social welfare, not to calculate the absolute amount of social welfare. Thus the downward bias in absolute average income (which is consistent in all the years under consideration) does not create a problem.

8 See Mukhopadhaya (2003d).

9 The value of β can be well above 1 for a more efficiency-prone person, however, whenever $\beta \geq 1$ the proposed SWF is Paretian (can easily be followed from the proof discussed next). As our argument is against Paretianity we are restricting ourselves to the upper limit 1, when it is the special case of Sen-SWF.

10 The mathematical derivation can be found in the Appendix to this chapter.

8 Conclusion

Over the past few decades, Singapore has experienced a rapid and very high growth rate, and along with that, its income inequality has worsened. The United Nations attempted to compute the inequality adjusted Human Development Index (IHDI) for several countries, but due to a lack of relevant information, this exercise is not possible for Singapore. Despite high rates of growth in national income, in terms of human development Singapore is below the average in very high human development groups. Besides national income, the Human Development Index (HDI) considers educational development and health. The reason for Singapore's relatively poorer rank in terms of HDI is its performance in education. However, expansion of the provision of educational facilities is one of the main policies the government of Singapore has followed since 1975. It is believed that human capital endowments have been crucial to the success of Singapore; education may raise the level of income of lower income groups at a higher proportion and thus could reduce the dispersion of income. It may also open up new opportunities for children from more deprived families, and thus act as a vehicle to social mobility. The United Nations use a multidimensional index (that includes health, empowerment and economic activity) to compare the status of gender inequality – Singapore is 160 per cent behind very high HDI countries in terms of this measure. Along with the achievement of high-income status, this is an aspect policy-makers should be concerned about.

This book has analysed the income distribution pattern in Singapore over a period of nearly 30 years (1984 to 2011), and observed that income inequality in Singapore has increased continuously from 0.470 (measured by Gini coefficient) in 1984 to 0.529 in 2011. Labour Force Survey data from various years were used for our measure of income inequality. As income data from this source is available for various income groups (as opposed to individual income data), there is a downward bias in the measurement. Moreover, the coverage of the survey is the working population, and therefore mostly excludes people aged over 60; however, our calculations from the population surveys indicate that inequality is quite high among people in the older age groups. Thus, if older people were included in these measurements, income inequality in Singapore would be shown to be even higher. Furthermore, the data source excludes all income from rents, interest, dividends and royalties, and the consequence of these exclusions is evident from the low proportion (7–12 per cent) of non-employment income captured in the data. Had this information been included, the income inequality figure may actually be more than is computed in this book. Calculations from other sources (for example, Household Expenditure Surveys, General Household Surveys, Population Censuses and income tax data) confirm the upward trend of income inequality in Singapore.

Rising inequality is universal and Singapore's experience is no different. However, the income inequality in Singapore is higher than other neighbouring High Performing Economies (e.g., Taiwan, Thailand, Malaysia, Indonesia, Japan and Korea) with the exception of Hong Kong. Note, however, that this comparison does not mean much since the concept of earning used in our analysis for Singapore may be different in other countries. For a more comprehensive comparison, further refinement of the definition of income for all countries must be employed.

To analyse the inequality trend in further detail, a decomposition method is employed. This decomposition analysis (using the Theil index) has brought out some interesting facts as can be seen in the summary in Table 8.1.

Unlike many other countries, inequality across age groups is low in Singapore. In fact over the period under study, for the contribution of the between-group by age, inequality decreased. This manifests the erosion of age premium for earnings. Singapore's policy-makers have focused more on 'proactivity-based earnings', and it seems from our observations that with age (presumably that generates experience and maturity in production) there has not been much increase in productivity. The contribution of high within-age inequality is due to unequal distribution of education within age groups. In the age group 50+, less-educated people dominate.

We also observe that the disparity within occupational groups on average is high because of dispersed age groups in the same occupations with diverse educational attainments. The wage premium for top jobs has not changed much relative to low-income jobs; however, the change in population share plays a vital role in increasing inequality. The between-occupational disparity also has a strong impact on overall inequality. The contribution of between-occupational inequality is higher than between-age or between-education inequality.

Income distribution in Singapore is mainly affected by policies relating to human capital formation and recruitment of foreign workers. The introduction of

Table 8.1 Comparing between- and within-group contributions of inequality for age, occupation and education groups (%)

	Average between-group contribution (1984–2011)	Average within-group contribution (1984–2011)
Age	12.25	87.75
Occupation	45.16	54.84
Education	35.89	64.11

foreign workers at the upper end of income brackets aimed to exploit the 'foreign talent', and at the same time at the lower end of the income ladder, the recruitment of foreign workers such as construction and household maids contributed largely to the widening of the income gap. More ingredients for disparity in recent years are added through the flexi-wage policies. The personal income tax structure does not reduce any disparity of income in Singapore.

We have found that income disparities between educational groups contribute 36 per cent to the total inequality. This is the case despite the fact that the restructuring of the economy from the beginning of this study shifted educational wage differentials in favour of professionals and other skilled workers. The big contribution of within-educational group inequality is a result of an increase in population share in the high-earning groups and also due to income disparity in the same educational groups. We observe that in the age group 35–39 the occupational group 'managers in financial services' earn more than twice the monthly gross wage of the 'managers in accommodation and food services'. This shows that when two people with the same educational background are in the same occupational category, due to a variation in industrial classification (and this depends on the specific subjects chosen in secondary or tertiary education) incomes vary to a great extent. In low-wage jobs this variation is much less. With better educational entrants in the labour force, the population share increased in those educational and occupational groups where high income disparity is observed. This makes high within-group inequality in educational and occupational groups.

The achievement in education in Singapore is spectacular; almost 30 per cent of people in the labour force are now tertiary educated, while two decades ago the proportion was only 5 per cent. This has been achieved through well-developed education policies and investment. However, it has been observed that the proportion of public spending on education in Singapore is much lower than the OECD average, and even lower than neighbouring Malaysia. Furthermore, with increasing educational expenses, these policies are mostly supporting the more able students. While the bright and poor are aided by state-provided scholarship and bursary schemes, the rich and middle class benefit more. The government of Singapore needs to attend to the amount and tenure of these financial supports targeted to the needy so they too are able to utilize this support and therefore enhance future productivity.

One of the achievements of educational development is the increase in the female labour force participation rate; more women are now working in high-earning jobs. However, in the older age groups Singapore is still lagging behind other high-income countries in terms of female labour force participation. Singapore provides less opportunity for women to return to work after they have spent some time out of the labour force fulfilling family responsibilities. Certain occupations that have traditionally been considered 'women's work' are still dominated by women, while most of the high-earning jobs are dominated by men. This is because male and female tertiary students specialize in different fields of studies. Furthermore, females tend to look for more flexible jobs in order to balance multiple tasks at home and in the workplace, and often these jobs are less remunerative.

Income growth for women was higher than that for males in Singapore during the period we studied; however, women still earn less than men. Although on average women's income increased with better-educated entrants, the influx of skilled foreign male workers at the higher end of the income ladder pushed up the income of already high-income-earning males.

There is not equal treatment of women at the workplace in Singapore. Provision of unpaid/full paid childcare leave for women is limited to civil servants only. The provision of paternity leave is quite uncommon. Flexi/part-time employment opportunities are unavailable. The provision of childcare facilities is not sufficient to encourage women with young children to return to the workforce. All these issues considered, the work-life earnings for women remain much less than for men. The situation is aggravated for those in the older age groups because life expectancy is higher for females than males. Thus central provident fund savings turn out to be less sustainable for women. Therefore, to live on family support becomes the only option available to older women.

By creating equal opportunities through educational development, the Singapore government attempted to bring equity to the country. While doing so, specific problems for low income families were ignored. Also, insufficient support systems have been developed to create earning opportunities for those required to perform with multiple tasks (for example home making, income earning etc.). Old age support is also minimum, therefore for those who have earned an insufficient amount over their working life may face severe financial difficulty. A selective migration policy and a lenient income tax system works adversely on income distribution. The flexi-wage system on the productivity-based earning model has increased the gap between high and low wage earners. As Singapore achieved the status of a high-income economy quite some time ago, time has now come to reconsider the efficiency (or growth) and equity trade-off differently.

Bibliography

Aghion, P., E. Caroli and C. Garcia-Penalosa (1999) 'Inequality and Economic Growth: The Perspective of the New Growth Theories', *Journal of Economic Literature*, 37, 1615–60.

Aigner, D. J. and A. J. Heins (1967) 'A Social Welfare View of the Measurement of Income Inequality', *Review of Income and Wealth*, 13, 12–25.

Akita, T. (2000) 'Decomposing Regional Income Inequality in China and Indonesia using Two-stage Nested Theil Decomposition Method', paper presented at 7th Convention of the East Asian Economic Association, 17–18 November, Singapore.

Alesina, A. and D. Rodrik (1994) 'Distributive Politics and Economic Growth', *Quarterly Journal of Economics*, 109, 465–90.

Amiel, Y. and F. Cowell (1992) 'Measurement of Economic Inequality', *Journal of Public Economics*, 47, 3–26.

Anand, S. (1983) *Inequality and Poverty in Malaysia*. London: Oxford University Press.

Arasu, S. and S. Ooi (1984) 'Women Who Have Risen High', *The Sunday Times*, 4 November.

Arrow, K. J. (1973) 'Some Ordinalist-Utilitarian Notes on Rawls's Theory of Justice', *Journal of Philosophy*, 70(9), 245–63.

Asher, M. (1993) 'Planning for the Future: The Welfare System in a New Phase of Development', in G. Rodan (ed.), *Singapore Changes Guard: Social, Political and Economic Directions in the 1990s*. New York: St Martin's Press.

Asher, M. (2008) 'Social Security Reform Imperatives in Developing Asia', *Indian Economic Journal*, April–June, 56(1), 112–23.

Asher, M G. and A. Nandy (2011) 'Singapore: Pension System Overview and Reform Directions', in D. Park (ed.), *Pension System and Old-age Income Support in East and Southeast Asia*. London and New York: Routledge, pp. 152–75.

Asher, M. and G. Shantakumar (1996) 'Financing Old Age through the National Provident Fund Mechanism', in G. Gaburro and B. O. Pettman (eds), *Social Economies in Transition*. UK: International Institute of Social Economics, pp. 132–46.

Ashton, D. and F. Green (1996) *Education, Training and the Global Economy*. Cheltenham, UK: Edward Elgar.

Ashton, D. N. and J. Sung (1994) *The State Economic Development and Skill Formation: A New East Asian Model*. Working Paper Number 3, University of Leicester, Centre for Labour Market Studies.

AsiaOne (2010) '540 Tuition Centres in Singapore – and growing', online article available at: http://www.edvantage.com.sg/content/540-tuition-centres-singapore-and-growing [accessed 5 November 2013].

Aslaksen, I. and C. Koren (1995) 'Unpaid Household Work: Actual and Potential Consequences for Social Security Entitlements', presented at the conference on 'The Cost of Being a Mother, the Cost of Being a Father', Florence.

Atkinson, A. B. (1970) 'On the Measurement of Inequality', *Journal of Economic Theory*, 2, 244–63.

Atkinson, A. B. (1980) 'Horizontal Equity and Distribution of Tax Burden', in H. Aaron and M. Boskin (eds), *The Economics of Taxation*. Washington, DC: Brookings Institution.

Atkinson, A. B. (1983) *The Economics of Inequality*, 2nd edn. Oxford: Clarendon Press.

Atolia, M., S. Chatterjee and S. J. Turnovsky (2012) 'Growth and Inequality: Dependence on the Time Path of Productivity Increases (and Other Structural Changes)', *Journal of Economic Dynamics and Control*, 36, 331–48.

Bailliu, J. and H. Reisen (1997) 'Do Funded Pensions Contribute to Higher Aggregate Savings? A Cross-Country Analysis', in H. Reisen (ed.), *Pensions, Savings, and Capital Flows: From Ageing to Emerging Markets*. Paris: OECD, pp. 113–31.

Balakrishnan, N. (1989) 'Battle of the Sexes', *Far Eastern Economic Review*, 145(31), 34–5.

Banerjee, A. V. and E. Duflo (2003) 'Inequality and Growth: What Can the Data Say?', *Journal of Economic Growth*, 8, 267–99.

Banerjee, A. V. and A. F. Newman (1993) 'Occupational Choice and the Process of Development', *Journal of Political Economy*, 101, 274–98.

Barro, R. J. (2000) 'Inequality and Growth in a Panel of Countries', *Journal of Economic Growth*, 5, 5–32.

Bartel, H. and Daly, M. (1980) 'Reverse Annuity Mortgages as a Source of Retirement Income', *Canadian Public Policy*, 6(4), 584–90.

Beach, C. M. and R. Davidson (1983) 'Distribution free statistical inference with Lorenz curves and income shares', *Review of Economic Studies*, 50, 723–35.

Becker, G. S. (1964) *Human Capital: A Theoretical and Empirical Analysis*. New York: National Bureau of Economic Research.

Becker, G. S. and B. R. Chiswick (1966) 'Education and the Distribution of Income', *American Economic Review*, 56(2), 358–69.

Behrman, J. E. and Taubman, P. (1990) 'The Intergenerational Correlation between Children's Adult Earnings and their Parents': Results from the Michigan Panel Survey and Income Dynamics', *Review of Income Wealth*, 36(2), 115–28.

Behrman, J. R. and B. L. Wolfe (1987) 'Investments in Schooling in Two Generations in Pre-revolutionary Nicaragua: The Roles of Family Background and School Supply', *Journal of Development Economics*, 27(1–2), 395–419.

Benn, S. I. (1967) 'Egalitarianism and the equal consideration of interests', in J. R. Pennock and J. W. Chapman (eds), *Equality: NOMOS IX*. New York: Atherton Press, pp. 61–78.

Berge, C. (1963) *Topological Spaces*. London: Oliver and Boyd.

Bergson, A. (1938) 'A reformulation of certain aspects of welfare economics', *Quarterly Journal of Economics*, 52, 310–34.

Berliant, M. and R. Strauss (1985) 'The Horizontal and Vertical Equity Characteristics of the Federal Income Tax, 1966–1977', in M. David and T. Smeeding (eds), *Horizontal Equity, Uncertainty and Economic Well-being*. Chicago: University of Chicago Press, pp. 179–211.

Berlin, I. (1980) *Concepts and Categories: Philosophical Essays*. Oxford: Oxford University Press.

Bertoli, S. and F. Farina (2007) *The Functional Distribution of Income: a Review of the Theoretical Literature and of the Empirical Evidence around its Recent Pattern in European Countries*. Siena: Department of Economic Policy, Finance and Development (DEPFID), University of Siena.

Bhattacharya, N. and B. Mahalanobis (1967) 'Regional Disparity in Household Consumption in India', *Journal of American Statistical Association*, 62, 143–61.

Bishop, J. A., S. Chakravorty and P. D. Thistle (1989) 'Asymptotically Distribution Free Statistical Inference for Generalized Lorenz Curves', *Review of Economics and Statistics*, 71, 725–77.

Blackorby, C., D. Donaldson and M. Auersperg (1981) 'A New Procedure for the Measurement of Inequality Within and among Population Subgroups', *Canadian Journal of Economics*, 14, 665–85.

Blaug, M. (1989) 'Review of Economics of Education', *Journal of Human Resources*, 24(2), 331–5.

Blaug, M., C. Dougherty and G. Psacharopoulos (1982) 'The Distribution of Schooling and the Distribution of Earnings: Raising School Leaving Age in 1972', *The Manchester School* (March), 24–39.

Blinder, A. S. (1973) 'Wage Discrimination: Reduced Forms and Structural Estimates', *Journal of Human Resources*, 8(4), 463–55.

Blumberg, R. (1988) 'Income under Female Versus Male Control', *Journal of Family Issues*, 9(1), 51–84.

Boix, C. (2009) 'The Conditional Relationship between Inequality and Development', *PS: Political Science & Politics*, 42, 645–9, available from http://www.princeton.edu/~cboix/conditional-relationship-growth-inequality.pdf [accessed 5 November 2013].

Bossert, W. and A. Pfingsten (1989) 'Intermediate Inequality: Concepts, Indices and Welfare Implications', *Mathematical Social Sciences*, 19, 117–34.

Bourguignon, F. (1979) 'Decomposition of Inequality Measures', *Econometrica*, 47, 901–20.

Bowles, S. (1972) 'Schooling and Inequality from Generation to Generation', *Journal of Political Economy*, 80(3), S219–51. Supplement.

Bowles, S. and Nelson, V. (1974) 'The Inheritance of IQ and the Intergenerational Reproduction of Economic Inequality', *Review of Economics and Statistics*, 56(1), 39–51.

Bridsall, N., N. Lustig and D. McLeod (2011) *Declining Inequality in Latin America: Some Economics, Some Politics*. Centre for Global Development, Working Paper no. 251. http://papers.ssrn.com/sol3/papers.cfm?abstract_id=1888348 [accessed 5 November 2013].

Broome, J. (1989) 'What is the Good of Equality?', in J. D. Hey (ed.), *Current Issues in Microeconomics*. London: Macmillan, pp. 236–62.

Buhmann, B., L. Rainwater, G. Schmaus and T. Smeeding (1988) 'Equivalence Scales, Well-being, Inequality and Poverty: Sensitive Estimates Across Ten Countries Using the Luxembourg Income Study (LIS) Database', *Review of Income and Wealth*, 34, 115–42.

Cancian, M., S. Danziger and P. Gottschalk (1993) 'Working Wives and Family Income Inequality among Married Couples', in S. Danziger and P. Gottschalk (eds), *Uneven Tides: Rising Inequality in America*. New York: Russell Sage Foundation.

Cannan, E. (1930) *Elementary Political Economy*. New York: Macmillan.

Castelló-Climent, A. (2010) 'Inequality and Growth in Advanced Economies: An Empirical Investigation', *Journal of Economic Inequality*, 8, 293–321.

Castells, M. (1992) 'Four Asian Tigers with a Dragon Head: A Comparative Analysis of the State, Economy and the Society in the Asian Pacific Rim', in R. P. Appelbaum and J. Henderson (eds), *State and Development in the Asia Pacific Rim*. London: Sage Publications, pp. 33–70.

Chatterjee, S. and N. Podder (2007) 'Some Ethnic Dimensions of Income Distribution from Pre- to Post-reform New Zealand *1984–98*', *Economic Record*, 83(262), 275–86.

Chee, C. H. (1989) 'The PAP and the Structuring of the Political System', in Sandhu, K. S. and P. Wheatley (eds), *Management Success: The Moulding of Modern Singapore*. Singapore: ISEAS, pp. 70–89

Cigno, A. (1994) 'Social Security, the Tax Treatment of Couples, and the Position of Women', presented in the World Bank Gender Symposium, Washington, DC.

ComCare (2009) *Annual Report*, available at: http://app1.mcys.gov.sg/Portals/0/Summary/publication/CSSD/Comcare%20FY2009.pdf. [accessed 29 August 2011].

Coulter, F. A. E., F. Cowell and S. Jenkins (1992) 'Equivalence Scale Relativities and the Extent of Inequality and Poverty', *Economic Journal*, 102(414), 1067–82.

Cowell, F. A. (1995) *Measuring Inequality*, 2nd edn. London, New York: Prentice Hall Harvester Wheatsheaf

Cowell, F. A. and K. Kuga (1981) 'Additivity and the Entropy Concept: An Axiomatic Approach to Inequality Measurement', *Journal of Economic Theory*, 25, 131–43.

CPF (various years) *Central Provident Fund Board Annual Report*, Singapore Government.

CPRC (2004) *Chronic Poverty Report 2004–05*. Manchester/London: Chronic Poverty Research Centre.

Dagum, C. (1977) 'A New Model for Personal Income Distribution: Specification and Estimation', *Economie Appliquée*, 30, 413–37.

Dagum, C. (1990) 'Relationship between Income Inequality Measures and Social Welfare Functions', *Journal of Econometrics*, 43, 91–102.

Dagum, C. (1993) 'The Social Welfare Bases of Gini and Other Inequality Measures', *Statistica*, 53, 3–30

Dagum, C. (1996) 'A Systemic Approach to the Generation of Income Distribution Models', *Journal of Income Distribution*, 6, 105–26.

Dalton, H. (1920) 'The Measurement of the Inequality of Incomes', *Economic Journal*, 30, 348–61.

Dalton, H. (1925) *Inequalities of Income*. London: Routledge and Kegan Paul.

Dasgupta, P., A. K. Sen and D. Starett (1973) 'Notes on the Measurement of Inequality', *Journal of Economic Theory*, 6, 180–7.

Davis, E. P. and Y. Hu (2004) *Is There a Link between Pension Funded Assets and Economic Growth? A Cross–Country Study*. London: Brunel University.

Deininger, K. and L. Squire. (1996) 'A New Data Set Measuring Income Inequality'. *World Bank Economic Review*, 10(3) 565–91.

De-Mesa, A. A. (2005) 'Fiscal and Institutional Considerations of Pension Reform: Lessons Learnt from Chile', in C. A. Crabbe (ed.), *A Quarter Century Pension Reform in Latin America and Caribbean*. Washington, DC: Inter-America Development Bank, Sustainable Development Department, pp. 83–125.

Donaldson, D. and J. A. Weymark (1980) 'A Single Parameter Generalisation of the Gini Indices of Inequality', *Journal of Economic Theory*, 22, 67–86.

DOS (1998) *Social Progress of Singapore Women: A Statistical Assessment*, Occasional Paper on Social Statistics, Singapore: Singapore Department of Statistics.

DOS (2000) *Is Income Disparity Increasing in Singapore?* Occasional Paper, Singapore: Singapore Department of Statistics.

DOS (2002) *Statistical Highlights*. Singapore: Singapore Department of Statistics.

DOS (2005) 'Trends in Household Income and Expenditure, 1993–2003', *Statistics Singapore News Letter*, September, Singapore: Singapore Department of Statistics.

DOS (2011) *Singapore Yearbook of Statistics*. Singapore: Singapore Department of Statistics.

DOS (2012) *Population Trends 2012*. Singapore: Singapore Department of Statistics.

Dover, K. J. (1974) *Greek Popular Morality in the Time of Plato and Aristotle*. Oxford: Blackwell.

Duggan, L. (1992) 'The Impact of Population Policies on Women in Eastern Europe: The German Democratic Republic', in N. Folbre, B. Bergmann, B. Agarwal and M. Floro (eds), *Issues in Contemporary Economics*, Vol. 4: *Women's Work in the World Economy*. London: Macmillan, pp. 250–64.

Duggan, L. (1995) 'Restacking the Deck: Family Policy and Women's Fall-Back Position in Germany Before and After Unification', *Feminist Economics*, 1(1), 175–94.

Dwyer, D. and J. Bruce (eds), (1988) *A Home Divided: Women and Income in the Third World*. Stanford, CA: Stanford University Press.

Early Childhood and Development Agency (2012) *Statistics on Childcare Services*. Singapore, ECDA, available at: http://www.childcarelink.gov.sg/ccls/uploads/Statistics_on_child_care(STENT).pdf [accessed 9 November 2012].

Easterly, W. (2007) 'Inequality does Cause Underdevelopment', *Journal of Development Economics*, 84(2), 755–76.

Economic Review Committee (2003) *Reports of the Economic Review Committee*. Singapore: Ministry of Trade and Industry.

Eichhorn, W. (1988) 'On a Class of Inequality Measures', *Social Choice and Welfare*, 5, 171–7.

Elson, D. (1991) 'Male Bias in Macroeconomics: The Case of Structural Adjustment', in D. Elson (ed.), *Male Bias in Development Process*. Manchester: Manchester University Press, pp. 164–90.

Fei, J. C. H. and G. Ranis (1974): 'Income Inequality by Additive Factor Components', Economic Growth Center, Yale University, Center Discussion Paper no. 207, June.

Fei, J. C. and G. Ranis (1997) *Growth and Development From an Evolutionary Perspective*. Malden, USA and Oxford: Blackwell.

Fei, J. C., G. Ranis and S. Kuo (1978) 'Growth and the Family Distribution of Income by Factor Components', *Quarterly Journal of Economics*, 29(1), 17–53.

Felstead, A., D. Ashton, F. Green and J. Sung (1994) *International Study of Vocational Education and Training in the Federal Republic of Germany, France, Japan, Singapore and the United States*. Leicester: Centre of Labour Market Studies, University of Leicester.

Fields, G. S. (1980) *Poverty, Inequality and Development*. Cambridge: Cambridge University Press.

Finance Canada (1996) *The Senior's Benefit: Securing the Future*. Ottawa: Ministry of Supply and Services Canada.

Fontana, R. A., A. Geuna and M. Matt (2006) 'Factors Affecting University-Industry R&D Projects: the Importance of Searching, Screening and Signalling, *Research Policy*, 35(2), 309–23.

Forbes, K. J. (2000) 'A Reassessment of the Relationship between Inequality and Growth', *American Economic Review*, 90, 869–87.

Formby, J. P., H. Kim and W. J. Smith (1997) *On Interpreting Gini Decompositions with Applications to White and Non-white Populations, 1962–1994*, Working Paper no. 269, Working Paper Series, Department of Economics, Finance and Legal Studies, The University of Alabama.

Foster, J. E. (1983) 'An Axiomatic Characterisation of the Theil Measure of Income Inequality', *Journal of Economic Theory*, 31, 105–21.

Foster, J. E. (1985) 'Inequality Measurement', in H. Payton Young (ed.), *Fair Allocation*. Proceedings in Symposia in Applied Mathematics. Providence, RI: American Mathematical Society, Providence, RI, 33, pp. 31–68.

Foster, J. E. and A. K. Sen (1997) *On Economic Inequality*, 2nd edn. London: Clarendon Press.

Frank, M. (2008) 'Inequality and Growth in the United States: Evidence from a New State-level Panel of Income Inequality Measures', *Economic Inquiry*, 47(1), 55–68.

Frazer, G. (2006) 'Inequality and Development across and within Countries', *World Development*, 34(9), 1459–81.

Freeman, R. (1991) *How much has De-Unionization Contributed to the Rise in Male Earning Inequality?*, National Bureau of Economic Research Working Paper no. 3826.

Fry, V. C. (1984) 'Inequality in Family Earnings', *Fiscal Studies*, 53, 54–61.

Fultz, E. and M. Ruck (2001) 'Pension Reform in Central and Eastern Europe: Emerging Issues and Patterns', *International Labour Review*, 140(1), 19–43.

Galbraith, J. K. and H. Kum (2003) 'Inequality and Economic Growth: A Global View Based on Measures of Pay', *CESifo Economic Studies*, 49, 527–56.

Garner, J. D. and S. O. Mercer (eds) (1989) *Women as they Age: Challenge, Opportunity and Triumph*. New York: Haworth Press.

Gasparini, L., J. Alejo, F. Haimovich, S. Olivieri, and L. Tornarolli (2007) *Poverty among the Elderly in Latin America and Caribbean*, Background paper for the World Economy and Social Survey.

Gastwirth, J. L. (1974) *A New Index of Income Inequality*. Proceedings of the 39th ISI Meeting, August 1973, pp. 437–41.

GHS (2005) *General Household Survey*. Singapore: Singapore Department of Statistics.

Gibrat, R. (1931) *Les Inégalités Économiques*. Paris: Librairie du Recueil Sirey.

Gill, I., T. Packard and J. Yermo (2005) *Keeping the Promise of Social Security in Latin America*. Stanford, CA: Stanford University Press.

Gittleman, M. and E. N. Wolff (1993) 'International Comparisons of Inter-industry Wage Differentials', *Review of Income and Wealth*, 39(3), 295–312.

Goldberg, G. S. (1991) 'Women on the Verge: Winners and Losers in German Unification', *Social Policy*, 22 (2), 35–44.

Goldberg, S. (1987) 'Mixed Messages: Public Policy and Women in Singapore', *Commentary: Journal of National University of Singapore Society*, 7(2–3), 25–37.

Gomez, J. (1997) 'Proportionalizing Political Representation in Singapore: Problems and Prospects', *Commentary*, 13, 118–30.

Gordon, M. S. (1988) *Social Security Policies in Industrial Countries: A Comparative Analysis*. New York: Cambridge University Press.

Gottschalk, P. and M. Joyce (1992) 'Is Earning Inequality also rising in other industrialized countries?', LIS/CEPS Working Paper no. 66, October.

Gottschalk, P. and T. M. Smeedings (1997) 'Cross National Comparisons of Earnings and Income Inequality', *Journal of Economic Literature*, 35, 633–87.

Graduate Employment Survey (1991) *NUS and NTU Graduate Employment Survey*. Singapore: National University of Singapore.

Gruber, J. (1994) 'The Incidence of Payroll Taxation: Evidence from Chile', presented at the Labor Markets Workshop, The World Bank, July 6–8.

Guest, R. S. (2006) 'Demographic Change in the Asia-Pacific: On Average Living Standard', *Journal of Asia Pacific Economy*, 11(3), 229–48.

Gustafsson, S., Jan-Dirk Vlasbom and C. Wetzels (1995) 'Women's Labor Force Transitions in Connection with Child Birth: A Comparison between Germany and Sweden', paper presented at the 1995 European Society for Population Economics Conference, Lisbon.

Haddad, L. and R. Kanbur (1990) 'How Serious is the Neglect of Intra-Household Inequality?', *The Economic Journal*, 100(402), 866–81.

Hamada, K. (1973) 'A Simple Majority Rule on the Distribution of Income', *Journal of Economic Theory*, 6, 243–64.

Harris, N. (1992) 'States, Economic Development and the Pacific Rim', in R. P. Appelbaum and J. Henderson (eds), *State and Development in the Asia Pacific Rim*. London: Sage Publications, pp. 71–84.

Harrison, E. and C. Seidl (1994) 'Proportional Inequality and Preferential Judgement: an Empirical Examination of Distributional Axioms', *Public Choice*, 79, 61–81.

Harsanyi, J. C. (1975) 'Can the Maximin Principle Serve as a Basis Of Morality? A Critique of John Rawls's Theory', *The American Political Science Review*, 69, 594–606.

Harsanyi, J. C. (1977) *Rational Behaviour and Bargaining Equilibrium in Games and Social Situations*. Cambridge: Cambridge University Press.

Hateley, L. and G. Tan (2003) *The Greying of Asia: Causes and Consequences of Rapid Ageing in Asia*. Singapore: Eastern University Press.

HelpAge International (2004) *Age and Security: An Analysis of the Role of Social Pensions in Tackling Chronic Poverty among Older People and their Families*, available at: http://www.chronicpoverty.org/uploads/publication_files/PB_2.pdf [accessed 5 November 2013].

HelpAge International (2011) *Aging in Motion*, available at: http://www.helpage.org/resources/ageing-data/ageing-in-motion/ [accessed 5 Novemebr 2013]

Heng, S. H. (2001) 'Life Tables by Ethnic Group, Age and Sex: Singapore 1990–1999', Honours thesis, National University of Singapore.

Herrnstein, R. (1971) 'I.Q.', *Atlantic Monthly*, 228(3), 43–64.

Hey, J. H. and P. Lambert (1980) 'Relative Deprivation and the Gini Coefficient: Comment', *Quarterly Journal of Economics*, 94, 567–73.

Hinrichs, K. (2000) 'Elephants on the Move: Pattern of Public Pension Reform in OECD Countries', *European Review*, 8(3), 353–78.

Holzmann, R. (1997a) 'On the Economic Benefits and Fiscal Requirements of Moving from Unfunded to Funded Pensions', in *The Future of the Welfare State: Challenges and Reforms*, ed. Commission of the European Union, European Economy Report and Studies 4. Brussels: Commission of the European Union, pp. 121–63.

Holzmann, R. (1997b) 'Pension Reform, Financial Market Development and Economic Growth: Preliminary Evidence from Chile', *IMF Staff Papers*, 44(2), 149–78.

Holzmann, R., R. Hinz, H. von Gersdorff, I. Gill, G. Impavido, A. R. Musalem, R. Palacios, D. Robolino, M. Rutkowski, A. Schwarz, Y. Sin and K. Subbarao (2005) *Old-Age Income Support in the 21st Century: An International Perspective on Pension Systems and Reform*. Washington, DC: The World Bank.

HRD (2010) *Human Development Report 2010*, UNDP, available at: http://hdr.undp.org/en/media/HDR_2010_EN_Tables_reprint.pdf [accessed 5 Novemebr 2013].

Islam, I. and C. Kirkpatrick (1986) 'Export-led Development, Labour-market Conditions and Distribution of Income: The Case of Singapore', *Cambridge Journal of Economics*, 10, 113–27.

Jarvis, S. (1995) 'Taxation as a Targeting Mechanism: The Case of Family Allowance in Hungary', presented at the 1995 European Society of Population Economics Conference, Lisbon.

Jenkins, S. (1988) 'Empirical Measurement of Horizontal Inequity', *Journal of Public Economics*, 37(3) 305–29.

Jenkins, S. P. (1995) 'Accounting for Inequality Trends: Decomposition Analyses for the UK, 1971–86', *Economica*, 62, 29–63.

Jensen, A. (1969) 'How Much can we Boost IQ and Scholastic Achievement?', *Harvard Educational Review*, 39, 1–123.

Jones, G. and E. Savage (1995) 'Should Income Splitting Replace Australia's Personal Income Tax?', Working Paper in Economics and Econometrics no 295. Canberra, Australia: Australian National University.

Joshi, H. and H. Davies (1992) 'Pensions, Divorce and Wives' Double Burden', *International Journal of Law and the Family*, 6, 289–320.

Juhn, C., K. M. Murphy and B. Pierce (1993) 'Wage Inequality and Rise in Return to Skill', *Journal of Political Economy*, 10(3), 410–42.

Kakwani, N. C. (1980) *Income Inequality and Poverty*. New York: Oxford University Press, World Bank Publication.

Kakwani, N. C. (1984a) 'On the Measurement of Tax Progressivity and Redistribution Effect of Taxes with Application to Horizontal and Vertical Equity', *Advances in Econometrics*, 3, 149–68.

Kakwani, N. C. (1984b) 'Welfare ranking in income distribution, in inequality, measurement and Policy', *Advances in Econometrics*, 3, 191–215.

Kakwani, N. C. (1984c) 'Issues in measuring poverty', *Advances in Econometrics*, 3, 253–82.

Kakwani, N. C. (1986) *Analysing Redistributive Policies: A Study Using Australian Data*. Cambridge: Cambridge University Press.

Kakwani, N. C. (1995) 'Income Inequality, Welfare and Poverty: An Illustration using Ukrainian Data', Policy Research Working Paper no. 1411, The World Bank.

Kay, J. S. and T. Sinha (eds) (2008) *Lessons from Pension Reform in Americas*. Oxford: Oxford University Press.

Khan A. R. and C. Riskin (2001) *Inequality and Poverty in China in the Age of Globalization*. New York: Oxford University Press.

Khan, A. R., K. Griffin, C. Riskin and Z. Renwei (1993) 'Sources of Income Inequality in Post-reform China', *China Economic Review*, 4(1), 19–35.

Kidd, S. and E. Whitehouse (2012) *Pension and Old Age Poverty*, in Robalino, D., R. Holzmann and T. Takayama (eds), *Closing the Coverage Gap: The Role of Social Pensions*. Washington, DC: World Bank, pp. 41–56, available at: http://www.cis.ier.hit-u.ac.jp/Japanese/society/workshop0802/kidd-whitehouse-paper.pdf [accessed 1 August 2012].

King, E. M. and L. Lillard (1987) 'Education Policy and Schooling Attainment in Malaysia and the Philippines', *Economics of Education Review*, 6(2), 167–81.

Knowles, S. (2005) 'Inequality and Economic Growth: The Empirical Relationship Reconsidered in the Light of Comparable Data', *The Journal of Development Studies*, 41(1), 135–57.

Koh E. C. (2001) 'Measuring Old Age Health Expectancy in Singapore', *Statistics Singapore Newsletter*, Department of Statistics, Government of Singapore.

Kolm, S.-Ch. (1966) 'The Optimal Production of Social Justice', in H. Guitton and J. Margolis (eds), *Proceedings of International Economic Association Conference on Public Economics, Biarritz. Economie Publique.* Paris: CNRS, 1968, 109–77. Reprinted in *Public Economics.* London: Macmillan, 1969, 145–200.

Kolm S.-Ch. (1976a) 'Unequal Inequalities: I', *Journal of Economic Theory*, 12, 416–42.

Kolm S.-Ch. (1976b) 'Unequal Inequalities: II', *Journal of Economic Theory*, 13, 82–111.

Kolm S.-Ch. (1996) *Modern Theories of Justice.* Cambridge, MA: The MIT Press.

Kolm, S.-Ch. (1999) 'Rational Measurement of Income Inequality', unpublished mimeo.

Kondo N, G. Sembajwe, I. Kawachi, R. M. van Dam, S. V. Subramanian and Z. Yamagata (2009) 'Income Inequality, Mortality, and Self Rated Health: Meta-analysis of Multilevel Studies', *British Medical Journal*, 339, b4471, doi: 10.1136/bmj.b4471.

Kuznets, S. (1955) 'Economic Growth and Income Inequality', *American Economic Review*, 45, 1–28.

Kuznets, S. (1963) 'Quantitative Aspects of the Economic Growth of Nations: VIII. Distribution of Income by Size', *Economic Development and Cultural Change*, 11(2) 1–80.

Kwang, H. F., W. Fernandez and S. Tan (1998). *Lee Kuan Yew: The Man and his Ideas.* Singapore: The Straits Times.

Lambert, P. J. and J. R. Aronson (1993) 'Inequality Decomposition Analysis and the Gini Coefficient Revisited', *Economic Journal*, 103, 1221–7.

Layard, R. and A. Zabalza (1979) 'Family Income Distribution: Explanation and Policy Evaluation', *Journal of Political Economy*, 87, 133–61.

Lee, M. M. (1990) 'Trends in Longevity and Working Life Tables for Singapore 1957–1987', Honours thesis, Department of Economics and Statistics, National University of Singapore.

Lee, J. S. K. and J. C. L. Pow (1999) 'Human Resource Policies for Women: A Study in Singapore', *Journal of Management Development*, 18(4), 326–41.

Lee, J. S. K., K. Campbell and A. Chia (1999) 'The Three Paradoxes: Working Women in Singapore', *AWARE*, Singapore.

Lerman, R. I. and S. Yitzhaki (1985) 'Income Inequality Effects by Income Source: A New Approach and Application to the United States', *Review of Economics and Statistics*, 67, 151–6.

Lewis, G. H. (1963) *Unionism and Relative Wages in United States.* Chicago: University of Chicago Press.

LFS (various years) *Report on Labour Force in Singapore*, Ministry of Manpower.

Li, H. and H. Zou (1998) 'Income Inequality is not Harmful for Growth: Theory and Evidence', *Review of Development Economics*, 2, 318–34.

Lim, K. L. (2002) 'Enhancing the Financial Security of Older Singaporean', in A. T. Koh, K. L. Lim, W.T. Hui, V. V. B. Rao and M. K. Chng (eds), *Singapore Economy in 21st Century: Issues and Strategies.* Singapore: McGraw-Hill, pp. 95–111.

Liu, P. and Y. Wong (1981) 'Human Capital and Inequality in Singapore', *Economic Development and Cultural Change*, 29(2), 275–93.

López-Murphy, P. and A. R. Musalem (2004) 'Contractual Savings and National Saving', Policy Research Working Paper 3410, Washington, DC: World Bank.

Love, R. and M. C. Wolfson (1976) *Income Inequality: Statistical Methodology and Canadian Illustrations*, Catalogue 13-559 Occasional. Ottawa: Statistics Canada.

Low, L., T. M. Heng and S. T. Wong (1991) *Economics of Education and Manpower Development: Issues and Policies in Singapore.* Singapore, New York: McGraw-Hill.

McCarthy, D., Mitchell, O. S. and Piggot, J (2002) 'Asset Rich and Cash Poor: Retirement Provision and Housing Policy in Singapore', *Journal of Pensions, Economics and Finance*, 1, 197–222.

Madrid Plan of Action (2002) *Report of the Second World Assembly on Ageing, Madrid 8–12 April, 2002*. New York: United Nations, available at: http://www.c-fam.org/docLib/20080625_Madrid_Ageing_Conference.pdf [accessed 5 November 2013].

Majumdar, S. and M. D. Partridge (2009) 'Impact of Economic Growth on Income Inequality: A Regional Perspective', annual meeting, July 26–28, Milwaukee, Wisconsin 49270, Agricultural and Applied Economics Association.

Malinen, T. (2012) 'Estimating the Long-Run Relationship Between Income Inequality and Economic Development', *Empirical Economics*, 42, 209–33.

Mandelbrot, B. (1962) 'Paretian Distribution and Income Maximization', *Quarterly Journal of Economics*, 76(1), 57–85.

Marginson, S. (1993) *Education and Public Policy in Australia*. Cambridge: Cambridge University Press.

Marshall, A. W. and I. Olkin (1979) *Inequalities: Theory of Majorisation and its Applications*. New York: Academic Press.

Mawhinney, P. (2010) 'Ethnic Minorities at High Risk of Poverty in Old Age'. Press release by Runnymede Trust, available at: http://www.runnymedetrust.org/uploads/PressReleases/ReadyForRetirementPressRelease.pdf [accessed 5 November 2013].

MCD (2004) *National Survey on Senior Citizens in Singapore*. Singapore: Ministry of Community Development, Youth and Sports.

Meade, J. E. (1976) *The Just Economy*. London: Allen & Unwin.

Mehran, F. (1975) 'A Statistical Analysis of Income Inequality Based on a Decomposition of Gini Index', contributed paper 40th session ISI, Warsaw.

Mehran, F. (1976) 'Linear Measures of Income Inequality', *Econometrica*, 44, 805–9.

Mehta, K. (ed.) (1997) *Untapped Resources: Women in Ageing Societies across Asia*. Singapore: Times Academic Press.

Mesa-Lago, C. (1989) *Ascent and Bankruptcy: Financing Social Security in Latin America*. Pittsburgh, PA: University of Pittsburgh Press.

Milanvac, B. (1997) 'A Simple Way to Calculate the Gini Coefficient, and some Implications', *Economic Letters*, 45–9.

Mincer, J. (1970) 'The Distribution of Labour Incomes: A Survey with Special Reference to the Human Capital Approach', *Journal of Economic Literature*, 8(1), 1–26.

Mincer, J. (1974) *Schooling, Experience and Earnings*. New York: National Bureau of Economic Research.

Mirza, H. (1986) *Multinationals and Growth of the Singapore Economy*. London: Croom Helm.

Mitchell, O. S. (1998) 'Building and Environment for Pension Reform in Developing Countries', Social Protection Discussion Paper Series, no. 9803. The World Bank.

MOH (2002) *Information and Statistics on Healthcare*, http://www.moh.gov.sg, 15 January, Ministry of Health, Government of Singapore.

MOM (2000) *Occupational Segregation: A Gender Perspective, paper no 1/00*. Singapore: Ministry of Manpower and Statistics Department, April.

MOM (2011) *Report on Wages in Singapore 2011*. Singapore: Ministry of Manpower, Government of Singapore.

MOM (2013a) 'Levies and Quotas for hiring Foreign Workers [online]', available at: http://www.mom.gov.sg/foreign-manpower/foreign-worker-levies/Pages/levies-quotas-for-hiring-foreign-workers.aspx [accessed 5 November 2013].

MOM (2013b) 'Foreign Workforce Numbers [online]', available at: http://www.mom.gov.sg/statistics-publications/others/statistics/Pages/ForeignWorkforceNumbers.aspx [accessed 5 November 2013].

Mookherjee, D. and A. F. Shorrocks (1982) 'A Decomposition Analysis of the Trend in UK Income Inequality', *Economic Journal*, 92, 886–902.

Mukhopadhaya, P. (2001a) 'Changing Labour Force Gender Composition and Male–Female Income Disparity in Singapore', *Journal of Asian Economics*, 12(4), 547–68.

Mukhopadhaya, P. (2001b) 'Distribution of Income and Expansion of Education in some East Asian Countries', *Journal of Interdisciplinary Economics*, 12, 327–57.

Mukhopadhaya, P. (2003a) 'Trends in Income Disparity and Equality Enhancing (?) Education Policies in the Development Stages of Singapore', *International Journal of Educational Development*, 23(1), 37–56.

Mukhopadhaya, P. (2003b) 'Trends in Subgroup Income Inequality in the Singaporean Workforce', *Asian Economic Journal*, 17(3), 243–64.

Mukhopadhaya, P. (2003c) 'The Ordinal and Cardinal Judgment of Social Welfare Changes in Singapore, 1982–99', *The Developing Economies*, 41(1), 65–87.

Mukhopadhaya, P. (2003d) 'Generalized Social Welfare Function and its Disaggregation by Components of Income: The Method and Application', in Y. Amiel and J. Bishop (eds), *Research on Economic Inequality* Vol. 9. Amsterdam: JAI, pp. 245–64.

Mukhopadhaya, P. (2004a) 'Wage Policy and its Effect on the Social Sector in Singapore', *Problems and Perspectives in Management*, 2004(3), 103–110.

Mukhopadhaya, P. (2004b) 'Trends in Total and Subgroup Inequality in Singaporean Work Force', *Asian Economic Journal*, 17(3), 243–64.

Mukhopadhaya, P. (2004c) 'World Income Inequality Data Base (WIID) Review', *Journal of Economic Inequality*, 2(3), 229–34

Mukhopadhaya, P. (2005) 'Crisis, Social Sector and Income Distribution in Singapore and Thailand', in F. Sjoholm and J. Tongzon (eds), *Institutional Change in Southeast Asia*. London and New York: RoutledgeCurzon, pp. 91–126.

Mukhopadhaya, P. (2006) 'Income Disparity Trends and Data Problems in Singapore: Some Myths and Realities', *Journal of Interdisciplinary Economics*, 17(4), 401–24.

Mukhopadhaya, P. (2013) 'Trends in Income Inequality in China: the Effect of Various Sources of Income', *Journal of Asia Pacific Economy*, 18(2), 304–17.

Mukhopadhaya, P. and Y. Chung (2007) 'Inequality During an Economic Crisis: Evidence from Singapore', in Clem Tisdell (ed.), *Poverty, Poverty Alleviation and Social Disadvantage: Analysis, Case studies and Policies*, Vol. 3. New Delhi: Serial Publications, pp. 784–97.

Mukhopadhaya, P. and V. V. B. Rao (2002) 'Income Inequality', in A. T. Koh, K. L. Lim, W.T. Hui, V. V. B. Rao and M. K. Chng (eds), *Singapore Economy in 21st Century: Issues and Strategies*. Singapore: McGraw-Hill, pp. 95–111.

Mukhopadhaya, P. and G. Shantakumar (2009) 'Economics of Gender: The Case of Singapore', *Journal of Interdisciplinary Economics*, 21(4), 339–77.

Mukhopadhaya, P., G. Shantakumar and V. V. B. Rao (2011) *Economic Growth and Income Inequality in China, India and Singapore: Trends and Policy Implications*. London and New York: Routledge.

Murphy, K. M., A. Schleifer and R. Vishny (1989) 'Income Distribution, Market Size and Industrialization', *Quarterly Journal of Economics*, 104(3), 537–64.

Nelson, J. (1996) *Feminism, Objectivity and Economics*. London and New York: Routledge.

Newbery, D. (1970) 'A Theorem on the Measurement of Inequality', *Journal of Economic Theory*, 2, 264–6.

Nielsen, K. (1985) *Equality and Liberty: A Defence of Radical Egalitarianism.* Totowa, NJ: Rowman and Allanheld.

Nygard, F. and A. Sandstrom (1982) *Measuring Income Inequality.* Stockholm: Almqvist & Wiksell.

Oaxaca, R. (1973) 'Male–Female Wage Differentials in Urban Labour Markets', *International Economic Review*, 14(3), 693–709.

OECD (2002) *Regulating Private Pension Schemes, Trends and Challenges.* Paris: OECD.

OECD (2009) *Pensions at a Glance: Public Policies across OECD Countries, 2009 Edition.* Paris: OECD Publishing.

OECD (2012) *Education at a Glance 2012: OECD Indicators*, available at: http://www. oecd.org/edu/EAG%202012_e-book_EN_200912.pdf [accessed 5 Novemebr 2013].

Ofori, G. (1995) 'Foreign Construction Workers in Singapore', ILO working paper SAP 2.57/WP. 106, ILO, Geneva.

O'Higgins, M., G. Schmaus and G. Stephenson (1990) 'Income Distribution and Redistribution: A Microdata Analysis for Seven Countries', in T. M. Smeeding, M. O'Higgins and L. Rainwater (eds), *Poverty, Inequality and Income Distribution in Comparative Perspective.* Washington, DC: Urban Institute Press, pp. 20–56.

Ontario Fair Tax Commission (1992) *Women and Taxation.* Toronto: Toronto University Press.

Ontario Fair Tax Commission (1993) *Fair Taxation in a Changing World: Highlights of the Report of the Ontario Fair Tax Commission.* Toronto: Toronto University Press.

Paglin, M. (1975) 'The Measurement of Trend of Inequality a Basic Revision', *American Economic Review*, 65(4), 598–609.

Paglin, M. (1977) 'The Measurement of Trend of Inequality: Reply', *American Economic Review*, 67(3), 520–31.

Pang, E. F. (1975) 'Growth, Inequality and Race in Singapore', *International Labour Review*, 111(1), 15–28.

Peebles, G. and P. Wilson (1996) *The Singapore Economy.* Cheltenham, UK and Brookfield, US: Edward Elgar.

Pérez-Moreno, S. (2009) An Assessment of the Causal Relationship between Growth and Inequality in Spanish Regions, European Planning Studies, 17(3), 389–400.

Pfahler, W. (1987) 'Redistributive Effects of Tax Progressivity: Evaluating a General Class of Aggregate Measure', *Public Finance/Finances Publiques*, 37, 1–31.

Phipps, S. and P. S. Burton (1994) 'Sharing Within Families: Implication for the Distribution of Individual Well-Being in Canada', Department of Economics Working Paper no. 94-07. Halifax, NS: Dalhousie University.

Piggott, J. and E. Whitehouse (2000) *Pensions in Paradise: Modernizing the Mauritius Retirement Income Schemes.* Washington, DC: The World Bank.

Podder, N. (1993a) 'A New Method of Disaggregating the Gini Index by Groups', *Sankhya*, Series B, 55, 262–71.

Podder, N. (1993b) 'The Disaggregation of the Gini Coefficient by Factor Components and its Application to Australia', *Review of Income and Wealth*, 39, 51–61.

Podder, N. (1996) 'Relative Deprivation, Envy and Economic Inequality', *Kyklos*, 49, 353–76.

Podder, N. and P. Mukhopadhaya (2001) 'The Changing Pattern of Income and its Impact on Inequality: The Method and its Application to Australia, 1975–94', *The Economic Record*, 77 (238), 242–51.

Popper, K. (1962) *The Open Society and its Enemies*, 4th edn. London: Routledge and Kegan Paul.

Pratt, J. (1964) 'Risk Aversion in the Small and in the Large', *Econometrica*, 32, 122–36.

Psacharopoulos, G. (1985) 'Returns to Education: A Further International Update and Implications', *Journal of Human Resources*, 20(4), 583–604.

Psacharopoulos, G. and Z. Tzannatos (1989) 'Female Labour Force Participation: An International Perspective', *World Bank Research Observer*, 4, 187–201.

Pyatt, G. (1976) 'On the Interpretation and Disaggregation of Gini Coefficient', *Economic Journal*, 86, 243–55.

Pyatt, G. (1987) 'Measuring Welfare, Poverty and Inequality', *Economic Journal*, 97(386), 459–67.

Pyatt, G., C. Chen and J. Fei (1980) 'The Distribution of Income by Factor Components', *Quarterly Journal of Economics*, 95(3), 451–73.

Quah, S. R. (1993) 'Marriage and Family', in A. K. Wong and W. K. Leong (eds), *Singapore Women: Three Decades of Change*. Singapore: Academic Times Press, pp. 69–93.

Rao, V. M. (1969) 'Two Decomposition of Concentration Ratio', *Journal of the Royal Statistical Society*, Ser A, 132, 428–425.

Rao, V. V. B. (1990) 'Income Distribution in Singapore: Trends and Issues', *Singapore Economic Review*, 35, 143–60.

Rao, V. V. B. (1996) 'Income Inequality in Singapore: Facts and Policies', in Lim Chong Yah (ed.), *Economic Policy Management in Singapore*. Singapore: Addison-Wesley, pp. 383–96.

Rao, V. V. B. (1999) 'East Asian Economies: Trends in Poverty and Income Inequality', *Economic and Political Weekly*, 34(18), 1029–39.

Rao, V. V. B. (2001) *East Asian Economies: The Miracle, a Crisis and the Future*. Singapore: McGraw-Hill.

Rao, V. V. B. and M. K. Ramakrishnan (1980) *Income Inequality in Singapore*. Singapore: Singapore University Press.

Rao, V. V. B., D. S. Banerjee and P. Mukhopadhaya (2003) 'Earnings Inequality: The Singapore Case, 1974–98', *Journal of Asia Pacific Economy*, 8(2), 210–28.

Rashdall, H. (1907) *The Theory of Good and Evil*. Oxford: Oxford University Press.

Rawls, J. (1971) *A Theory of Justice*. Cambridge, MA: Harvard University Press and Oxford: Clarendon Press.

Richards, P. and M. Leonor (1981) *Education and Distribution in Asia: A Study Prepared for the International Labour Organization Within the Framework of World Employment Program*. London: Croom Helm.

Rodan, G. (1989) *Political Economy of Singapore's Industrialization: State and International Capital*. Basingstoke: Macmillan.

Rodríguez-Pose, A. and V. Tselios (2010) 'Inequalities in Income and Education and Regional Economic Growth in Western Europe', *The Annals of Regional Science*, 44(2), 349–75.

Roy, A. D. (1950) 'The Distribution of Earnings and of Individual Output', *Economic Journal*, 60, 489–505.

Sahota, G. (1978) 'Theories of Personal Income Distribution: A Survey', *Journal of Economic Literature*, 16, 1–55.

St. John, S. and Willmore, L. (2001) 'Two Legs are Better than Three: New Zealand as a Model for Old Age Pension', *World Development*, 29(8), 1291–305.

Sakellariou, C. (2006) 'Benefits of General vs Vocational/Technical Education in Singapore Using Quantile Regressions', *International Journal of Manpower*, 27(4), 358–76.

Samuelson, P. A. (1947) *Foundation of Economic Analysis*. Cambridge, MA: Harvard University Press.

Scherman, K. G. (1998) 'The Social Insurance Reform Debate: in Search of a New Consensus', in L. Thompson (ed.), *Older and Wiser: the Economics of Public Pensions*. Sydney: Ashgate.

Schokkaert, E. and B. Overlaet (1989) 'Moral Intuition and Economic Model of Distributive Justice', *Social Choice and Welfare*, 6, 19–31.

Sebastian, E. (1995) 'Why are Saving Rates so Different across Countries? An International Comparative Analysis', NBER Working Paper 5097. Cambridge, MA: National Bureau of Economic Research.

Selowsky, M. (1976) 'A Note on Preschool-Age Investment in Human Capital in Developing Countries', *Economics Development and Cultural Change*, 24(4), 707–20.

Sen, A. K. (1973a) *On Economic Inequality*. Oxford: Clarendon Press.

Sen, A. K. (1973b) 'On Ignorance of Equal Distribution', *American Economic Review*, 63, 1022–4.

Sen, A. K. (1974) 'Information Bases of Alternative Welfare Approaches' *Journal of Public Economics*, 3, 387–403.

Sen, A. K. (1976) 'Real National Income', *Review of Economic Studies*, 43, 19–39.

Sen, A. K. (1979) 'Utilitarianism and Welfarism', *Journal of Philosophy*, 76, 463–88.

Sen, A. K. (1981) *Poverty and Famines: An Essay on Entitlement and Deprivation*. Oxford: Clarendon Press.

Sen, A. K. (1990) 'Gender and Cooperative Conflicts', in I. Tinker (ed.), *Persistent Inequalities: Rethinking Assumptions about Development and Women*. New York: Oxford University Press, pp. 123–49.

Shantakumar, G. (1993) 'Demographic and Socio-economic Characteristics of Older Women: Issues and Policy Implications', in Aline K. Wong and Leong Wai Kum (eds), *Singapore Women: Three Decades of Change*. Singapore: Times Academic Press, pp. 208–51.

Shantakumar, G. (1994a) *The Aged Population of Singapore 1990*. Monograph No 1, Department of Statistics, Government of Singapore.

Shantakumar, G. (1994b) 'Senior Citizens in Singapore: Now and Their Future', Proceedings of International Conference on the Elderly. Singapore: SAGE and International Federation on Ageing, pp. 299–312.

Shantakumar, G. and P. Mukhopadhaya (2001) *Economic Crisis and Higher Education in Singapore*. International Institute for Educational Planning Monograph. Paris: UNESCO.

Shantakumar, G. and P. Mukhopadhaya (2002) 'Impact of the Economic Crisis on Higher Education in Singapore', in N.V. Varghese (ed.), *Impact of the Economic Crisis on Higher Education in East Asia: Country Experiences*. Paris: UNESCO, International Institute of Educational Planning, pp. 157–81.

Shantakumar, G. and P. Mukhopadhaya (2008) 'Demographics, Incomes and Development Issues Amongst Indians in Singapore', in K. Kesavpany, A. Mani and P. Ramasamy (eds), *Rising India and Indian Communities in East Asia*. Singapore: Institute of South East Asian Studies, pp. 568–601.

Sharp, R. and R. Broomhill (1995) 'Women and Economic Restructuring in Australia', presented at the International Association for Feminist Economics Conference, Tours, France.

Shen, C. and J. B. Williamson (2010) 'China's New Rural Pension Scheme: Can it be Improved?', *International Journal of Sociology and Social Policy*, 30(5), 239–50.

Sheshinski, E. (1972) 'Relation Between Social Welfare and the Gini Index of Inequality', *Journal of Economic Theory*, 4, 98–100.

Shorrocks, A. F. (1980) 'The Class of Additively Decomposable Inequality Measures', *Econometrica*, 48, 613–25.

Shorrocks, A. F. (1982) 'Inequality Decomposition by Factor Components', *Econometrica*, 50, 1337–9.

Shorrocks, A. F. (1983a) 'The Impact of Income Components on the Distribution of Family Incomes', *Quarterly Journal of Economics*, 98, 311–26.

Shorrocks, A. F. (1983b) 'Ranking Income Distributions', *Economica*, 50, 3–17.

Shorrocks, A. F. (1984) 'Inequality Decomposition by Population Subgroups', *Econometrica*, 52, 1369–85.

Shorrocks, A. F. (1988) 'Aggregation Issues in Inequality Measurement', in W. Eichhorn (ed.), *Measurement in Economics: Theory and Application of Economic Indices*. Heidelberg: Physica-Verlag, pp. 429–52.

Silber, J. (1989) 'Factor Components, Population Subgroups and the Computation of the Gini Index of Inequality', *The Review of Economics and Statistics*, 71(1), 107–15.

Silber, J. (1993) 'Inequality Decomposition by Income Source: A Note', *Review of Economics and Statistics*, 75(3), 545–7.

Singapore Annual Report, EESS (2011/12) *The Education Endowment and Savings Schemes, Annual Report for Financial Year 2011/2012*, Government of Singapore.

Singapore Census of Population (2010) available at: http://www.singstat.gov.sg/Publications/publications_and_papers/cop2010/ssnsep09-pg23-28.pdf [accessed 5 November 2013].

Singapore Central Provident Fund (CPF) (2009) *Annual Report Annexes*, available at: http://mycpf.cpf.gov.sg/NR/rdonlyres/CA5FDA33-97E5-4FD1-9AE7-2787F9A578A4/0/Annexes.pdf [accessed 29 August 2011].

Smith, P. (1993) 'Measuring Human Development', *Asian Economic Journal*, 7(1), 89–106.

Sukiassyan, G. (2007) 'Inequality and Growth: What does the Transition Economy Data Say?', *Journal of Comparative Economics*, 35, 35–56.

Tan, T. (1986) *Economic Change and the Foundation of Education Policy*. Singapore: Information Division, Ministry of Communication and Information.

Taussing, F. W. (1915) *Principles of Economics*. New York: Macmillan.

Taussing, F. W. (1939) *Principles of Economics*, 4th edn. New York: Macmillan.

Tawney, R. H. (1961[1931]) *Equality*. New York: Capricon Books.

Temkin, L. S. (1986) 'Inequality', *Philosophy and Public Affairs*, 15, 99–121.

Temkin, L. S. (1993) *Inequality*. New York/Oxford: Oxford University Press.

Theil, H. R. (1967) *Economics and Information Theory*. Amsterdam: North-Holland.

Tilak, J. B. G. (1989a) *Education and its Relation to Economic Growth, Poverty and income Distribution* (World Bank Discussion Paper). Washington, DC: The World Bank.

Tilak, J. B. G. (1989b). 'Rates of Return to Education and Income Distribution'. *De Economist*, 137(4), 454–65.

Toh, M. (2008) 'Tuition Nation', *Asiaone [The Straits Times]*, 15/17 June, available at: http://news.asiaone.com/News/Education/Story/A1Story20080616-71121.html http://en.wikipedia.org/wiki/Education_in_Singapore [accessed 5 November 2013].

Tridico, P. (2010) 'Growth, Inequality and Poverty in Emerging and Transition Economies', *Transition Study Review*, 16, 979–1001.

UNDP (1996) *Human Development Report: Economic Growth and Human Development.* Oxford: Oxford University Press.

UNDP (1999) *United Nations Development Programme Annual Report.* New York: UNDP.

UNDP (2000) *United Nations Development Programnme Annual Report.* New York: UNDP.

UNDP (2011) *Human Development Report, 2011, Singapore*, available at: http://hdrstats.undp.org/images/explanations/SGP.pdf [accessed 9 November 2013].

UNESCO (2008) *Education Statistics: Malaysia*, UNESCO Institute for Statistics, Data Centre, available at: http://stats.uis.unesco.org/unesco/ReportFolders/ReportFolders.aspx [accessed 5 November 2013].

Valtos, G. (1962) 'Justice and Equality', in R. B. Brandt (ed.), *Social Justice.* Englewood Cliff, NJ: Prentice-Hall.

Voitchovsky, S. (2005) 'Does the Profile of Income Inequality Matter for Economic Growth?: Distinguishing Between the Effects of Inequality in Different Parts of the Income Distribution', *Journal of Economic Growth*, 10, 273–96.

Vu, H. and P. Mukhopadhaya (2011) 'Reassessing the Relationship between Economic Growth and Inequality', *Economic Papers*, 30(2), 265–72.

WDI (2012) *World Development Indicators 2012.* Washington, DC: The World Bank.

Weiss, A. (1995) 'Human Capital vs. Signalling Explanation of Wages', *Journal of Economic Perspectives*, 9(4), 133–54.

Weymark, J. A. (1981) 'Generalized Gini Inequality Indices', *Mathematical Social Sciences*, 1, 409–30.

Williams, B. (1962) 'The Idea of Equality', in P. Laslett and W. G. Runciman (eds), *Philosophy, Politics and Society.* Oxford: Basil Blackwell, pp. 110–31.

Williamson, J. B., M. Price and C. Shen (2012) 'Pension Policy in China, Singapore and South Korea: An Assessment of the Potential Value of Notional Defined Contribution Model', *Journal of Aging Studies*, 26, 79–89.

Willmore, L. and S. Kidd (2008) *Tackling Poverty in Old Age: A Universal Pension for Sri Lanka.* London: HelpAge International.

Wirtz, J. and T. Menkhoff (1998) 'From Entrepot to NIC: Economy and Structural Policy Aspects of Singapore's Development', *Sasin Journal of Management*, 4(1), 112–23.

Wong, S. T. (1993) 'Education and Human Resource Development', in L. Low, T. M. H. Heng, T. W. Wong, T. K. Yam and H. Highes (eds), *Challenges and Responses: Thirty Years of Economic Development Board.* Singapore: Times Academic Press.

Woolley, F. (1993) 'The Feminist Challenge to Neoclassical Economics', *Cambridge Journal of Economics*, 17(4), 485–500.

World Bank (1992) 'Hungary: Reform of Social Policy and Expenditures', A World Bank Country Study. Washington, DC: The World Bank.

World Bank (1993) *The East Asian Miracle: Economic Growth and Public Policy.* New York: Oxford University Press.

World Bank (1994) *Averting the Old Age Crisis: Policies to Protect the Old and Promote Growth.* Washington, DC: The World Bank.

World Bank (2011) 'World Development Indicators', available at: http://data.worldbank.org/indicator [accessed 30 July 2011].

World Development Report (2011) *World Development Report 2011*. The World Bank, available at: http://wdr2011.worldbank.org/ [accessed 30 July 2011].

World Health Organization (2004) 'World Health Report, Singapore', available at: http://www.who.int/whr/2004/annex/country/sgp/en/index.html [accessed 31 October 2013].

Yitzhaki, S. (1979) 'Relative Deprivation and the Gini Coefficient', *Quarterly Journal of Economics*, 93, 321–4.

Yitzhaki, S. (1982) 'Relative deprivation and economic welfare', *European Economic Review*, 17, 99–113.

Yitzhaki, S. (1983) 'On the Extension of Gini Index', *International Economic Review*, 24, 617–28.

Zaman, K., I. A. Shah, M. M. Khan and M. Ahmad (2012) 'The Growth, Inequality and Poverty Triangle: New Evidence from a Panel of SAARC countries', *International Journal of Economics and Business Research*, 4, 485–500

Index

For Product Safety Concerns and Information please contact our EU
representative GPSR@taylorandfrancis.com
Taylor & Francis Verlag GmbH, Kaufingerstraße 24, 80331 München, Germany

www.ingramcontent.com/pod-product-compliance
Ingram Content Group UK Ltd.
Pitfield, Milton Keynes, MK11 3LW, UK
UKHW021828240425
457818UK00006B/112